Public Management and Vulnerability

This book locates the issue of 'vulnerability' in an international context, within public-sector reform processes, and goes beyond the conceptualization of existing concepts of policing and vulnerability to include multi- and intra-agency working. It uncovers many competing and contradictory conceptualisations of the phenomenon and shows how a variety of agencies in different jurisdictions prioritise and operationalise this escalating 21st-century social problem.

Two recurring themes of this edited collection are the ways in which non-state organisations and agencies have become an acknowledged feature of modern service delivery, and how the withdrawal of the state has heralded a perceptive shift from collective or community provision towards the stigmatization of individuals. Increasingly, public service professionals and 'street level bureaucrats' work in collaboration with non-state agents to attempt to ameliorate vulnerability. Chapter contributions were deliberately drawn from combinatory empirical, theoretical, policy and practice fields, and diverse academic and policy/professional authors. Editors and authors deliberately cast their nets widely to provide integrative scholarship, and contributions from international perspectives to confirm the complexity; and how socio/cultural, political and historic antecedents shape the definitions and responses to vulnerability.

This collection will appeal to academics, policy makers and practitioners in a wide variety of disciplines, such as public management and leadership, criminology, policing, social policy, social work, and business management, and any others with an interest in or responsibility for dealing with the issue of vulnerability.

Gareth David Addidle is a Senior Lecturer in Policing at Teesside University, UK, where he teaches on the undergraduate and postgraduate Policing and Criminology programmes.

Joyce Liddle is Professor of Public Leadership and Enterprise, Director of Research and KE, Newcastle BS, Northumbria, UK.

Routledge Advances in Management and Business Studies

Improving Competitiveness through Human Resources Development in China
The Role of Vocational Education
Min Min and Ying Zhu

Collaborative Research in the United States
Policies and Institutions for Cooperation among Firms
Albert N. Link

Green Human Resource Management in Chinese Enterprises
Jie Shen, Jenny Dumont and Xin Deng

Developing the Workforce in an Emerging Economy
The Case of Indonesia
Edited by Kantha Dayaram, Linda Lambey, John Burgess and Tri Wulida Afrianty

Cross-Cultural Leadership
Being Effective in an Era of Globalization, Digital Transformation and Disruptive Innovation
Ahmad M. Salih

The Global Pharmaceutical Industry
The Demise and the Path to Recovery
Daniel Hoffman and Allan Bowditch

Public Management and Vulnerability
Contextualising Change
Edited by Gareth David Addidle and Joyce Liddle

For more information about this series, please visit www.routledge.com/Routledge-Advances-in-Management-and-Business-Studies/book-series/SE0305

Public Management and Vulnerability

Contextualising Change

Edited by
Gareth David Addidle and Joyce Liddle

Routledge
Taylor & Francis Group

NEW YORK AND LONDON

First published 2021
by Routledge
605 Third Avenue, New York, NY 10017

and by Routledge
2 Park Square, Milton Park, Abingdon, Oxon, OX14 4RN

First issued in paperback 2022

Routledge is an imprint of the Taylor & Francis Group, an informa business

Library of Congress Cataloging-in-Publication Data
Names: Addidle, Gareth David, editor. | Liddle, Joyce, 1952– editor.
Title: Public management and vulnerability : contextualising change / edited by Gareth David Addidle and Joyce Liddle.
Description: New York, NY : Routledge, 2021. |
Series: Routledge advances in management and business studies | Includes bibliographical references and index.
Identifiers: LCCN 2020013031 (print) | LCCN 2020013032 (ebook) | ISBN 9780367371012 (hardback) | ISBN 9780429352683 (ebook)
Subjects: LCSH: Public welfare. | Human services. | Social service. | Marginality, Social—Government policy. | Poor—Services for. | Social policy.
Classification: LCC HV95 .P775 2021 (print) | LCC HV95 (ebook) | DDC 361—dc23
LC record available at https://lccn.loc.gov/2020013031
LC ebook record available at https://lccn.loc.gov/2020013032

ISBN 13: 978-0-367-53708-1 (pbk)
ISBN 13: 978-0-367-37101-2 (hbk)
ISBN 13: 978-0-429-35268-3 (ebk)

DOI: 10.4324/9780429352683

Typeset in Sabon
by codeMantra

Contents

Contributors

Dr Gareth David Addidle is a Senior Lecturer in Policing at Teesside University, where he teaches on the undergraduate and postgraduate Policing and Criminology programmes. He is the Programme Leader for the MSc Evidence-based Policing postgraduate degree and is a Teaching Fellow of the Higher Education Academy. He is a graduate of Glasgow Caledonian University; received Doctorate from Plymouth University; and has held previous academic roles at Open University, Plymouth University and the University of Derby. His research and publications are in the areas of policing, governance, community safety and partnership working. Dr Addidle has worked with a number of police services across the UK and has been involved in research projects with Police Scotland (formerly Strathclyde Police); Devon and Cornwall Police; Her Majestys Inspectorate of Constabulary (HMIC); and, more recently, with Newcastle Business School.

Professor Stephen Barber is Professor of Global Affairs at Regent's University London, where he is also Assistant Dean for Programmes. The author of numerous books, articles and papers, he is Co-Editor of the International Public Management Review and is a Senior Research Fellow of the Global Policy Institute.

Professor Emma Bond is Director of Research, Head of the Graduate School and Professor of Socio-Technical Research at the University of Suffolk. She has extensive research experience, focussing on online risk and vulnerable groups, especially in relation to domestic abuse, revenge pornography, sexual abuse and image-based abuse. Emma has 17 years of teaching experience in social science undergraduate and post-graduate courses, and is a Senior Fellow of the Higher Education Academy. Her research on virtual environments, mobile technologies and risk has attracted much national and international acclaim, and she has been interviewed for BBC Breakfast, ITV, The Today Programme on Radio 4, Woman's Hour on Radio 4 and Channel 4's Sex Education Show, and various national media channels in the UK, America and Canada.

Dr Stephen Brookes QPM is a Senior Lecturer (Associate Professor) in public policy and management at the University of Manchester (Alliance Manchester Business School). His research interests focus on public leadership and organisational development, and he was the Founding Editor for the *International Journal of Public Leadership (IJPL)* until 2018. He has published three books, including *The New Public Leadership Challenge* (2010) and *The Selfless Leader* (2016). He is an experienced Programme Director in health-care management and leadership, and teaches negotiations skills on the Global MBA programme, with most of his teaching taking place internationally. Before joining Alliance Manchester Business School (AMBS) Stephen had a unique blend of experience at a senior level in the police, central and regional government, and local government. He was awarded the Queens Police Medal in the Jubilee Birthday Honours in June 2002 for distinguished police service. Immediately prior to his academic appointment Stephen was the Home Office Director for the Government Office for the East Midlands, which he undertook for almost six years. During this time he had considerable experience in working with partnerships and supporting both performance improvement programmes and facilitating and leading change. He is a Fellow of the Chartered Management Institute (FCMI) and a Fellow of the Royal Society of Arts (FRSA).

Dr Brian Brown was an engineer in the coal mining industry and experienced first-hand the miner's strike in 1984/85. He saw how vulnerable people can become when exposed to stress-provoking situations. Before leaving the coal industry, Dr Brown studied with the Open University and then the University of Durham, where he graduated with a BA Hons in Social and Public Administration. Dr Brown then undertook a social work qualification and Master's in Social Work at the University of York. As a social work professional for four years and manager for 20 years working in Local Authority Children's Services Dr Brown was able to gain in-depth insight into the daily pressures experienced by social workers involved in safeguarding children. He undertook doctoral research with the University of Teesside Business School, relating to managing in turbulent public organisations, with a focus on Children and Family Court Advisory and Support Service (CAFCASS), where he was a senior manager. In 2012 he was awarded a Doctorate in Business Administration (DBA) and subsequently established a management consultancy company focussing on supporting Local Authority Children's Services who had failed Ofsted Inspection. The majority of this work was specifically with front-line managers and social work practitioners in a number of different Local Authority settings, providing a broad insight into the high levels of vulnerability experienced by these professionals and how extensive the issue actually is.

Rachel Close is a qualified Social Worker, currently working thera-peutically with children and families. Rachel was adopted as a baby from Romania by British parents. During adolescence, following a breakdown in family relationships at home, Rachel was placed in emergency foster care before living independently from the age of 18. Rachel went on to study social work and postgraduate systemic practice in the hope of supporting children and families experiencing relational difficulties.

Mr David Cook completed five years with the Open University then undertook a Bachelor's Degree in Sociology and Social Policy at the University of Durham. His career in social care included two years as a personal tutor in a secure unit with young offenders and two years as a social work assistant in adult community mental health, during which he completed a Diploma in Social Work and an MA in Applied Social Studies (also at the University of Durham). Since qualifying as a Social Worker, he has worked in several Local Authorities as a Social Worker, Senior Practitioner and Team Manager. He then moved into an Independent Fostering Agency and became a Child Protection Training coordinator, followed by a role as an Organisational Devel-opment Advisor and Manager for both Children and Adult Services. For the past five years he has acted as Tutor/Lecturer and Placement Coordinator at New College FE/HE College, Durham, UK.

Mr Stephen Down is a qualified Social Worker who worked for most of his career in Local Authorities across the North-East and in Brent, London. Most of his career has been spent working with adults with mental health issues or in various Safeguarding Adults roles. He is an experienced Independent Best Interest Assessor under the Deprivation of Liberty Safeguards framework and regularly travels around England and Wales assessing vulnerable people in a variety of placements. Stephen also runs his own training business, providing bespoke training, conferencing and consultancy support to a wide range of professionals from the National Health Service (NHS), Local Authority and Private Care sector. His areas of interest include the Mental Capacity Act, Deprivation of Liberty Safeguarding (DoLS), Mental Health and Safeguarding Adults. Stephen is an associate trainer for Social Care Institute for Excellence (SCIE) and has been a Guest Lecturer at Northumbria University. He currently works as Mental Health Lead for the North East Ambulance Service (NEAS) and previously held the Safeguarding Adults Lead post with NEAS. In his private life, he loves spending time with his family, friends and pet dog Milo. He loves Cricket and is a long suffering Sunderland football supporter.

Dr Ian Fitzgerald is a Reader in Employment Relations and Associate Professor. He is Head of the Human Resource Management, Work and Employment subject group and Unit of Assessment Lead for the Department of Leadership and Human Resource Management at Newcastle Business School, Northumbria University. His migration research involves 13 projects as a principle investigator and two as a co-investigator, and led to a REF2014 impact case study. These projects included being invited to be a national UK expert with regard to the Posting of Workers Directive 96/71/EC and the Posting of Workers Enforcement Directive 2014/67/EU. This pioneering research has produced over 50 peer-reviewed publications, keynote contributions and practitioner publications that have been cited over 650 times.

Dr Sirak Berhe Hagos is a specialist on Entrepreneurship and SMEs, and his research interest includes Business Studies, Consumer Behaviour, Cross-Cultural Management, Integration of Refugees and Asylum Seekers, and Ethnic Conflict & Management. He is a freelance researcher and consultant, offering acculturation and integrating solutions to academic and government units. Dr Hagos also works as Visiting Lecturer at Durham University, where he delivers lectures occasionally on Culture Understanding, and offers coaching on Culture and Inter-Cultural Understanding through his consultancy company. He has been appointed all over the UK to speak on the topic of the cultural Adaptation and Integration of refugees and asylum seekers.

Stephanie Hunter qualified as a Social Worker in 1997. She has worked in Local Authority Children's Services, CAFCASS and Child and Adolescent Mental Health Services (CAMHS), and substance misuse services. In 2002 she set up a mental health service for children in care and adopted children. This won three national awards and accolades, including Beacon Status (2002) and Young Minds Exemplar (2006), and the team was highly commended in the 2006 Positive Practice Awards. It also won three local NHS awards. Stephanie is trained in Eye Movement and Desensitisaton and Reprocessing, North East (EMDR), Dyadic Developmental Psychotherapy, Theraplay and Family Therapy. From 2015 to June 2019 she was a Senior Lecturer at Sunderland University.

Stephanie has spoken nationally and internationally at Conferences. Currently working independently, Stephanie has a wide portfolio of work, chairing fostering panels, evaluating service effectiveness; adoption support funded therapies and bespoke packages of work including two books developed with and for children. Stephanie has also undertaken media work, including numerous media interviews and many regional newspaper articles. Stephanie is a Trustee of the Institute of Recovery from Trauma, which delivers best practice events at the House of Lords and EMDR North East and British Association of Social Work (BASW). Stephanie Hunter Dip S/W. BA. BSC, MA, Advanced Award in Social Work, PGCE, FHEA.

Dr Jonathan Knox is Head of Commercial Development for NEAS. Most of his career (more than 20 years) has been in a range of commercial roles, including sales, marketing, new product/service development, innovation and project management. With 15 years of private-sector experience across a range of industries, including oil and gas, electronics and fast-moving consumer goods (FMCG), and ten years of public-sector experience in NEAS, Jonathan has a passion for developing innovative solutions to problems and a special interest in developing better care for patients through improved service provision, new clinical interventions and the potential of digital care and big data implications for disease management and cure. Specialising in organisational strategy, innovation, business development and competitive tendering/bidding, Jonathan completed a Doctorate in Business Administration in 2017 with Northumbria University. The focus of his study was public-sector organisational bidding strategy. Jonathan is also an Associate Lecturer at Northumbria University, working principally on the BA in Leadership and Management (BALM).

Professor Joyce Liddle is Professor of Public Leadership and Enterprise, Director of Research and KE, Newcastle BS, Northumbria. She was Professor of Public Leadership and Management at Institut de Management Publique Gouvernance Territoriale (IMPGT), Aix-Marseille Université, France. She was a graduate of the University of Durham; received a Doctorate from the University of Warwick; and held previous senior academic roles at Nottingham Business School, NTU, University of Nottingham, University of Durham, Sunderland and Teesside Business Schools. She was Hon Chair of the UK Joint University Council and Fellow of UK Academy of Social Sciences, Regional Studies Association, Joint University Council. She holds (or has held) Visiting Professorships at the Universities of Eastern Finland, Tor Vergata, Rome, Paul Cezanne, France, Northumbria, Edge Hill and Glasgow Caledonian. She has published over 200 articles, 25 book chapters and 12 books; co-edits an Annual Book series on Critical Perspectives on International Public Sector Management; chairs the Editorial Advisory Board (EAB), International Journal of Public Sector Management (was Editor in Chief and Book Review Editor for 14 years); and is Consulting Editor or EAB member on six international journals.

Susan McKenna is a 39-year-old woman who was placed in Local Authority Care on two occasions, once at 10 years of age and then from 14 years until joining HM Forces at 18 years. Susan aspired to employment within the Police and as a Social Worker to support those affected by child abuse and domestic violence. She has attained those life goals within the specific roles she has undertaken and continues to undertake within the HM Forces.

Helen McMillan is Assistant Chief Constable, Northumbria Police. Helen joined Northumbria in June 2017, having previously worked for Durham Constabulary in a variety of roles, most recently as Assistant Chief Constable. She has experience working in many operational roles and in training and professional standards departments, and is an experienced firearms and public order commander. Assistant Chief Constable McMillian is responsible for Territorial Policing and Operations.

Professor Alex Murdock is Professor Emeritus at London South Bank University, where he was Head of the Centre for Government and Charity Management. He is also Visiting Professor at various universities, including Northumbria, Cagliari (Italy) and Potsdam (Germany). He has taught and researched for long periods at The Sorbonne, Paris, and Copenhagen Business School, and has published six books and numerous articles. His research interests focus on the intersection of the public, private and third sector, together with social innovation, especially related to responses to food insecurity and ageing demographics. Previously he was a professional and senior manager in Local Government. He has been Chair of social business and charities, and is Co-Editor of the International Public Management Review.

Professor Peter Murphy is Professor of Public Policy and Management, and Head of Research at Nottingham Business School in Nottingham Trent University. He is a member of the Advisory Board of the Centre for Public Scrutiny. Prior to joining the business school in 2009, he was a senior civil servant in four Whitehall departments and a Director of the Government Office for the East Midlands, and he is a former Chief Executive of Melton Borough Council in Leicestershire. He was responsible for emergency planning and co-ordinating the response to emergencies at local, regional and national levels for over 30 years. His recent books include *Fire and Rescue Services: Leadership and Management Perspectives*, edited with Kirsten Greenhalgh, and *Rebuilding the Fire and Rescue Services: Policy, Delivery and Assurance*, with Kasia Lakoma, Pete Eckersley and Russ Glennon.

Professor Andy Phippen is a Professor of Digital Rights at Bournemouth University, working between issues of legislation, rights and behaviours in digital technology. He has specialised in the use of ICTs in social contexts for almost 10 years, carrying out a large amount of grass roots research on issues such as attitudes toward privacy and data protection, and internet safety as well as contemporary issues such as sexting, peer abuse and the impact of digital technology on well-being. In more recent times, he has focussed on the failures of legislation to protect the rights of the vulnerable: for example young people and those with mental capacity issues. In particular he has been a vocal opponent of the use of digital technology to track and monitor individuals in order to keep them 'safe'. He has presented written and oral evidence to parliamentary inquiries related to the use of ICTs in society, is widely published in the area and is a frequent media commentator on these issues. His latest book '*Child Protection and Safeguarding Technologies – Appropriate or Excessive "Solutions" to Social Problems?* is published by Routledge.

Rachel Woodley is a 29-year-old woman living in Essex. She was born and raised in Darlington. Rachel was raised in the care system from the age of 3 to 21 as she stayed in higher education until the age of 21. Rachel works full time in accounts and studies part time for a degree in criminology and law, with the aspiration to work as a police detective within the field of domestic abuse.

Dr Xiaojian Wu is a Senior Lecturer at Newcastle Business School, Northumbria University in the UK, where he manages and teaches on the undergraduate Business Management Programmes. He was educated in China and has been actively involved in collaboration works at various international universities in fields such as information systems management, comparative policing, knowledge and learning. His research and publications are in areas of management learning in public organisation contexts, cross boarder knowledge transfer, competences matrix and comparative management study. Dr Wu is recipient of a number of research grants from international agencies, including the British Council, National Foreign Experts Administration in China, and is particularly interested in multidisciplinary enquiries on international policing. He is also the visiting Professor at the Zhongnan University of Economics and Law, of Wuhan, China, and University of Lyon, France.

1 Introduction

Contested Perspectives on Vulnerability: Which Groups Are Vulnerable and Why?

Gareth David Addidle and Joyce Liddle

The overall collection of chapters addresses a number of important policy questions, such as

- Why is Vulnerability an important topic for academic enquiry, for policy makers and for professionals who are dealing with the consequential rise in individuals and groups now categorised as Vulnerable?
- Why is it a contentious and slippery concept to define? Which definitions make more sense?
- Which groups and individuals are now defined as Vulnerable and why?
- Where are there gaps in knowledge and understanding of the concept?
- What historical legacies are there?
- Which agencies have traditionally dealt with Vulnerable groups? Has the coverage and ability to deal with Vulnerable individuals and groups changed, and if so why?

This introductory chapter sets the context for the discussions in subsequent chapters by analysing some literature on conceptualising vulnerability, as well as examining the types of individuals and groups now defined as Vulnerable. There are many and varied definitions on this very contentious and politically charged concept, and historically different individuals and groups have been categorised as Vulnerable from different professional, policy and academic perspectives. As editors we are interested in drawing out the antecedents and ways of analysing what it is to be Vulnerable in 2020 in different contexts and examining why it is an important topic for academic enquiry. Moreover, we want contributors to consider how policy makers and front-line professionals respond to the rise in Vulnerable individuals, depending on the specific context under the microscope, who is attempting to define it, but more importantly, the types of policies and decisions to be implemented in dealing with a 'wicked issue', that has many unintended consequences of policy action (or inaction).

The two editors demonstrate integrative scholarship by drawing on their expertise in criminology and public management and leadership to bring together a wide range of current academic, policy and practitioner understandings of vulnerability; a key issue within 21st century society (*Home Secretary Sajid Javid's 2018 speech to the Police Federation, 23rd May 2018, Integrated Communities Strategy Green Paper Building stronger, more united communities, March 2018*).

Vulnerability is a complex concept that can result from a set of primary vulnerabilities, such as economic, housing, physical, family, cultural, and for each individual or group a set of variables can be used to define varying levels of vulnerability. It is also influenced by age, class, occupation, gender, ethnicity and disability, and adverse events of natural hazards within the broader social, economic, political and institutional structures can produce differential outcomes for different individual groups. Vulnerability can be manifested as poverty, marginalisation and lack of assets. It arises at many levels and over time as many varied and different processes deprive people of coping and leave them physically weak, economically impoverished, social dependent, humiliated and psychologically harmed. Organisation for Economic Co-operation and Development (OECD) define vulnerability as

> The exposure to contingencies and stress, and difficulty in coping with them. Vulnerability thus has two sides- an **external** side of risks, shocks and stress to which an individual or household is subject- and an **internal** side which is defencelessness, meaning a lack of means to cope without damaging loss.
>
> (Freyssinet, OECD, 2019)

But the concept has also been defined in numerous global reports and statements (e.g., The World Bank, IMF and EU), and national, regional and local agencies have also tried to develop 'Vulnerability Indices' to capture and measure economic, social and environmental vulnerability. Specific public agencies such as local authorities, social service departments, police and Mental Health Trusts have all developed their own definitions of the term to identify and classify disadvantaged groups. Moreover, some business organisations and companies have produced Vulnerability Assessment Tools (VSAT, Birmingham Resilience, UK, 2019), but there is no universally agreed definition. To add to the confusion, in some literature it is linked to sustainability, resilience, continuity management and risk management agendas. The 2010 UK Government led by Prime Minister David Cameron produced a National Well Being Index, but this was superseded by a Vulnerability Index based on a variety of models to measure the incidence of vulnerability across various professional environments.

Vulnerability, if not dealt with effectively across society, has potential to affect overall economic, businesses and service productivity and performance, and can bring disastrous ramifications for societal cohesion and integration across communities. In response to turbulent environmental forces and globalisation, many businesses have strategies to cope with emergencies and risks such as terrorism, pandemics and other such threats they also recognise the need for better deployment of human resources because Vulnerable citizens and workforces can have detrimental effects on personnel issues such as absenteeism, sickness and mental health issues. Mental health issues are now prevalent across society, and worryingly in the UK, at least, there is evidence to suggest that children as young as five years of age in primary schools are experiencing vulnerability and anxiety. Indeed, the current Prime Minister Johnston's predecessor, Teresa May introduced a policy of placing mental health nurses in every primary and secondary school, such was the scale of the identified problem. In communities too, many families are feeling Vulnerable due to instability, loss of employment, general safety and other significant forces impacting on their lives.

To respond to the increasing number of calls surrounding public welfare, tackling vulnerability through early intervention has emerged as a key theme in contemporary policing (Bartkowiak-The´ron and Asquith, 2012). Indeed, police forces in the UK are individually graded on how effective they are at protecting Vulnerable people from harm by Her Majesty's Inspectorate of Constabulary (HMIC, 2016). However, the way to do this remains ambiguous. Whilst some working definitions do exist in policing (Rogers and Coliandris, 2015), HMIC noted that there is no accepted definition of vulnerability across all police forces of England and Wales as each 'continues to define a Vulnerable victim in different ways' (2016: 74). To compound this, there is limited guidance as to who merits intervention, and the types of interventions to be made. As we shall see in the practice chapter in this collection, Emergency and Blue Light Services have all adopted different mechanisms appropriate to their operational capacities and strategies to decide when and when, not to intervene.

The concept of vulnerability is very complex with fleeting contours and is expressed differently in the USA, Europe and China as later chapters will demonstrate. The debate was largely re-framed in the USA by the loss of life experienced during the September 11th atrocity, but across Europe it has been defined as individual precarity and exclusion due to the abandonment of individuals to naked forces of the market. In China, as Wu in particular illustrates in his chapter, vulnerability is treated from a wholly different perspective by police who seek to maintain social order, above all else.

Vulnerability, apart from the case we include on China where different cultural norms apply, is generally characterised by instability, turbulence, insecurity and the fragility of individual relational integration in society (Ferrarese, 2016: 149–159). This is not to say that there is an absence of vulnerability in China because in fact the opposite is true as millions of people live precarious lives in poverty. However, vulnerability and protests are used interchangeably by academics in a Chinese context, and the need to maintain social order is paramount in such a non-democratic and authoritarian state.

Over the past ten years, research on community safety, and safety and security highlighted the fact that vulnerability moved from a 'collective' understanding, to the stigmatisation of the 'individual', as both contributions from Brookes and Hunter and co-authors confirm in their analysis of sex workers (prostitution), modern slavery, youth extremism and females experiences of care UK system. Both sets of authors urge professionals to understand the holistic nature of vulnerability, and the contextual drivers that lead people to become Vulnerable. This shift in emphasis has been underpinned by policies that shift focus from vulnerability as a broader societal concern to one in which individuals are blamed for their own pathological weaknesses. In turn, lack of state support for Vulnerable individuals and groups has been reflected in numerous attempts to enforce 'self-help' due to withdrawal of state forms of support, and front-line responses by 'street level' bureaucrats. Lipsky's highly influential work on street-level bureaucracy (30th Ann. Ed, 2010), Goodsell (1981), Hupe et al. (2016), Maynard-Moody and Musheno (2003), Zacka (2017) and others have taken an ethnographic approach to studying frontline work, in police, social work and education. Bartel (2015) collection of institutional ethnographies of changing front-line work, and communication in public encounters have both informed theoretical and practice debates.

In responding to vulnerability, there are numerous Australian examples of policing and multi-agency and inter-agency working (Bartkowak-Theron and Asquith, 2013, Asquith et al., 2017), whereas in the USA a merging of social work and policing has led to the creation of police social workers. In Western Europe, the changing context of public-sector reform has heightened the need to find solutions to the 'vulnerability' question, as indeed is true for all societal 'wicked issues' and governmental responses have been varied, as the varied chapters in this collection demonstrate. In China, however, as ably demonstrated by Wu, vulnerability has an altogether different connotation, and government officials deal with this problem in a culturally appropriate way to existing societal norms. In their day-to-day dealings with poor and Vulnerable people, Chinese police adopt what Wu refers to as 'relational repression'. Within a political system of centralised authority and under-developed legal standardisation, vulnerability is treated in a much more stringent fashion, in the interests of maintaining social order at any costs. This is facilitated by the use of informal and culturally grounded personal ties to impose constraints on the poor and Vulnerable, rather than the accepted Western adherence to the more formalised criminal justice systems and welfare organisations.

The articulation of strong historical narrative of how different individuals and groups have been categorised as Vulnerable from different professional, policy and academic perspectives, elucidates what it is to be considered Vulnerable in 2020. As all chapters demonstrate, policy makers and front-line professionals respond to the rise in Vulnerable individuals and groups in very diverse ways, and the choice of policies and decisions to be implemented in dealing with such a 'wicked issue' can also have numerous intended and unintended consequences of policy action (or inaction). However, in lesson drawing within, and between varied policy responses we can usefully highlight key issues, and in some cases enable learning in other jurisdictions.

In the UK public service budgets have been severely constrained for over ten years, and despite Prime Minister Johnston's promises since the December 2019 General Election to relax stringent spending targets, local authorities, police and other statutory services on the front line, those dealing with Vulnerable groups have suffered the most Draconian cuts. Indeed, local authorities will be required to be almost self-sufficient over the medium to long term. A Better Care Fund has also been introduced to integrate health and social care (as demands on mental health services continue to grow). Furthermore, all local councils can now set a precept for social care on council tax bills. Many of the new Combined Authorities (UK-specific combinations of Local Authorities) are developing health and social care strategies at the same time as individual local authorities are reducing the support they have traditionally provided for charities, third sector and community organisations. Paradoxically, just as traditional state providers withdraw from direct service provision for Vulnerable people, they no longer have the capacity to fund arms-length service deliverers such as third and community and charities. There is evidence, as shown throughout this collection that nowadays many non-statutory agencies are stepping into the breach as state agencies withdraw, or severely limit their coverage in dealing with social policy problems. Investigating the scale of Vulnerability, as one the most challenging social policy problems of the early 21st century reveals that many state agencies lack sufficient capacity to deliver services and cope with the growing demands placed upon them.

State officials increasingly work alongside a multitude of stakeholders to deal with numerous global and internal environmental forces; primarily amongst these, as we argue throughout this collection, are on-going budgetary and fiscal constraints. The pressures for reform, from above and below, have forced them to work in partnership with other agencies and actors to develop novel ways of determining delivery, evaluation and measurement of services. Creating public and social value is now an essential part of a comprehensive approach to thinking about continuous improvement and understanding how modern governance can deliver effective public services to wider society. One way of ensuring that this happens is to be open to new ways of transforming governance and public service delivery in co-production with stakeholders. Moreover, there is an expectation of on-going re-invention, re-assessment and re-imagining a future public service, due to the likelihood of further limited state intervention, and a need to a rethink all operations, systems and ways of doing things. Public services have changed cultures, behaviours and ways of doing things to become more akin to private and commercial sectors of the economy, but more recently, have involved civic and community/voluntary sectors in working together to solve 'wicked' issues such as vulnerability. There is general acceptance that no one agency alone can solve the huge economic, social and environmental problems across the globe, and that states must look beyond their narrow confines to seek collaborative solutions to societal ills. There are few ready-made answers to some of the urgent and critical issues facing society, and the rising numbers of Vulnerable groups and individuals is a very pressing issue, one that is taking up a huge amount of resources, both financial and non-financial as there are no longer 'one size fits all' universal solutions to complex social problems. Vulnerability is a very complex 'wicked' issue with many causal factors.

Citizens are no longer passive consumers but empowered individuals who expect state agencies to provide more personalised services and choice (Mau and Katsonins, 2008, cited in Schofield, 2008), either those more akin to private provision, or increasingly through a wider range of civic providers. An iPod generation that expects personalised service delivery (Harle, 2008, cited in Schofield, 2008) and rapid responses to problems needs to be set against a backdrop of 'finite resources and infinite demands' meaning that innovative approaches to societal ills become even more crucial. Nowadays a plurality of inter-relationships between state, market and civic institutions have become the focal point for co-production and co-responsibility of public service delivery and production of public value. These new relational forms of governance are not only a challenge to the role of government in advanced democracies in the 21st century because but they raise questions on what type of institutions, organisational and leadership capacities are needed in future to synergise the state's own resources, capacities and knowledge with those of the market and civic institutions. This calls for less hierarchical, top down, bureaucratic governance, and more horizontal, bottom up, facilitative or enabling forms of engagement with citizens experiencing vulnerability.

We took as a starting point two key publications (Bartkowiak-Theron and Asquith, 2013, Asquith et al., 2017) with a focus on Australian policing and police to identify a clear market gap internationally associated with front-line responses (policing and multi-agency and intra-agency). The editors encouraged al chapter authors to build on existing knowledge but also develop a much broader conceptualisation of both contemporary policing and vulnerability, more generally. Drawing on extant literature on comparative international research on multi-agency approaches to the phenomenon, and on contested perspectives on vulnerability, the chapters as a whole illustrate convergence and highly varied responses to Vulnerable and marginalised individuals and groups within society.

This collection of chapters attempts to goes further than earlier works because it surfaces many different meanings and usages of the concept of vulnerability, it captures how professionals, practitioners and policy makers and academics identify, define and prioritise activities to respond to vulnerability, but more significantly it shows how shifting responsibilities and fragmentation across the public service system are revealing major gaps in coverage in 21st century public service provision.

Clayton, Donovan and Merchant (2015) highlighted that Vulnerable groups became demonised after 2010 in the UK Welfare System to justify some of the changes being driven in, but there was a concomitant effect on stresses, strains and increased vulnerability of professionals working with Vulnerable and disadvantaged groups. Many of the chapters include findings that confirm this stigmatisation and demonisation of the Vulnerable, as the 'problem' has shifted focus from a societal issue towards blaming individuals for their plight. It is important to think about whether vulnerability is a collective and therefore a societal issue or the responsibility of the individual, who is increasingly blamed, demonised and stigmatised. Brookes eloquently uses examples of sex work (prostitution), modern slavery and youth extremism to demonstrate how these issues not only transcends the criminal justice system but can only be understood more fully within the context of social, political and economic determinants. Unless these are appreciated, then framing vulnerability remains contentious. Fitzgerald and Hagos also use the examples of asylum seekers and refugees to illustrate the notion of 'deserving' and 'undeserving' Vulnerable people and their treatment at the hands of public officials. Many experience hostility and difficult journeys to safety, as they face in some cases, detention, destitution, health issues and potential slave labour. Furthermore, Hunter and colleagues' chapter give voice to the ways that individuals feel judged and stigmatised.

By also inviting contributions from practitioners, we show the scale of stress and need for support and training needs within a variety of professional settings. Undoubtedly, as Brown and Cook suggest, the escalation in the numbers of Vulnerable people is causing untold misery to many front-line service deliverers in their daily encounters. Social workers, unlike other emergency service professionals such as police officers, fire and rescue workers, prisons and National Health Service personnel who had been defined by central government as Vulnerable, experience higher levels of stress-related illness and absenteeism, in comparison with other professional groups. Excessive working hours, low staff coverage, poor support mechanisms lead to negative work/life balances and mental health issues. Brown and Cook found social workers who are as Vulnerable as the Vulnerable individuals and client groups they joined their respective professions to support.

In the practice chapter, with contribution written from the perspective of professionals working in Ambulance, Police and Fire and Rescue services, the findings do indeed confirm the challenging nature of front-line service delivery, as all services are coping with increasing demands from Vulnerable people. Each Emergency or Blue Light service attempts to respond to those who are in need of safeguarding, who are at risk or in danger of potential harm. They must all adhere to European and national policy imperatives, within given statutory requirements and available resources, in any response they make. Increasingly they are unable to respond without working in partnership with other state and non-state agencies, and all services are under-represented (in current personnel terms) with respect to the balance of minority and ethnic employees, in relation to the overall population.

While many Vulnerable people still have face to face encounters with front-line professionals as Phippen and Bond argue social media and virtual space have led to key questions on who is now Vulnerable, and where vulnerability can be seen. Abuse and a rise in Vulnerable individuals can take place anywhere in the world now, and the anonymity afforded by the World Wide Web allows abusers to access potentially millions of Vulnerable people through a multitude of personas. This challenge to criminological norms and the inability to 'police' or regulate/legislate the web is, it is argued, failing victims as the internet has reshaped the environment in which abuse of Vulnerable individuals takes place.

Multi-disciplinary contributions examine some of the more conventional approaches to social work provision for Vulnerable individuals and groups, but as Hunter et al. show in the narratives of Vulnerable females exposed to the social care system, many children who go through the system are seriously damaged and may experience mental health difficulties, poor educational outcomes, homelessness, suicide. They are also more likely to end up in prison than going to university. For Hunter this throws up many inadequacies in social work training, and she pleads for more support in helping Vulnerable individuals to navigate the system and lead valuable lives afterwards, without fear that stigmatisation will follow them into adulthood. In earlier research on complex pathways into care, Ellis (2018: 156–163) also found that females in care rejected the label of being 'vulnerable' and 'troublesome' as their experiences seriously disenfranchised them from services designed to help them.

A recurrent theme throughout the collection is the correlation between the changing nature of social work, subtle changes to police operational activities and the growing importance of non-crime social interventions. In particular, many authors stress how vulnerability, marginalisation and associated social problems have much wider, societal significance than those witnessed in the realms of social work and policing. Contributing chapters from widely different academic, policy and practice fields within social science and business and management enable authors to explain how rapidly changing socio-political and economic contexts increase the scale, visibility and need for action. Brookes confirms this in his call for all public leaders to collectively tackle the contextual social, political and economic determinants of vulnerability, and the historical contours of situations, based on a strong evidence base. In his chapter vulnerability, he argues, should be firmly at the centre of community safety strategies, through a collective form of community-based leadership because of the belief that agency leaders have a duty of care to victims, and must solve these societal and 'wicked issues'; as public interest and public value should be at the very core of all strategies and plans.

The changing context of public-sector reforms is usefully employed as a framework for analysis on how governments pursue policies for the 'vulnerable' in society, and it would be unwise to discuss the changing approaches without some acknowledgement of the antecedents of policy shifts. Contemporary public-sector reform was initiated in the 1980s in advanced capitalist democracies as a response to public-sector expansion after the Second World War to assess how well various programmes were operating. However, not only was it focussed on improving performance and reshaping the structural configuration of states, it was also the starting point for a complete questioning of the role of Welfare States in societies (Lane, 1997). This questioning of how welfare services should be delivered is playing out with regards to the vulnerability agenda as provision moves beyond the conventional social work and policing roles towards more multi and intra-agency approaches.

In Western countries, in particular, demographic shifts have increased the numbers of isolated, lonely and Vulnerable elderly and young people. There are also more homeless people sleeping on the streets of many cities across Europe, and poverty levels are impacting on mental health issues, together with associated problems of alcohol, drug dependency and domestic violence. Murdock's chapter on ageing provides an excellent exploration of the elderly demographic, and though he puts a positive spin on the phenomenon, it is clear to see that the numbers of individuals living to a grand old age can create both positive and negative effects, and help to reshape social policies. Fitzgerald and Hagos in considering the difficulties facing asylum seekers and refugees, and Brookes in introducing cases of sex workers (prostitutes), modern slavery and youth extremism all succeed in isolating particular groups of Vulnerable people for deeper investigation.

Added to the aforementioned discussion, changing employment and migration patterns, growing prison populations, increased fear of crime, climatic events or terrorist threats, as well as a growth in Vulnerable and problem families have all contributed to changing perceptions of vulnerability. All the chapters written from a professional perspective confirm the huge increase in calls that front-line workers are responding to, from people experiencing mental health issues. On any particular evening, in any city across the UK, all emergency and blue light services will be straining under the pressure on operations capacities, as demonstrated in practice chapter contributors, and the Brown and Cook chapter.

Across the globe, in many states, on-going austerity and financial stringency since the 2008 meltdown have led governments to re-evaluate their policies for ameliorating the resultant escalation in social problems. Even the Brexit negotiations between the UK and Europe partners are having repercussions across the world and adding to feelings of uncertainty and instability. As Liddle and Addidle found in their chapter, Brexit, and its potential aftermath, if analysed through a transnational lens can identify many local consequences and impacts on vulnerability. Some impoverished areas will feel the full force of Brexit and may be disproportionately affected during Brexit negotiations and future trade deals. Policing, security and criminal justice issues have largely been ignored in Brexit negotiations, and potential rises in terrorism, borderless crime, people trafficking, drug smuggling and other issues facing Police (and other Emergency and Blue Light) Leaders will challenge them even more on top of responding to on-going austerity, budget cuts and a multitude of other domestic safety and security issues. There are numerous social commentators who believe that three years of Brexit negotiations, and the lengthy period ahead, may have stimulated numerous other criminal activities such as hate and race crime, Islamophobia, Anti-Semitism, and cyber-crime. Vulnerable groups, such as the homeless, rough sleepers, refugees and immigrants, are living in poverty, and many seek assistance from the authorities. There are so many imponderables arising from Brexit negotiations, so it is rather difficult for the Emergency and Blue Light services, and statutory social and welfare services, to predict how safety and security might be compromised. Some of the senior Emergency Service personnel referred to throughout this collection give voice to these very real concerns.

The phenomenon of vulnerability, as earlier argued is contested within international and public-sector reform contexts as policy shifts from collective/community approaches to stigmatization of the 'individual'; government responses include a variety of multi-agency partnerships and enlarged arenas for action but no-one really knows the full extent of how many non-state, charitable, voluntary, church and other civic organisations are stepping in to support the Vulnerable once the statutory agencies withdraw coverage. Issues of vulnerability and marginalisation were traditionally and firmly located in the domain of social work, but changes to police practices (coupled with changes to newer responsibilities and accountabilities), and problem escalation coupled with shrinking public service budgets has widened the scope for multi-agency action, in public, private and voluntary/community/charities and faith-based organisations. Barber and Murdock provide an excellent historical explanation as to how the scope for action is now broadened to numerous non state actors and agencies, and Fitzgerald and Hagos in discussing refugees and asylum seekers highlight the ways in which people are processed through a very complicated system before they can reach the safety away from their original destinations. They also highlight the role of charitable and voluntary sector Refugee and Asylum organisations providing extra non-state support, and in the concluding chapter Liddle and Addidle illustrate a selection from the very many thousands of examples of charitable, faith and voluntary sector activities aimed at the Vulnerable in society.

Front-line workers, those referred to by Lipsky (2010) as 'street level bureaucrats' across many public service organisations (including police, social workers and other public professionals) are facing an onslaught of increased demands in supporting Vulnerable individuals as testified by the findings from Wu, Brookes. Brown and Cook and highlighted in the practice chapters. Numerous ethnographic studies of front-line workers interactions with citizens' (Goodsell, 1981, Maynard-Moody and Musheno, 2003, Lipsky, 2010, Bartel, 2015, Hupe et al., 2016, Zacka, 2017) have added to our knowledge and understanding of front-line public service professionals responses to citizens' needs, but more are needed if we are to understand the complex interactions and problems arising for these bodies of professional front-line workers.

Competing and contestable definitions of vulnerability enable practitioners to identify, prioritise and operationalise the concept, as can be witnessed in the practice chapter but they do so within shifting policy and statutory agendas that create a whole variety of problems and issues in practice. Multiple issues and problems, such as blurring of organisational boundaries, competing responsibilities and accountabilities, differing cultural values and others, increase stress levels for front-line workers and street level bureaucrats, who are all aiming to satisfy the public interest and create public value in all of their interactions with citizens (Liddle, 2016). Interestingly, Barber and Murdock convincingly challenge earlier explanations of public-sector reform by suggesting that a new era of New Public Populism has arisen from citizen discontentment, largely (but not solely) from Vulnerable groups who depend on welfare services. Many individuals are vociferous in their condemnation of policies and more than prepared to take to the streets to protest. Civil disobedience is on an upward trajectory, driven by an anti-elitist and anti-establishment ideology, and this poses a challenge to governments across the Globe, as well as creating potential, further security threats and safety issues across many local communities.

Pragmatically, what works from a policy and practice perspective is a key factor in driving change and innovative ways of working, and we hope that this collection of chapters will prove to be of value to a wide range of readers such as politicians, civil servants, public-sector professionals, undergraduate, postgraduate and post experience students. Seeking out new ways of dealing with practical social problems is at the heart of good policy and practice, and the widely varied, though complimentary contributions contained in the following chapters offer useful pointers to examine this crucial, and ever-expanding topic of enquiry.

References

Asquith, N. L., Bartkowiak-Théron, I., and Roberts, K. A. (eds) (2017). *Policing Encounters with Vulnerability*, Palgrave Macmillan. www.palgrave.com/gb/book/9783319512273.

Bartel, K. P. R. (2015). *Communicative Capacity: Public Encounters in Participatory Theory and Practice*, Policy Press, Bristol.

Bartkowiak-Théron, I., and Asquith, N. (eds) (2012). *Policing Vulnerability*, Federation Press, Sydney.

Bartkowiak-Théron, I., and Asquith, N. L. (eds) (2013). *Policing Vulnerability*, Federation Press, www.federationpress.com.au/bookstore/book. asp?isbn=9781862878976.

Clayton, J., Donovan, C., and Merchant, J. (2015). Emotion and Austerity: Care and Commitment in Public Service Delivery in NE England. *Emotion, Space and Society*, 14, 24–32. www.sciencedirect.com/science/article/pii/S0195925513000802.

Ellis, K. (2018). Contested Vulnerability: A Case Study of Girls in Secure Care. *Children and Youth Services Review*, 28, 156–163.

Ferrarese, E. (2016). Vulnerability: A Concept with Which to Undo the World As It Is? *Critical Horizons*, 17(2), 149–159. DOI: 10.1080/14409917.2016.1153885.

Freyssinet, J. (2009). How Can Social Vulnerability Be Measured?: A Work in Progress: The 3rd OECD World Forum on Statistics, Knowledge and Policy, Busan, 27–30 October.

Goodsell, C. T. (1981). *Public Encounter: Where State and Citizen Meet*, Indiana University Press, Bloomington.

Harle, T., untitled essay cited in Schofield, C. P. (2008). Key Challenges Facing Public Sector Leaders: Themes from the Ashridge Public Leadership Centre Essay Competition 2007, Autumn 2008, The Ashridge Journal, UK.

HMIC. (2016). *PEEL: Police Effectiveness 2016: A National Overview*. www.justiceinspectorates.gov.uk/hmic/wp-content/uploads/peel-police-effectiveness-2016.pdf.

Home Secretary Sajid Javid's 2018 speech to the Police Federation, 23rd May 2018, Integrated Communities Strategy Green Paper Building stronger, more united communities, March 2018, London.

Hupe, P., Hill, M., and Buffat, A. (eds) (2016). *Understanding Street-Level Bureaucracy*, Policy Press, Bristol.

Lane, J. E. (1997). *Public Sector Reform: Rationale, Trends and Problems*, Sage, London.

Liddle, J. (2016). Public Value Management & New Public Governance: Key Traits, Issues and Developments, chapter in Ongaro, E. and van Thiel, S., *The Palgrave Handbook of Public Administration and Management in Europe*, 967–990, chapter 49 of 63.

Lipsky, M. (2010). *Street-Level Bureaucracy, 30th Ann. Ed.: Dilemmas of the Individual in Public Service*, Russell Sage Foundation, New York.

Mau, K., and Katsonis, M., untitled essay cited in Schofield, C. P. (2008). Key Challenges Facing Public Sector Leaders: Themes from the Ashridge Public Leadership Centre Essay Competition 2007, Autumn 2008, The Ashridge Journal, UK.

Maynard-Moody, S. W., Musheno, M., and Musheno, M. C. (eds) (2003). *Cops, Teachers, Counsellors: Stories from the Front Lines of Public Service*, Michigan Press, Ann Arbor.

Rogers, C., and Coliandris, G. (2015). 'Seeing Vulnerability'. Police Professional (No. 471, 03 September), Verdant Media, Aylesbury.

Vulnerability Self-Assessment Tool for Business (VSAT), Birmingham Resilience, Birmingham City Council, UK downloaded 11 November 2019, www.birminghamprepared.gov.uk/news/vulnerability-self-assessment-tool-for-businesses/.

Zacka, B. (2017). *When the State Meets the Street: Public Service and Moral Agency*, The Bellnap Press, Harvard University Press, Cambridge University Press, Cambridge.

2 Beyond Public Services
The Era of New Public Populism

Alex Murdock and Stephen Barber

Introduction

New Public Leadership represented a response to a period of 'austerity' where those responsible for managing public services attempted to do more (or at least the same) with squeezed financial resources. It was a development from the radicalism of an earlier time when New Public Management sought to re-cast the public sector from fat bureaucracies to efficient organisations modelled on a private-sector ideal. Today, the era of populism to have emerged in western democracies represents a different sort of challenge which invites a fresh appraisal of public services and the people who rely upon them most.

The challenge of political ideology in the 1980s was met logically by the creation of management structures, corporate governance and quasi-markets. The challenge of funding after the 2008 financial crisis was met rationally by the emergence of leadership at every level and a looser idea of what constituted public service agents. Disenchantment, social division and anti-elitism have given rise to simplistic answers and contradictory positions. Since populism is neither inherently logical nor rational, it is difficult to address in a coherent fashion. And yet it is inevitable that public services will be expected to tackle the broad array of social concerns which underpin the growth of populism. After all it is the most vulnerable in society who rely on heath, social care and welfare. These are the people who have been hit hardest by squeezed public finances and the consequent cuts to services. But they are also most likely to be part of the demographic which has begun to identify with populist rhetoric and vote for populist politicians.

New Public Populism represents a contradiction for the delivery of public services when the very citizens who need to be satisfied politically are in many cases also the most vulnerable and need to be cared for.

In considering this possible new paradigm, this chapter explores the concept of 'public services' using a simple concept of 'broad and narrow' definitions of what constitutes such services. It will briefly examine how different theoretical concepts have shaped the views of public services ranging from traditional public administration through to exploring the emerging implications of populism.

The chapter uses selected examples of populism and explores emerging models which may become more commonplace and be regarded as a response to continuing challenges to meet public needs in a context of limited traditional public-sector resources.

What Are Public Services and Who Are They For?

The concept of 'public services' can be defined in several ways. One is simply to consider it from the perspective of the provider as defining the service. Hence, under this 'public services' are services provided by the state or by a state agency or by a government department. At the very least, they exist because they are a public good resulting from market failure and as a consequence are provided across society though are relied upon most by those with the fewest resources or those who are vulnerable for other reasons including health, age and circumstances.

The traditional concept of public administration would focus not just upon the nature of the service provided but also upon who provides it – the state on behalf of its citizens (Pollitt 2016). This arguably 'narrow' conception of public services has been accepted for centuries and indeed underpinned the original discipline known as 'public administration' and inspired both a literature, a university education and the various journals which still bear the name 'public administration' in their title.

Starting with the seminal article by Hood (1991), the traditional definition of public administration was challenged by the concept of 'new public management', which identified and described a range of practices derived from the private sector that had been utilised in public service delivery. This resulted from a radical political decade in the 1980s when neo-liberal governments, notably that of Margaret Thatcher in the United Kingdom, set about reforming the economy and the state. It opened up a potential pandora's box in which the delivery of public services could be through agents other than public employees. In effect the 'provider' side of public services was no longer defined by a sector boundary and 'managerialism' became an increasingly commonplace term in the provision linked to concepts of efficiency and competition (Dunleavy and Hood 1994).

The subsequent developments of New Public Management highlighted the development of contracting out of services (both to the private and to the voluntary sector) and the changing nature of the basis of such contracts with the development of targets and outcome-based contracts (Hood 2006, Hyndman and Lapsey 2016). This meant a degree of competition for those servicing the needs of the most vulnerable in society.

The growth of contracting out led to academics talking of the 'hollowed out state' whereby the state had contracted out much of the delivery of public services (Rhodes 1994, Roberts and Devine 2003). The development of a 'language of partnership' which operated not just within a contract context but also in terms of a more complex and less hierarchical environment led to an examination of the governance implications for public services (Bovaird 2006).

However all these evolutions were based significantly upon a perception of public services which was 'narrow' in nature. The focus was upon services which were deemed to be legally the responsibility of the state to provide and where the state had changed the notion of whether such delivery was undertaken directly or indirectly through contract or partnership models.

In Table 2.1 we introduce the concept of public services which have a 'broad definition'. The table also shows the narrow definition which is characterised by the discussion of public administration and the subsequent emergence of new public management and public governance. It encompasses the range of possible 'public service' delivery modes but is focussed on those for which a legal requirement exists or where the state has deemed (whether at national or local level) that it should assume a direct or indirect responsibility. That is the responsibility can be delegated to others whether by contract or through a grant funding mechanism.

However, if a broad construct is assumed then the argument is based upon whether the service provided serves to address a public need. This public need is defined as something where the public sector could logically be deemed to have some responsibility if the service was

Table 2.1 Broad versus Narrow perceptions of Public Services

Broad: Based on the actual activity	*Narrow: Based on a legal obligation on the state*
Encompassed four sectors • The family (provision of care and meeting resource needs within a kinship setting) • The Private sector (providing services which divert or reduce the likelihood of pressures on the state) • The (broad) NFP sector (engaging in a range of provision which meets the criteria of 'public good'. This may include sports clubs, for example. NOT dependent on receiving any public money • The Public Sector (engaging in direct or indirect provision of public services. Not necessarily due to any legal requirement)	• Determined by a legal or similar determination of a state obligation to ensure provision • May be delivered directly or indirectly • May use contractual arrangements with private and NFP providers to ensure this • May also use grant mechanisms • Expectations of 'accountability, fairness and equity'

non-existent. Likewise, it is possible to determine that the existence of a state-provided service has the potential to 'crowd out' provision by other means. The family is clearly a source as it furnishes the primary base of care for many vulnerable children and adults. In most welfare states if the family fails in this role then the state is obligated to provide support. Many such tasks are undertaken out of a sense of voluntary obligation or from love and affection. It is widely acknowledged that care can be compared to that offered by state employees (Pickard and Glendinning 2002). State policy is often focussed upon encouraging more individual informal engagement in such activity. It is a possible recognition that the resources of the police and state security agencies are not adequate to guard against all the perceived and potential threats.

Similarly, the private sector has a role, in a market context, to provide services (such as food and housing). Where the private sector is unable – or unwilling – to furnish the essential needs of citizens this is sometimes described as 'market failure'. This may be associated with failure of other sectors (Salamon 1987). However, where core needs such as food and shelter are provided by the private sector in a functioning market context then the public sector does not need to intervene and yet has extended its reach.

The 'broad voluntary sector' also has a role in service provision. This is widely acknowledged in the literature which has examined the growth of engagement of Voluntary organisations in a wide range of provision which the state might otherwise have to assume (Bennett et al. 2003, Brandsen and Pestoff 2006). The role of charities in the provision of services such as education and social/health care is well accepted. Meanwhile, the importance of the broader civil society organisations such as sports and social clubs is perhaps less obvious. However, when factors such as the avoidance of loneliness or the promotion of healthy physical activity is concerned such organisations can serve an important function in reducing the likelihood of pressures on statutory services (Catalan et al. 1984, South et al. 2008).

Finally, the public sector itself is part of the 'the broad public sector provision'. In emergency services the encouragement of 'first responders' to intervene through, for example, the provision of defibrillators in public settings is such an instance. Community first responders in Scotland have been the subject of study. It shows that the public sector recognises that it needs to have an immediate response to emergencies in rural areas, but it does not have the resource to either staff such provision itself or contract for such provision. So, it works with local people to offer training and support such that they can function in a similar manner to a public-sector professional in an immediate response (Roberts 2014).

Consequently, while public services are provided for all citizens and in particular for those with the greatest need, the nature and concept of those services not only varies but has also long been in flux. For the most vulnerable, this could be seen as academic so long as those services continue to be provided. Inevitably, however, the separation of interests between commissioners, providers and users as well as pressures on funding and the wider socio-economic environment have knock on effects to both service users and service providers.

The Emergence of Discontent

Two big themes to have emerged in the 21st century not only elicited identifiable responses in the leadership and management of public services but can also be seen to have sown the seeds of discontent among service users. The first of these is a near agent principal dilemma where funders of public services are incentivised differently to delivers who are incentivised differently to users. The second is the dramatic effect the global financial crisis had in squeezing public spending at a time when recession meant greater demand for provision for the most vulnerable in society.

The growth of provision via non-governmental actors (whether by the private or not for profit sector) has been associated with a concern with the governance issues of such arrangements. When the service provided is not amenable to a 'product logic' but rather a 'service dominant' logic and the user or beneficiary of the service is not the actual purchaser then this creates a governance problem. In the market context if a service is regarded as poor value for money (and there is some aspect of consumer choice) then a poor service provider will generally fail. However, where the end user is NOT the actual purchaser then this is not necessarily the situation. The example of Serco which was charging the government for electronic tagging of individuals in a way which was found to involve fraudulent or false accounting.[1] The seriousness of the matter was reflected by later charges laid on former senior Serco staff.[2] This example clearly is an example at the radical end of concerns about outsourcing to the private sector but serves to illustrate the nature of concerns. It was not simply a matter of contractual compliance but raised some fundamental questions of the governance of outsourcing of public services.

The importance of governance to ensure that the service provided is being valued by the end user is an ongoing problem regardless of provider. One author, in their professional life, directly experienced the waste involved in local authority provision of equipment to disabled and elderly people; such equipment was never utilised by the intended beneficiaries and was typically eventually found in a non-useable condition when the beneficiary died or was admitted to a care facility. Arguably, when the provision is outsourced then the potential for this is even greater.

Osborne offered New Public Governance theory as a response to the need to have some sort of steering mechanism which operated in the absence of the direct management of services by the public sector or through the mechanisms of outsourcing via contract characterised through mechanisms such as networks which may be self-organising. This could be viewed as a further development from New Public Management. Osborne (2006) distinguishes it in disciplinary terms in that he views it as grounded in organisational sociology.

However, the move away from public services furnished directly by public bodies and the growth of network governance meant that the division between political and administration was becoming more diffuse. Public-sector 'managers' were increasingly needing to take on a leadership role in order to enable and influence public services which they did not directly control but which were spread amongst a range of providers only some of which were controlled via contract (Brookes and Grint 2010).

The issue of the application of 'product based' models to public services has been the subject of comment and discussion by researchers such as Osborne (Osborne et al. 2012, 2015, Osborne 2018). The argument, briefly, is that public goods are primarily service in nature, yet the history of public management has tended towards a product-based approach which is applicable to manufacturing contexts. Osborne and his colleagues argue that 'public services' are not amenable to an approach based on a product-dominated theory (Osborne at al 2013:136).

Osborne draws attention to what he identifies as a 'service dominant logic' stressing the aspects of services, such as their intangibility and the importance of process as opposed to simply the finished product. One is reminded of the comment about sausages that one enjoys the product so long as one is not aware of the process of their production. In a service-dominant logic the process is core to the experience and indeed may dominate over the actual outcome. Harold Shipman, an English family doctor, was one of the most prolific serial killers in history with possibly 250 or more patients as his victims. Yet he was much respected by his patients who initially were strongly supportive of him after his arrest. He was someone who, in the process of providing a service was viewed positively by his patients (Soothill and Wilson 2005). If the issue had been around a dangerous product which led to the death of many then it is questionable whether the users of such a product would have maintained a loyalty to it. Instead the level of support for a local doctor was such that local shopkeepers displayed signs stating support for Dr Shipman (Schechter 2003:110).

The issue for a service dominant logic is that production and consumption occur simultaneously. Also, typically the consumer of the service may participate in the production. So, a health club will require that its member actively engage in the delivery of the fitness regime which the health club offers.

This means that the nature of willingness to participate and also expectations are critical at the interaction between the service provider and the recipient. One author had the experience in a local authority of a dispute between the Director of Social Services and the Chief Executive of the official term to be used in documentation to describe those who received social services. The Director of Social Services adhered to the well-established term 'client', The Chief Executive preferred the then emerging term of 'customer'. The Director's argument was that some recipients of services had no choice because the services were the subject of, for example, a court proceeding or determination. The response of the Chief Executive was that 'precisely because they had no choice the term customer should be used in order to convey the nature of a 'service'.

New Public Service focus thus moved away from the concept of a managerial orientation. It has been given a particular orientation from US academics and it is worth drawing upon their work (Denhardt and Denhardt 2000, 2015). The focus is placed upon 'serving' as opposed to the 'steering' implicit in the outsourcing approach. It has been described as 'post-modern public administration' (Denhardt and Denhardt 2000). It has its roots in concepts of democratic citizenship, concepts of community and civil society. It also draws on organisational humanism which values people more than efficiency and productivity.

The importance of the public service concept in the evolution of public service delivery is that it moves the locus towards a 'value focus' which is not simply linked to 'public values' as represented by the concept of values inculcated into the recruitment and training of public-sector professionals (Perry and Hondeghem 2008). Rather it locates the values in a shared space which includes citizens and civil society. Though one may attribute a common basis to some of these values it cannot be assumed that the values espoused by 'career' public servants are automatically shared by those who do not work (and some cases probably never will work) in the public sector. For example, the concepts of both objective fairness and 'job security' may NOT be commonly shared by civil society where there may be a view that some are 'more deserving' than others and indeed some are not deserving of public services at all. The concept of civil service 'job security and assured pensions' may indeed be regarded with askance by those elements of civil society who do not enjoy such benefits and may see no reason why civil servants should be so favoured. In particular such benefits are not usually found in civil society organisations involved in public service delivery. It was a theme to emerge much more strongly in the second decade of the 21st century.

The global economic crisis which started in 2008 represented the longest and deepest economic downturn since the Great Depression itself. It had a profound impact on public services and the society's most vulnerable, who were most likely to both be impacted by recession and require the support of those services; however they are delivered. Most developed economies suffered from the crisis which required an injection of public funds into the economy to support the collapsing banking sector and eventually a squeeze on public finances meaning an erosion in public service delivery.

The subsequent impact on public finances in the UK led to major cuts in budgets (Clarke and Newman 2012, O'Hara 2015, Youdell and McGimpsey 2015). These cuts led to quite dramatic re-assessment of what services, traditionally within the remit of publicly funded and staffed (such as libraries and public spaces), might move out of this domain and be entrusted to community groups with a focus upon voluntary effort supported by a certain level of grant funding. The level of cuts required particularly of local government meant that there were radical changes in nature of public-sector employment (Bach, S., 2012). To some extent this can be seen as a continuation of a trend towards what has been described as a 'hollowing out of the state' arising from contracting out (Skelcher 2000).

Some of the changes associated with austerity had a synergy with the concepts of co-production which predated the financial crisis (Brudney, and England 1983, Crowley 2013). The arguments for involvement of service users in the co-production agenda (co-design, co-delivery, co-evaluation) originally focussed upon aspects of improvement and consultation (Steen et al. 2019). However austerity brought about an argument also based upon financial stringency (Lowndes and Pratchett 2012, Taylor-Gooby 2012). There were implications for service governance which ensued from the de facto withdrawal or reduction of the public sector in terms of directly managed or contractually funded provision (Davies and Pill 2012, Pollitt et al. 2016).

In a review of the book by Brookes and Grint, Liddle notes that the nature of this austerity post the 2008 financial crisis was possibly associated with the emergence of public leadership. In effect as public-sector budgets were cut or squeezed then pressure was upon public managers to offer leadership where public resource was simply not available to meet the demand (Liddle 2011). This period of austerity, however, further eroded public trust in policy makers since many reliant on public services felt they were suffering disproportionately.

When Discontent Turns to Populism

The story so far has been about external economic and political developments which have led to not only identifiable responses in public service delivery but also the emergence of discontent among the most vulnerable. Each period has an associated public service paradigm with a shift in emphasis, governance mechanism and value base. These are set out for comparison in Table 2.2. Most recently a more illogical and irrational social political environment has emerged with the potential to develop a new, unpredictable, paradigm to which public services must inevitably respond.

The last decade has seen the growth of what has been described as 'populism' in a number of western countries. The election of Donald Trump has been associated with this together with the evidence of the growth of populism in other countries such as Britain, France, Italy and Poland. Such populism is not simply a matter of the 'Far Right' and is also exemplified by instances from the Left (Mair 2013, Mudde 2016, Mudde and Kaltwasser 2017, Eatwell and Goodwin 2018). However, for reasons beyond the remit of this chapter the majority of the academic literature has focussed on the populism of the 'Right'. In discussing the implications for public service delivery we will not restrict our remit to that of simply examining one side.

Populism has largely been analysed and described from the perspective of politics and psychology (Hawkins and Chavismo 2010). The concept is viewed as one in which society is divided into two distinctly separate groups which are seen as oppositional to each other. One group is defined typically as 'the people' and the other group is the existing 'elite' which is regarded as self-interested and self-serving. The 'elite' is seen as encompassing the current representational institutions such as political parties and even bodies such as trade unions and industrial associations.

For a populist movement (whether of Left or Right) such existing intermediate institutions have a tendency to be corrupting of the will of the 'people' as defined by the populist. Hence, populism does not seek to change through some gradualist means those existing institutions. Rather the aim is to 'overthrow the establishment' and to enable the will of the people to be directly put into effect. Mair described this as amounting to a 'partyless democracy' (Mair 2000). This may be mediated by a division between parties which are normally in power and parties which present a populist vision (based on a conflict model in which the establishment is seen as frustrating the will of the people) but which do not have a reasonable chance of attaining power through the conventional political processes. Mudde, Mair and others describe the rise typically of Right Wing populism in both Europe and the USA in such a manner.

For those familiar with events in the USA and in the UK this account of populism may have a familiar resonance. Politics in both countries has taken on a 'populist hue' with a perceived void in the middle ground and an unwillingness to accept the validity of the arguments offered by the 'other'. That can involve the disparaging of the views of 'experts' (Clarke and Newman 2017). The phenomena of 'unfriending' on social media on the basis of how people voted in the Brexit referendum has also drawn comment (Carl 2018).[3]

Table 2.2 New Public Populism in context (© Alex Murdock 2020), bringing it all together (derived from Osborne and Dickinson – Murdock 2020)

Paradigm	Theory	Nature of state	Focus	Emphasis	External relations	Governance mechanism	Value base
Public Admin	Political Science and Public Policy	Unitary	How policy is made	Policy implement	Policy system	Hierarchy	Public sector ethos
NPM	Economics (rational choice)	Disaggregated	Intra Org Management	Service output and input	Contracts and market	Market via contract	Competition
New Public Governance	Org Sociology and Network	Plural	Inter Org Management	Service processes and outcomes	Preferred suppliers and agents	Trust or relational contract	Neo-Corporatist
New Public Leadership	Motivation and Public value	Plural	Achieving change	Value creation	Stakeholders	Leadership and change	Public value
New Public Service	Post Modern PA Democratic theory	Plural	Service	Value people	Citizens	Democracy and citizen accountability	Public interest
New Public Populism	Politics and Psychology	Target for change/ takeover	Nation and localism	Anti-elite/ establishment	Conflict	Citizen movement	Oppositional

The Emergence of New Public Populism

We propose to examine the implications through the lens of three recent and tangible examples. One of these has a largely UK focus, one has a primary focus in France and the third has a wider implication extending to a large number of countries.

The first example which has a particular focus on the UK is the populism associated with Brexit. The second example is that of the (Gilets Jaunes or Yellow Vest) movement in France. The final example is of Extinction Rebellion, which whilst having its origin in the UK has demonstrably far wider implications (Rebellion 2019).

Brexit

The last years in the UK have seen the dominance of the Brexit agenda, which has been significantly linked to populism (Norris and Inglehart 2019). The populist argument (for the 'leaver' vote) was linked to arguments about people feeling 'left behind' and ignored and as a consequence seeking to send a message to the political elite which was seen as responsible for this situation (Barber 2017). There is a strong suggestion that there was a populist motivation behind the vote outcome and the subsequent anger at the lack of progress in carrying out the decision of the referendum (Iakhnis et al. 2018).

The Parliamentary Election of December 2019 which led to a very substantial Conservative majority was seen as significantly a consequence of voters whose natural allegiance to the Labour party in working class constituencies of the Midlands and the North was overcome by a desire to not simply ensure that Brexit was carried out but as a reinforcement of the populist rhetoric of the campaign. It is the most vulnerable citizens who felt that they have never been listened to, who were left behind by globalisation and whose prospects were eroded by competition from foreign workers and a metropolitan elite who no longer shared their values. Potentially failure of both the major parties in the UK to address the concerns of those who felt disregarded and disadvantaged could lie behind the reasons for the Brexit vote. Public Services, seen in terms of our narrow definition of basic legal provision, would probably not have sufficed. The concerns were around the wider aspects including fears (whether valid or not) of a loss of a national identity (Iakhnis et al. 2018).

The implications of the Brexit vote and the level of resentment and concern which underpinned it is arguably likely to impact on public service provision particularly in the areas which voted heavily for leaving the EU. One such Northern England municipality, Hartlepool, (at the time of writing) has a mayor from the Brexit party and through independent councillors joining the Brexit party may be a possible indicator of what may be the implications for public services for a populist dominated local authority.[4] The town had been especially hard hit by austerity and funding cuts and ranked amongst the poorest communities in the UK.[5] Though the Labour MP retained his seat in the December 2019 election this was only on account of a strong showing for the Brexit party which in effect split the vote. Due to pre- and post-election promises made by Boris Johnson, the Conservative Prime Minister, areas such as Hartlepool have an expectation of better treatment in terms of public services that address their particular concerns, which are local in nature, and they perhaps view localism and 'Britishness' as taking precedence over any multi-cultural and 'equality' priorities, even if they are embedded in law.

These expectations which Boris Johnson, the Prime Minister has generated over promises to 'repay' the votes he describes as 'lent' to the Conservative Party by electors in previously Labour areas may well indicate a refocussing of public service delivery. Pundits have ascribed the failure of Labour as in part down to promises to restore welfare provision to such areas when what voters were seeking was a conscious rebalancing of economic opportunities to redress what had been lost. Welfare schemes manifestly may not do this and would have had the potential to trap the areas into welfare dependency. After the election, Goodwin regarded the result as demonstrating that the Labour party were no longer the party of the 'working class'.[6]

The implications of this is that – influenced by populism – public service delivery may need to respond to pressures which seek a focus upon addressing the needs for 'local people' interpreted in a way which is at variance with traditional public-sector values of professional detachment and which may also add an implicit need for reassurance that perceived 'imbalances' will be corrected.

The Gilet Jaunes

The disruption caused nationally in France by the 'Yellow Vest' movement was seen as a populist response to certain government policies (in particular the raising of fuel prices). The Yellow Vest nickname was derived from the legal requirement to have such a safety vest in a vehicle. The movement gathered force with both petitions and disruptive (and illegal) actions that closed city centres and prevented or impeded transportation.

The movement was seen as based in the smaller towns and more rural areas which, perhaps similarly to areas of the UK, saw themselves as left behind and ignored. Those involved were often lower paid but working people who saw themselves as losing ground economically. Analysis of the movement found that it had populist aspects of both the far right and far left in its demands.[7] Other analysis suggested that the protests were a function of not the poor – who took little part – but those who had some degree of work security and income but who saw themselves as potentially 'losing out' as a consequence of reforms particularly to pensions and reduced spending power.[8]

What is of little dispute, however, is the challenge to the 'state' it represented, and the fracturing of society revealed together with the circumvention of the normal channels of democratic policy discourse. Planned policies were disrupted and the government had to make promises in response. The Yellow Vest movement has demonstrated a malaise and concern about the failure of the state to address the demands of a substantial proportion of the population who then regard the normal democratic channels as insufficient (Chamorel 2019).

In public services terms the Yellow Vest movement represents a 'bottom up' quasi 'leaderless' phenomena, which, through sheer weight of numbers, combined with the ability to disrupt, can potentially influence policy agendas. It is not the same as the organised strikes which are not uncommon in France. In fact, the French Trade Unions stayed aloof from the Yellow Vest protests in part because they saw them as not 'led by' their membership. The Yellow Vests represent a sort of force of nature in themselves which, given mass support, can impact on public policy and resource allocation decisions. The protest involved not just civil disobedience but actual criminality (the destruction of speed cameras and burning of vehicles). At least ten people died as a direct consequence of the Yellow Vest protests.[9] Many more have been injured, some seriously. One estimate is that around 100 deaths are indirectly attributable in particular to the destruction of speed cameras and a subsequent increase in road fatalities attributed to this.[10]

There appears little evidence of serious prosecutions of 'leaders' of the Yellow Vest protests (a search found just one prosecution leading to a fine)[11] However a number of policemen were charged with offences arising from their actions and 174 such incidents were reported.[12] This potentially has significant implications in respect of public services in that 'populist' actions such as the Yellow Vests may bring more negative consequences for public employees tasked with trying to respond to them than is the case in more structured protest actions such as Trade Union organised strikes or formal demonstrations.

Extinction Rebellion

The third example of a populist movement is that of Extinction Rebellion which was established in the UK in May 2018. It was in form a grassroots movement which severely disrupted London in October and November 2018 by blocking streets and bridges. It is described as loosely networked and decentralised (Horton 2019).

The movement's aim is to achieve system change in particular in respect of climate change and loss of biodiversity. It draws its inspiration from previous movements against nuclear weapons and the civil rights movement. The use of mass protest is accompanied by an acceptance of acts which are illegal and may lead to arrest. However, it is non-violent in nature, and there have not been the same deaths and injuries associated with the activities of the Yellow Vest movement. However, the movement shares with the Yellow Vest the mechanism of major civil disruption particularly of transport systems.

It has rapidly spread to other countries particularly the US and Australia. The mass arrest as a tactic distinguishes it from the Yellow Vests and clearly is drawn from the Civil Rights movement strategies in India and the USA. However, it is arguably not diverse in nature with relatively little reach into the poorest sections of society. One UK think tank (Policy Exchange) defined them as an extremist group, noting that 'the underlying extremism of the campaign has been largely obscured from public view by what many see as the fundamental legitimacy of their stated cause'.[13]

The implications of Extinction Rebellion for public service delivery are considerable. Their objectives are based on what they view as the threat of climate change and loss of bio-diversity, the threat of which is seen as having a scientific basis (Gardner and Wordley 2019). An obvious impact is the actual cost of policing which has been estimated at over £37 million (or the equivalent of 1,000 police officers). It was reported that Extinction Rebellion cost was twice that of responding to violent crime over the period of the disruptions.[14] The implications for public service budgets of such mass populist actions are considerable and arguably have the predictable effect of 'de-prioritising' other public service activities.

Some protestors glued themselves to public transport (some of which was arguably environmentally friendly – an electric train). Their protests have been met with considerable sympathy (at least initially) by police who saw the participants as law abiding citizens exercising a right to protest – even if it caused major disruption and a degree of damage. The reaction of the courts to those arrested has been equally mild and even the protestors who glued themselves to public service vehicles were treated with sympathy.[15]

As with the Yellow Vests there have been complaints against the police with likely prosecutions for unlawful arrest and challenges to police bans or restrictions on protest.[16] Though these are not on the scale of what happened with the Yellow Vest in France nevertheless such a mass use of the court system by educated and well-resourced protestors must represent a concern to both the police and to the civil authorities. The likelihood of sympathetic juries may also weigh in the balance.

Thus, such civil disobedience on a large scale has the clear potential to disrupt public service delivery. Road or airport development schemes clearly would have the potential to arouse the ire of Extinction Rebellion and concerns about ecology could impact upon a wide range of public services. What currently is determined through democratic and professional decision processes could find that the determination is heavily affected by the actions of a mass movement whose members are, in some cases, indifferent to the strictures of law and willing to risk arrest and even incarceration for their cause. The potential for thousands of additional entrants to an already overcrowded prison system (if they refused to pay fines or to be 'bound over') would probably keep any Home Secretary awake at night. Extinction Rebellion in its essence challenges the very concept of conventional public-sector policy making by engaging in direct action which by-passes the normal democratic political processes.

These three examples bring out some common factors which all have implications for public services delivery. First, they all deny the notion of a mutually acceptable 'middle ground' or space for substantial compromise. They represent an 'either/or choice' between two radically different options. Public policy and public service decisions based on an incremental basis which authors such as Lindblom described have arguably no acceptable fit with this alternative of two perceived extremes (Dror 1964).

Allied to this is the rejection not only of rational debate but also of evidence. The notable riposte to an informed challenge during the UK EU Referendum campaign came from Cabinet Minister and Leave advocate Michael Gove: 'People in this country have had enough of experts' he told a television audience.

A further implication is a potential rejection of the usual mechanisms of democratic governance. A duly elected government (whether at a national or a local level) is viewed as illegitimate or unacceptable when making a decision which one side of the populist argument rejects. Indeed, a government seeking to find a compromise may well discover that both side of the argument dispute and reject their right to effect such consensus.

This lack of acceptance of traditional governance modes means that alternative methods of bringing about change are not only possible but are actively practiced. In effect as the electoral system is seen as having failed then the 'mob' becomes a legitimate alternative. There is nothing new about this and there is ample evidence of such a mechanism from the earliest history of Greek democracy to the present day (McClelland 2010).

This brings us to a further implication which is that of the growth of actual illegality as a means of bringing about change. The examples above have shown the willingness of populist activists to break the law in pursuit of their objective. Though such law breaking may lead to convictions and legal penalties, it may also be deliberately calculated to frustrate the process of justice. To arrest and convict a handful of people who are breaking the law is not a problem. When it becomes thousands of people then the system cannot cope unless it resorts to extreme measures such as are found in countries which eschew democratic process and hum rights. In effect such mass protest can represent a denial of the right of the state to function.

The implications of this for public services is considerable. Extinction Rebellion and the Yellow Vests in effect denied the freedom of movement of citizens and frustrated the operation of public services such as travel and arguably the movement of goods and services. When such action is targeted at specific aspects of public service delivery then it has the potential to deny or impede the operation of a particular service. In Germany a recent article noted the growth of terrorism in response to immigration and the fluidity of the nature of the involvement which included people who were public servants (Koehler 2018). When people have strong opinions and are willing to take extreme and illegal measures then the normal operation of public services can become difficult. Placing migrants in a geographical location where not only are they unwelcome among local inhabitants, but some are prepared to engage in law breaking is highly problematic. Extinction Rebellion could be seen in terms of an eco-activist known as Swampy who impeded road construction some 20 years ago through digging tunnels in the path of the proposed road and living in them.[17] We would argue that it is not whether one agrees or not with the nature of the populist extreme but rather the way that it can frustrate the operation of public services.

New Public Populism as a Response

Are there currently examples of how the public sector can respond to the phenomena of populism enabling public services to continue to be delivered to the most vulnerable? Rather than addressing the challenge in theoretical terms, in this final section we propose to offer and to critique an example of practice. In doing so, the chapter initiates a debate around the central tenets of what could be a 'New Public Populism' paradigm.

A natural concern people have is to 'protect' and safeguard themselves against a perceived outside threat. Localism is a well-established concept which recognises that people have a geographic affinity and that public policy should both acknowledge and support this (Davoudi and Madanipour 2015). This has found an example in practice of Community Wealth Building (CWB). It originated in Cleveland in the USA (Howard 2012). The principal behind CVB is to retain wealth locally and it is particularly applicable to cities or communities which have suffered decline. It represents a different approach to the traditional regeneration models in that it focusses on local initiatives and, in particular, procurement decisions. A recent think tank publication explores this as a way forward (Guinan and O'Neill 2019). Community Wealth Building is seen as an example of what is described as New Municipalism. The state is seen as a facilitating institution enabling collaboration and crossovers between sectors. The focus is upon building local wealth as opposed to redistributing wealth from those that have to those that are in need (McInroy 2018).

In the UK the town of Preston furnishes an example of this in practice. They note that the key elements of Community Wealth Building encompass the following elements: (CLES May 2019).[18]

- Plural Ownership of the local economy which focusses on co-ops and locally based organisations
- Making Finance work through local investment
- Fair employment and just Labour Markets
- Progressive procurement – dense local supply chains
- Socially productive use of land and property
- Identification and support of anchor institutions (such as local educational colleges and universities)

CLES (the Centre for Local Economic Strategies) has undertaken a great deal of work with local municipalities to enable such Community Wealth Building to develop and to be evaluated. The attraction of this for the future evolution of public services is significant. The retention of employment locally not just in terms of the actual earnings but also in respect of spending is key to community wealth building. The importance of local 'anchor institutions' which may be in any sector (Public, Private or Third Sector) is evident in enabling this to happen.

The implications of procurement and investment decisions which stress localism are that the usual commercial considerations of, for example, lowest cost may need to stand aside in the interests of retaining wealth within the community. Similarly, it has possible implications for 'fair employment' in that procurement may focus upon the employment of locally based residents as opposed to workers who are brought in from outside the defined locality. The concept of a 'living wage' may also be stressed with a focus upon employing people who are in need of work as opposed to those who may be best suited to the particular work. Social Enterprises are familiar with this concept of reaching out to those who are 'furthest away' from employment. However, it has not been characteristic of private sector companies whose focus has been upon 'maximising shareholder value'. In the UK the Public Services (Social Value) Act of 2012 provided a basis for social clauses in public-sector procurement.[19] However, Community Wealth Building aims to reach beyond just the use of municipal procurement by public bodies and encourage all local employers to consider local factors and to engage in 'fair and just' employment practices (Lockey and Glover 2019).

Community Wealth Building has obvious benefits and potentially may well address pressures arising from populism. The local focus and stress upon employment of residents would address some populist pressures particularly an antipathy to 'globalism'. However, some could suggest that if localism was taken to a logical extreme then it could lead to a zero-sum game situation where employment and investment becomes highly localised with the consequences of rigidity of both the labour and commercial markets.

In Ireland there have been very successful Citizens Assemblies which have considered complex and emotive issues: abortion, fixed term referendums, parliaments, aging and climate change. Established after the 2016 general election, they involved ordinary Irish citizens representative of the population who were asked to deliberate on these questions. Those deliberations were supported by a professional secretariat and expert witnesses.

Such localism can also serve to ameliorate the concerns of movements such as Extinction Rebellion if it focussed upon local sourcing of food and recycling schemes. Local 'ethical' generation of 'green' power would also find favour.

Conclusion

Public services exist to support the most vulnerable in society. Defining what actually constitutes 'public services' lies at the root of deciding on delivery. If a 'narrow' concept is applied, then such services can be limited to those which are mandated by legal obligation (such as police and fire services). Here the usual concept is either direct delivery by public servants or by fairly narrowly defined contractual arrangements. The broader concept of 'public services' brings with it constructions which may and will involve a range of actors – some of which may be informal. Such a broad construction is not at all dependent upon legal obligation and indeed may lie outside of significant regulation by the state.

The successive explanatory approaches from traditional public administration through to the emerging concept of populism have been set out in Diagram 2. Each approach is associated with particular conceptions of how public services are defined. The most recent and least researched (in terms of public management literature) is populism. The possible impact of populism for public services and public management is considerable and here we suggest the beginnings of a fresh paradigm in the form of New Public Populism.

The implications of populism pose a particular challenge to public service delivery. The nature of populism suggest it is not open to compromise or 'seeking a middle ground'. Neither is it tolerant of traditional democratic mechanisms (unless they lead to the outcomes which populism seeks) and it is accepting of means which do not respect the law.

However, we suggest that there may be routes which public service delivery may find which treads a possibly uneasy path in such uncertain times. Community Wealth Building is offered as such an example. With time and innovation others may emerge.

Notes

1 See www.bbc.co.uk/news/business-48853870 Accessed 1 December 2019.
2 See www.bbc.co.uk/news/uk-50806919 Accessed 20 December 2019.
3 Note: Figure 2 First 3 paradigms derived from Helen Dickinson in Butcher and Gilchrist (2016:44). The revised figure is the work of © Alex Murdock 2020.
4 Source: www.thenorthernecho.co.uk/news/17900531.brexit-party-takes-hold-hartlepool-borough-council/ Accessed 1 Dec 2019.
5 See www.newstatesman.com/politics/uk/2019/03/there-ll-be-uprising-hartlepool-life-brexit-town-no-deal-sight Accessed 20 Dec 2019.
6 See www.thetimes.co.uk/article/meet-the-new-left-behind-labours-middle-class-elite-g0w9scnd9 Accessed 24 Dec 2019.
7 Source: Mathilde Damgé; Anne-Aël Durand; Maxime Vaudano; Jérémie Baruch; Pierre Breteau (4 December 2018). "Sur un axe de Mélenchon à Le Pen, où se situent les revendications des 'gilets jaunes'?". *Le Monde* Accessed 22 Dec 2019.
8 Source: laviedesidees.fr/La-couleur-des-gilets-jaunes.html Accessed 22 Dec 2019.
9 Source www.telegraph.co.uk/news/2018/12/22/driver-killed-accident-yellow-vest-roadblock-southern-france/ Accessed 22 Dec 2019.
10 See www.thelocal.fr/20190404/opinion-how-the-gilets-jaunes-killed-over-100-people-in-four-months Accessed 22 Dec 2019.
11 See www.wsws.org/en/articles/2019/06/11/vest-j11.html Accessed 22 Dec 2019.
12 Source: www.telegraph.co.uk/news/2019/05/30/french-police-face-charges-yellow-vest-injuries/ Accessed 22 Dec 2019.
13 Source: policyexchange.org.uk/publication/extremism-rebellion/ Accessed 20 Dec 2019.
14 Source: www.theguardian.com/uk-news/2019/oct/22/extinction-rebellion-protests-cost-met-police-37m-so-far Accessed 21 Dec 2019.
15 Source: www.bbc.co.uk/news/uk-england-london-50839406 Accessed 20 Dec 2019.
16 Source: www.theguardian.com/environment/2019/nov/06/police-ban-on-extinction-rebellion-protests-ruled-illegal-by-high-court Accessed 20 Dec 2019.
17 Source: www.theguardian.com/environment/2019/oct/09/eco-warrior-swampy-on-extinction-rebellion-it-gives-me-hope Accessed 20 Dec 2019.
18 Source: www.preston.gov.uk/media/1792/How-we-built-community-wealth-in-Preston/pdf/CLES_Preston_Document_WEB_AW.pdf?m=636994067328930000 Accessed 20 Dec 2019.
19 Source: www.legislation.gov.uk/ukpga/2012/3/enacted Accessed 20 Dec 2019.

References

Bach, S., 2012. Shrinking the state or the Big Society? Public service employment relations in an era of austerity. *Industrial Relations Journal*, 43(5), pp. 399–415.
Barber, S., 2017. The Brexit environment demands that deliberative democracy meets inclusive growth. *Local Economy*, 32(3), pp. 219–239.
Bennett, J., Iossa, E. and Legrenzi, G., 2003. The role of commercial non-profit organizations in the provision of public services. *Oxford Review of Economic Policy*, 19(2), pp. 335–347.
Bovaird, T. 2006. Developing new forms of partnership with the 'Market' in the procurement of public services. *Public Administration*, 84(1), pp. 81–102.

Brandsen, T. and Pestoff, V., 2006. Co-production, the third sector and the delivery of public services: An introduction. *Public Management Review*, 8(4), pp. 493–501.

Brookes, S. and Grint, K., 2010. A new public leadership challenge? In Brookes, S. and Grint, K., (eds), *The new public leadership challenge* (pp. 1–15). London, Palgrave Macmillan.

Brudney, J.L. and England, R.E., 1983. Toward a definition of the coproduction concept. *Public Administration Review*, 43(1), pp. 59–65.

Butcher, J. and Gilchrist, D. eds., 2016. *The three sector solution: Delivering public policy in collaboration with not-for-profits and business.* Canberra, ANU Press.

Carl, N., 2018. Leavers have a better understanding of Remainers' motivations than vice versa. LSE Brexit Blog, London School of Economics, https://blogs.lse.ac.uk/brexit/2018/05/04/leavers-have-a-better-understanding-of-remainers-motivations-than-vice-versa/.

Catalan, J., Gath, D., Edmonds, G. and Ennis, J., 1984. The effects of non-prescribing of anxiolytics in general practice: I. Controlled evaluation of psychiatric and social outcome. *The British Journal of Psychiatry*, 144(6), pp. 593–602.

Chamorel, P., 2019. Macron versus the yellow vests. *Journal of Democracy*, 30(4), pp. 48–62.

Clarke, J. and Newman, J., 2012. The alchemy of austerity. *Critical Social Policy*, 32(3), pp. 299–319.

Clarke, J. and Newman, J., 2017. 'People in this country have had enough of experts': Brexit and the paradoxes of populism. *Critical Policy Studies*, 11(1), pp. 101–116.

CLES, May 2019. How we built community wealth in Preston Council and CLES. Manchester, Centre for Local Economic Strategies.

Crowley, N., 2013. Lost in austerity: Rethinking the community sector. *Community Development Journal*, 48(1), pp. 151–157.

Davies, J.S. and Pill, M., 2012. Hollowing out neighbourhood governance? Rescaling revitalisation in Baltimore and Bristol. *Urban Studies*, 49(10), pp. 2199–2217.

Davoudi, S. and Madanipour, A. eds., 2015. *Reconsidering localism.* Abingdon, Routledge.

Delpirou, A., 2018. La couleur des Gilets jaunes. *La vie des idées, en ligne.* https://laviedesidees.fr/IMG/pdf/20181123_giletsjaunes-3.pdf (Accessed 20 December 2019)

Denhardt, R.B. and Denhardt, J.V., 2000. The new public service: Serving rather than steering. *Public Administration Review*, 60(6), 549–559.

Denhardt, J.V. and Denhardt, R.B., 2015. *The new public service: Serving, not steering.* Abingdon, Routledge.

Dror, Y., 1964. Muddling through- "Science" or inertia? *Public Administration Review*, 24(3), 153–157.

Dunleavy, P. and Hood, C., 1994. From old public administration to new public management. *Public Money & Management*, 14(3), pp. 9–16.

Eatwell, R. and Goodwin, M., 2018. *National populism: The revolt against liberal democracy.* London, Penguin Publishers.

Gardner, C.J. and Wordley, C.F., 2019. Scientists must act on our own warnings to humanity. *Nature Ecology & Evolution*, 3(9), pp. 1271–1272.

Guinan, J. and O'Neill, M., 2019. From community wealth-building to system change. *IPPR Progressive Review*, *25*(4), pp. 382–392.

Hawkins, K.A. and Chavismo, V.S., 2010. *Populism in comparative perspective*. Cambridge, Cambridge University Press.

Hood, C., 1991. A public management for all seasons? *Public Administration*, *69*(1), pp. 3–19.

Hood, C., 1995. Contemporary public management: A new global paradigm? *Public Policy and Administration*, *10*(2), pp. 104–117.

Hood, C. and Peters, G., 2004. The middle aging of new public management: Into the age of paradox? *Journal of Public Administration Research and Theory*, *14*(3), pp. 267–282.

Hood, C., 2006. Gaming in targetworld: The targets approach to managing British public services. *Public Administration Review*, *66*(4), pp. 515–521.

Horton, R., 2019. Offline: Extinction or rebellion? *The Lancet*, *394*(10205), p. 1216.

Howard, T., 2012. Owning your own job is a beautiful thing: Community wealth building in Cleveland, Ohio. Investing in What Works for America's Communities. Essays on People, Place & Purpose, *Democracy Collaborative*, pp. 204–214.

Hyndman, N. and Lapsley, I., 2016. New public management: The story continues. *Financial Accountability & Management*, *32*(4), pp. 385–408.

Iakhnis, E., Rathbun, B., Reifler, J. and Scotto, T.J., 2018. Populist referendum: Was 'Brexit' an expression of nativist and anti-elitist sentiment? *Research & Politics*, *5*(2), pp. 1–7.

Koehler, D., 2018. Recent trends in German right-wing violence and terrorism: What are the contextual factors behind 'hive terrorism'? *Perspectives on Terrorism*, *12*(6), pp. 72–88.

Liddle, J., 2011. The new public leadership challenge. *International Journal of Public Sector Management*, *24*(1), pp. 97–98. doi: 10.1108/09513551111099244.

Lockey, A. and Glover, B., 2019. The wealth within. Source: www.demos.co.uk

Lowndes, V. and Pratchett, L., 2012. Local governance under the coalition government: Austerity, localism and the 'Big Society'. *Local Government Studies*, *38*(1), pp. 21–40.

Mair, P., 2013. *Ruling the void: The hollowing of Western democracy*. Brooklyn, NY, Verso Trade.

McClelland, J.S., 2010. *The crowd and the mob (Routledge revivals): From Plato to Canetti*. Abingdon, Routledge.

McDonnell, J., 2019. *Economics for the many*. Brooklyn, NY, Verso.

McInroy, N., 2018. Wealth for all: Building new local economies. *Local Economy*, *33*(6), pp. 678–687.

Mudde, C. ed., 2016. *The populist radical right: A reader*. Abingdon, Taylor & Francis, Routledge.

Mudde, C. and Kaltwasser, C.R., 2017. *Populism: A very short introduction*. Oxford, Oxford University Press.

Norris, P. and Inglehart, R., 2019. *Cultural backlash: Trump, Brexit, and authoritarian populism*. Cambridge, Cambridge University Press.

O'Hara, M., 2015. *Austerity bites: A journey to the sharp end of cuts in the UK*. Bristol, Policy Press.

O'Neill, M., 2018. INTERVIEW: Beyond extraction: The political power of community wealth building. *Renewal: A Journal of Labour Politics*, *26*(2), pp. 46–53.

Osborne, S.P. 2006. The new public governance? *Public Management Review*, 8(3), 377–387.

Osborne, S.P., Radnor, Z. and Nasi, G., 2013. A new theory for public service management? Toward a (public) service-dominant approach. *The American Review of Public Administration*, 43(2), pp. 135–158.

Osborne, S.P., Radnor, Z., Kinder, T. and Vidal, I., 2015. The SERVICE framework: A public-service-dominant approach to sustainable public services. *British Journal of Management*, 26(3), pp. 424–438.

Osborne, S.P., 2018. *From public service-dominant logic to public service logic: Are public service organizations capable of co-production and value co-creation?* Abingdon, Routledge, Taylor and Francis

Perry, J.L. and Hondeghem, A. eds., 2008. *Motivation in public management: The call of public service*. Oxford, Oxford University Press on Demand.

Pickard, S. and Glendinning, C., 2002. Comparing and contrasting the role of family carers and nurses in the domestic health care of frail older people. *Health & Social Care in the Community*, 10(3), pp. 144–150.

Pollitt, C., 2016. *Advanced introduction to public management and administration*. Cheltenham, Edward Elgar Publishing.

Pollitt, C., Birchall, J. and Putman, K., 2016. *Decentralising public service management*. London, Macmillan International Higher Education.

Rebellion, D.E., 2019. An open letter to Extinction Rebellion. *Journal of Global Faultlines*, 6(1), pp. 109–112.

Rhodes, R.A., 1994. The hollowing out of the state: The changing nature of the public service in Britain. *The Political Quarterly*, 65(2), pp. 138–151.

Roberts, J.M. and Devine, F., 2003. The hollowing out of the welfare state and social capital. *Social Policy and Society*, 2(4), pp. 309–318.

Roberts, A., Nimegeer, A., Farmer, J. and Heaney, D.J., 2014. The experience of community first responders in co-producing rural health care: In the liminal gap between citizen and professional. *BMC Health Services Research*, 14(1), p. 460.

Salamon, L.M., 1987. Of market failure, voluntary failure, and third-party government: Toward a theory of government-nonprofit relations in the modern welfare state. *Journal of Voluntary Action Research*, 16(1–2), pp. 29–49.

Schechter, H., 2003. *The Serial Killer Files*. New York, Ballanntine Books.

Skelcher, C., 2000. Changing images of the state: Overloaded, hollowed-out, congested. *Public Policy and Administration*, 15(3), pp. 3–19.

Soothill, K. and Wilson, D., 2005. Theorising the puzzle that is Harold Shipman. *Journal of Forensic Psychiatry & Psychology*, 16(4), pp. 685–698.

South, J., Higgins, T.J., Woodall, J. and White, S.M., 2008. Can social prescribing provide the missing link? *Primary Health Care Research & Development*, 9(4), pp. 310–318.

Steen, T., Brandsen, T. and Verschuere, B., 2019. Public administration into the wild: Grappling with co-production and social innovation. In *A Research Agenda for Public Administration*. Cheltenham, Edward Elgar Publishing.

Taylor-Gooby, P., 2012. 'Hollowing out' versus the new interventionism: Public attitudes and welfare futures. In Svallfors, S. and Taylor-Gooby, P. (eds), *The End of the Welfare State?* (pp. 13–24). Abingdon, Routledge.

Youdell, D. and McGimpsey, I., 2015. Assembling, disassembling and reassembling 'youth services' in Austerity Britain. *Critical Studies in Education*, 56(1), pp. 116–130.

3 The Impact of Brexit on Vulnerability

Using a Theoretical Lens of Transnational and Local Linkages

Joyce Liddle and Gareth David Addidle

Introduction

On Thursday, 23rd June, the United Kingdom voted to leave the European Union. Since then, there has been relatively little public discussion, or analysis of, the likely implications for policing, criminal justice or security. Almost without exception, discussion and debate has focussed on Brexit's economic implications (Rix, 2016). Most academic literature and policy research has been focussed on the local and regional consequences of Brexit within regional economic development (Barber, 2017, 219–239, North, 2017, 204–218, Levell et al., 2018, HOC, HCLG, 2019), but there has been relatively little attention paid to the transnational challenges and local consequences for UK policing, security and criminal justice, and few works have examined how the Police (and other Emergency and Blue Light Service Leaders) will maintain pan-European and transnational relationships or deal with the local impacts and consequences in a post-Brexit world. According to a recent report the extent to which the European Union (EU) and the UK will work together on policing, security and criminal justice remains a crucial, but under-discussed aspect of the future relationship between the two sides (Durrant et al., ILG, 2018).

In the first section of this chapter there is a broad context setting of Brexit drawing on literature and relevant policy documentary source materials. Then a short examination of some extant politics, geography, cultural, sociology and business/strategy literature on transnational linkages and local connections to frame the later discussion of findings, on what the consequences arising from Brexit might mean for UK policing and security (and other emergency and blue light services) and the criminal justice system.

The findings are discussed through the lens of transnational theory, which has not previously been adopted to examine this specific policy field. Discussion of the findings at both transnational and local scales are analysed separately to identify the transnational challenges and local consequences, and then a synthetic section links the transnational to the local scale to show that relationships and inter-connections across spatial levels within policing, security and criminal justice may have detrimental impacts on how agencies respond to an escalation in vulnerable individuals and groups at local levels. We conclude by suggesting that policing, security and criminal justice have hitherto, been largely absent from political and academic discussions on Brexit; the implications of Brexit will have far reaching and long term consequences in this policy domain with a severe potential knock-on effect of a rise in 'wicked' social issues. Therefore there is a greater need for future research in this important field if we are to fill gaps in current knowledge and understandings of not only transnational-local linkages, connections and consequences, but also to increase the knowledge base of some of the major, underlying and contested explanations of who the vulnerable individuals and groups in society are, how to interrogate the causes and consequences of a rise in Vulnerability, and more significantly how police and security agencies might address these growing problems.

Context

As the UK heads towards Brexit, and once the dust settles following the outcome of the December 2019 UK General Election, new elected Members of Parliament will reflect on how the seismic shift in public opinion led to the election of a Conservative Party with a large majority to take control of the country. Despite many contested arguments and recriminations on what exactly went wrong for the Labour Party in its traditional (poorer) heartlands, it is clear that the Conservative Government led by Prime Minister Boris Johnson, with his vow to 'get Brexit done by the end of January 2020' will face many unknowns. The future of many deprived and de-industrialised areas of the UK is far from certain because after the Brexit Withdrawal Bill goes through Parliament Brexit negotiations may not commence proper until the end of 2020. The overall economic situation is difficult to predict, despite a rise in sterling in the immediate aftermath of the General Election, and the investment plans of large manufacturers such as Nissan, Komatsu and others hang in the balance. The full consequences of Brexit may take years to play out and much is unknown on the types of trade deals the British Government may secure in future negotiations. It is also unclear if, and how, any future negotiations could directly benefit deprived regions, because recently elected Conservative MPs representing the former Northern Labour heartlands may have limited input into the Brexit process. Moreover, some regions with poor social and economic legacies, which are therefore dominated by public services, may disproportionately feel the economic effects of Brexit in comparison to some southern regions: for example in terms of recruitment into the NHS and other services. Moreover, there could be unpredicted consequences for vulnerable groups and individuals.

In a recent (2019) publication 'The North East after Brexit: Impact and Policy' Liddle and Shutt argue on the importance of city leaders developing a stronger regional and sub regional voice in the decade ahead. Brexit cannot be regarded as a one-off episode but part of an on-going process that will require both caution and continued vigilance if the UK Government is to deliver on its declared promises to the British people. Newly elected MPs representing, in particular poorer, Northern regions have a duty on behalf of their constituents to continue to lobby central government on the shape of a future UK Spending Review, on the distribution mechanism for the UK Shared Prosperity Fund (the declared replacement fund to make up the shortfall in EU funding) and on the specific policy levers such as the UK Industrial Strategy that will rebalance the national economy and bring industry and new investment to Northern areas, and away from its concentration in London and the SE. The Johnson Government has made assurances that key policies on transport, economic development, health, education and crime will rebalance the North/South divide and deal with the legacy of 'wicked' problems. The need for decent homes, good quality schools, health and social care, reduced crime and increased community resilience and cohesion, plus good air quality and environmental security are all essential to future national and regional development. However, despite the electoral promises to spend more on policing, the health service (especially mental health), adult and social care (Conservative Party Manifesto, November 2019), it remains unclear as to how spending plans can be achieved without a rise in either income tax, national Insurance or VAT.

Localities, including those where deprivation and disadvantage are more evident must now compete for new investment funds, such as the UK Shared Prosperity Fund, Industrial Strategy Challenge Funds, forthcoming transformative funds for transport, housing and health. All of these will stem from the next UK major Spending Review which apparently is aimed at lifting the UK away from the austerity age into a new age of public services reform and commitment, any impacts may have far reaching consequences in localities where vulnerable individual and groups live and work.

Many city and regional leaders are concerned at the continuing incidences of economic and social decay and escalation in vulnerable individuals, with consequential repercussions for the criminal justice system, police and other public service providers. There is a prevailing view that without the promised investment, even greater levels of social discord and disharmony may destabilise the country as a whole. City leaders have already deployed existing powers and resources to build homes, invest in infrastructure and introduce local policies to enhance the skills base needed for labour markets. However, there is no doubt that the challenges ahead for the UK's cities and regions could be immense, unless there is some real recognition of the deep seated and long-term structural issues brought on by de-industrialisation and the loss of key employment opportunities in local areas.

In deprived areas of the country public service provision is hugely important, and for numerous fractured localities, there has been an undoubted rise in social problems and an increased need for public services to deal with vulnerable groups. The emergency and blue light services, social services, care organisations, mental health, food bank providers, those dealing with immigrants, refugees, or rough sleepers are all facing increased demands. All public, private and other civic and social sectors have been transformed over the more recent past, as each sought to improve their capabilities on collaborative working in developing new approaches in response to a changing world. There is much evidence to show that where the local state has retreated from direct service provision many third sector, private sector, civic, voluntary and faith-based groups and charities have stepped into the breach and are providing many of the services for vulnerable groups that were once the sole preserve of local public agencies.

Brexit was indeed an external and unexpected shock to Parliamentary systems in the UK and other EU states, with on-going issues surrounding democratic legitimacy of decision making, but raises much wider issues on whether or not current parliamentary and participatory processes have the capacity to deal with extraordinary events and crises (Christiansen and Fromage, 2019), but more significant is the fact that while the protracted Brexit negotiations will continue for some considerable time

> at home, social services are falling apart due to austerity cuts, death rates arising among infants and the elderly since 2014, state schools budgets slashed, fewer homes for those who need them, a rapid rise in street homelessness, larger numbers of children spending Christmas in bed and breakfast accommodation, with entire families occupying one room. These are indeed desperate times.
>
> (Dorling and Tomlinson, 2019)

Despite the Conservative Party promised on increased spending on policing, National Health Service, Social Care and Schools, there is general agreement that after over ten years of austerity and budget cuts to local services any new funding will hardly replace the earlier cuts to service provision, including those to the police and criminal justice system.

Global shifts are impacting greatly on local economies with rises in terrorism, international crime, people trafficking, drug smuggling and many other issues facing Police Leaders who are already dealing with a multitude of domestic policy issues. The loss of European Funds, especially in deprived areas will hit local economies very harshly, and the lack of alternative sources of inward investment, it is argued, could exacerbate the North/South divide (Liddle and Shutt, 2019a). Many city and regional leaders are not convinced that the Conservative Government, or any future UK Government will be committed to make up the shortfall in European funding, in the short term at least, and recent statements from Northern leaders have raised concerns on the levels of inclusive growth and equality that can be achieved in response to a diminution of European financial support packages (Gibney, Liddle and Shutt, forthcoming, 2020). The long-term deprivation and deep-seated economic, social and environmental problems of older industrial areas may be set to continue without drastic policy interventions (see a wider discussion in Shutt and Liddle, 2019b). Indeed, many of those working in UK public services generally accord with the view that the system is in crisis, and it will take more than a short-term injection of investment to solve the long-standing 'wicked issues' such as a rise in Vulnerability.

The decision to leave the EU could have long-term ramifications beyond British shores, in terms of maintaining trading relations, or seeking out alternative markets for goods and services; and the ability to attract labour, skills and foreign direct investment; and develop commercial relationships across national boundaries. If, as it seems likely from recent Ministerial and Prime Ministerial statements that the British will gain agreement to withdrawing from both the Single Market and the Custom's Union, many city and regional leaders are developing more proactive and entrepreneurial strategies for seeking new trading relationships, with either Commonwealth countries directly, or building on existing relationships they may have developed over the past few years.

There is also uncertainty on whether or not there will be continued engagement in numerous European and international decision-making forums, and if local and regional economies are sufficiently resilient, or possess the necessary tools, capacities and resources to compete in a global economy. Nowhere is this more true than in policing and criminal justice, with the Director of Europol, claiming that 'leaving the EU means that the UK will become a second tier member of our club' (Wainwright, The Guardian, 22 June 2016).

In most other European countries beyond the UK, cities and regions have constitutional rights, freedoms and policy levers to achieve their social and economic development potential and build their infrastructure to support growth and development. This is not the case in the UK where leaders already facing severe austerity and budgetary constraints have major concerns about their capacity to continue to deliver services efficiently, effectively and economically. Considerable time and effort have already been expended in the period preceding the Brexit Referendum in developing entrepreneurial and innovative public services for citizens, and boosting local economies, but Brexit may undo much of the good work that local agencies (local government and police) have instigated. The potential consequences of Brexit could have far reaching impacts on safety and security in local areas, or how police and other agencies deal with a potential rise in Vulnerability. However, before discussing these consequences in detail we now turn our attention to the theoretical lens through which the findings will be analysed.

Transnational-Local Linkages: The Theoretical Lens

The concept of 'Transnationalism' has, more usually been applied to the sphere of economics, business and strategy literature to examine how the world's largest companies compete in response to global pressures and develop strategies within turbulent environments. For Bartlett and Ghosal (2002) leaders of companies have long recognised what they need to do in the face of international forces and continuous flux, and how to develop organisational strategies to execute their strategies. Studies have also examined transferring strategic organisational practices within multi-national companies (Kostova, 1999, 308–324); who owns and controls major corporations; how globalised bureaucrats, politicians and professional elites interact to form a 'Transnational Capitalist Class' (Sklair, 2002, 114–150); transnational international relations (Cowling and Sugden, 1987, Van der Pijl, 2005); international policy development and transnational governance (Tarrow, 2001, 1–20); transnational citizenship and social movements (Vertovec, 2009); and how advocacy networks develop transnationally (Keck and Sikkink, 2001, 89–101).

Geographers assert how social relations are increasingly stretched across national borders, linking the local to the global (Jackson et al., 2004), as relationships become stretched over space in the flux of real historical time (Harvey, 1982). In 2000 Smith examined ways that immigrants, refugees, political activists and institutions maintain social relations, and processes/connections as distinctive national boundaries become less important and increasingly varied (Schiller et al., 1995, 48–63).

This relational approach provides a way of thinking that challenges the view of localities as coherent bounded territorial entities, instead places exist within a complex and unbounded lattice of articulations constructed through, and around relations of power and inequality, and each social network mutually reinforces and influences others. The issue, therefore, is not how, and whether to draw lines around localities but to seek to understand the processes through which they are produced and reproduced (Hudson, 1990, Amin, 2004, Hudson, 2007). The interdependent and highly relational nature of complex social- and environment-related (and public-private-third sector) policy problems require a refreshed conceptualising of a relational-type leadership for a non-prejudicial exchange of knowledge and collaborative learning, as is the case in connecting the transnational and local in policing, security and criminal justice.

It is acknowledged that earlier political economists and management theories on transnational corporate companies, with their emphasis on competition and strategizing across national boundaries may have slightly less relevance for theorising about the links between transnational and local scales within policing, security and criminal justice due the numerous co-operative agreements in existence (but possibly now in jeopardy due to Brexit-see later discussion) between agencies across the EU. However more recent analyses on relational approaches linking the transnational to the local offer more resonance in examining social relations, processes/connections as distinctive national boundaries become less important, increasingly varied and pervasive across national boundaries. In summary a distillation of the aforementioned theories across multiple disciplines, broadly under the umbrella of 'transnationalism', all have in common the following features that help us analyse how transnational and local linkages are relevant to policing, security and criminal justice:

- How states and non-state agencies use institutional channels to broker cross border connectivity
- The need to facilitate communications and information exchange across national borders and develop cross-boundary linkages to connect transnational processes to local processes
- How partnerships and networks are created that cross national boundaries
- The importance of non-state actors interacting at different spatial levels within state agencies and across transnational boundaries

Despite the proliferation in social scientific research studies on transnationalism, there has been an absence of similar work in the fields of police, security and criminal justice, and Brexit and its potential impacts allow us to adopt a 'transnational lens' for identification of key interconnections, inter-linkages and processes to bring the transnational and local spaces into focus. It enables us to investigate some of the local consequences of transnational linkages, and to better understand some of the underlying forces that may, in some way, contribute to an escalation of Vulnerability in local areas. In the two sections to follow, findings on some transnational challenges for policing, security and criminal justice and local consequences for dealing with Vulnerability introduce examples drawn from the four territories of England, Scotland, Wales and Northern Ireland. Then a discussion and analysis linking the transnational and the local ensues is followed by some conclusive remarks and areas for future research.

Transnational Challenges for Policing, Security and Criminal Justice

In the wake of the EU Referendum and subsequent invocation of Article 50, the formal notification of the UK's intent to withdraw membership of the EU, as already articulated earlier in this piece, much academic work has concentrated on the implications of Brexit on industry and the economy, and despite a plethora of media and news coverage, voices from the fields of policing, security and criminal justice or criminology have been strangely absent from the debate (James, 2019, introduction).

One of the many areas of law to be affected by Brexit is police and criminal justice, and on a more practical level the issues of *extradition*, *police cooperation* and the capacity to negotiate in future with *EU counterpart agencies* may present transnational problems for the future. Although the UK has always had a looser relationship with the EU than other member states within policing and criminal justice, due in part to signing up to the Schengen measures on police cooperation, it is fair to say that there has always been a great deal of flexibility and an a *la carte* approach to EU measures, opting in and out on an individual basis, as and when necessary (Williams, 2016). However, despite this flexibility, the UK chose to opt into a series of instruments, to which it remains bound; largely those designed to foster police cooperation, notably the controversial *European Arrest Warrant*, which under 'mutual recognition' measures was regarded by House of Lords Select Committee members as 'the single most important police and criminal justice measure' (HOL Select Committee, 2016).

In addition to the *European Arrest Warrant*, and Under Article 13 of the European Council Act 2000, establishing the Convention on Mutual Assistance in Criminal Matters between Member States of the EU, OJ, 197 (12 July 2000) the UK Government also signed up to rejoin measures including mutual recognition of financial penalties, confiscation orders, taking account of convictions in other member states, establishing organised crime evaluation mechanisms, asset freezing and recovery, security at international football maths, sharing of criminal records and information, Joint Investigation Teams, a European Image Archiving System, European Judicial Network, managing internet pornography and others (Wright and Cooper, 2016). These measures were facilitated and managed mainly through EU Agencies such as EUROPOL and EUROJUST; both were created to support cooperation between EU Law Enforcement Agencies. It is evident that UK police and security chiefs are keen to maintain these cross-border connections and continue their support for European and International Crime Agencies in the fight against global crime because 'lack of access to European Law enforcement data bases could put the public at risk, and we may need to quickly replace them so that quickly extradite and arrest criminals' (Cressida Dick, 27.11.18).

The UK's departure from the EU will involve negotiations leading to an exit treaty, and this could allow parts of EU criminal law to continue, but if any settlement involves a 'clean break' the UK will be freed from EU burdens, but also deprived of its benefits (Spencer J R, 2016). Some of the downsides of withdrawal would be, first, the free movement of goods and people (which EU criminal Law was created to deal with) because it could increase the movement of criminals and crime, depending on what an exit treaty includes and the extent to which free movement continues or is curtailed.

If the UK pulled out of EU crime fighting and information sharing agencies such as EUROPOL EUROJUST or ECRIS and withdrew from 'mutual recognition' deals and police cooperation, which seems very unlikely if the voices of UK senior police and criminal justice spokespeople are to believed, it remains the case that the UK will have no say in how these organisations operate, develop their strategies or plan their future activities. Suggestions that mutual recognition instruments and existing cooperation could be replaced by individual negotiated 'inter-governmental' agreements with EU member state would involve very lengthy and complex arrangements indeed. The UK already cooperates with EU and non- EU states through the Council of Europe on a series of Extradition Conventions, so there is a basis for future business with the 27 member states on extradition, at least. In terms of extradition of criminals from one state to another, existing EU rules state that a criminal can be extradited even if the criminal activity in another state is not an offence in the UK. Member states currently recognise warrants and permit extradition even in cases where there is no equivalent criminality in that state because the state is also able to issue arrest warrants to other Member states who will recognise them in return. However, there is no guarantee that this reciprocity will continue once the UK leaves the EU and it may require individual bi-lateral treaties with different states. On sharing of data on, for example air passengers, post Brexit, the UK may have to seek and negotiate individual agreements with other states.

From a Scottish policing perspective, Ian Livingston the Chief Constable of Police Scotland regards the biggest challenge of Brexit as the loss of existing legal powers such as the European Arrest Warrant and membership of EUROPOL. In his opinion 'Police Scotland have been a 'great beneficiary' of joint investigation teams through EUROPOL, particularly regarding people trafficking and organised crime threats to Scotland, as well as from intelligence sharing networks and using European Arrest Warrants'. Scotland is therefore creating bi-lateral deals with Poland, the Baltic countries, Latvia, parts of Scandinavia, Spain and Portugal. Brexit, argues Livingston, has the potential for disruption at ports as well as the Irish border, and public disorder and disruption to food and medical supplies are among scenarios and contingencies currently being planned for (Livingston, 2019). In Wales, Brexit risks putting the UK and North Wales in jeopardy, 'because co-operation with the rest of Europe is used to help North Wales police guard against terrorism, serious organised crime including modern slavery and human and drugs trafficking' (Williams, 2018). The threats to policing from a Brexit fallout in Northern Ireland are even more profound than not having access to European data bases or involvement in mutual working alongside European Crime Agencies. Since 1949, citizens from the Republic of Ireland have had the right to freely enter, reside and work in the UK and even at the height of the Troubles there was still significant cross-border movement between Northern Ireland and the Republic of Ireland. Moreover, between 1969 and the Anglo-Irish Agreement in 1985, the British authorities found it difficult to police the Irish border, checkpoints were costly to run, and the border remained vulnerable to attack by the Irish Republican Army. Any establishment of a strict border system between the two Irelands would be greatly detrimental to the 1998 peace agreement and wider Anglo-Irish relations (Kearney, 2016, Tannam, 2018).

It is clear that the UK, post Brexit, will need to establish on-going relationships within the policing, security and criminal justice systems and individually negotiate extradition and other criminal exchanges of data, information and other cross border activities involving crime. Any future Treaty will need to protect and preserve existing measures and instruments that aid European and UK crime agencies in carrying out their responses to criminal activities. However, what does seem clear is that, much as in other policy arenas, the UK will no longer be at the table in European decisions, nor will they be able to influence the development of new instruments and measures to fight criminality. As the Head of EUROPOL suggested 'by sitting at the negotiating table the UK has consistently demonstrated its ability to ensure that joint measures reflect its own policies'. Moreover, withdrawal from EU could lead to the UK criminal justice authorities no longer being in a position whereby they can extend full cooperation to EU member states, and consequentially no longer benefit from cooperation with other Member states. As crime become ever more borderless and many criminal activities more international in nature, new technology allows greater cooperation across policing, security and criminal justice agencies but without a seat at the 'European table' it makes it more difficult for UK policing and criminal justice agencies to fight the escalation in cross-border criminal activities, with many repercussions being played out in localities across the UK, as the next section will illustrate.

Local Consequences for Dealing with Vulnerability

The EU Referendum on Brexit was a terrific shock as the British electorate, either those voting 'Leave' or 'Remain' soon began to realise the inevitable destabilising effects on constitutional principles and national and local decision making, institutional structures and international relationships (Marnoch, 2018, 1–7). Leaving the free trade and custom union have the potential to impose huge damage on manufacturing and service industries, as well as public services too. Many of the social, economic and environmental impacts of Brexit remain to be seen in coming decades, but the challenges facing many localities across the UK are arising at a time when many deprived areas are yet to recover from the 2008 Global economic downturn and fiscal crisis, let alone those still reeling from the demise of traditional industries in the 1970/80s (e.g., coal mining in Wales, the North-East, heavy engineering in the West Midlands and Shipbuilding in Belfast or on the Clyde). In the past 12 months alone, Tees Valley has lost most of its steel making facilities to China, and Middlesbrough, on the recent IMD (Index of Multiple Deprivation, September, 2019), is not only ranked as the poorest and most deprived place in the country – it is also the most unsafe and insecure locality to reside in. In a recent study on the Brexit vote, Telford and Wistow (2019, 1–20) highlighted the strength of feeling about political abandonment and social dislocation among sections of working-class voters in Teesside.

The challenges posed by Brexit for impoverished localities where the coal, iron and steel industries shaped the industrial and social/political landscape are daunting, because in such areas shipbuilding, heavy engineering and chemicals, some new advanced manufacturing and digital industries are developing, though in insufficient volume to compensate for the loss of traditional industries. City and local leaders are debating how best to advance the interests of localities within new global and transnational economic realities, and how best to respond to Brexit and build and secure employment in the advanced industries of the future (Liddle and Shutt, 2019a).

Public services, including local government, health and social care, education and policing are not part of the competencies of the EU, but instead all are delivered at local level by a mixture of central Block Grant and locally raised taxes. Nevertheless, it is clear that local areas could experience numerous consequences and on-going ripple effects attributable to an EU exit, and the type of Brexit deal that can be agreed. Uncertainty is increasing, UK inequalities are rising and the incidences of Vulnerability more prevalent. Public service leaders across all agencies including the NHS, social care, police and local government are used to dealing with uncertainties, but rarely on the scale created by Brexit. Moreover, as the agencies in the front line dealing with Vulnerable groups, all will face different uncertainties around many of the financial consequences of Brexit; continuing EU legal obligations and institutions; sequencing and impacts of Brexit negotiations, but more significantly for the difficulties in delivering services for vulnerable people, with many largely dependent on a migrant EU workforce to deliver key public services.

Police services have suffered greatly from cuts to public expenditure, as have local government services (in some cases by up to 40 percent of budgets year on year) (Liddle and Murphy, 2012: 83–87), and whereas the NHS has recently received a boost in finances, mainly to reduce waiting lists, it is clear that the most crucial implications for NHS and social care providers is the shortage of doctors, nurses and ancillary workers, many who were born in other EU Member states and who came to the UK to man the health and social service departments and respond to the vulnerable in society.

Local authorities (and in some case Universities working in collaboration with local authorities) have been significant beneficiaries of EU Funding sources through programmes such as ERDF and ESF, many of them used to enhance programmes for long-term unemployed, disadvantaged and poor groups. Local Government Association and others representing the interests of local government have been pressurising central government to ring fence monies and make up the shortfall in EU funding through the UK Shared Prosperity Fund, and although warms words have emanated from Whitehall and Westminster, thus far the Consultation exercise on UKSPF has stalled twice in the past two years.

In some ways, the obsession with Brexit over the past two and half years has meant that national politicians and civil servants have taken 'their eyes of the ball' of the domestic agenda, and this deflected attention away from key public policy issues and the need to improve public services for tackling some of the persistent 'wicked issues' in poorer communities, especially with a rise in those groups and individuals considered to be more 'vulnerable'.

It is also arguable that any negotiated deal may in fact accelerate the break-up of the United Kingdom with Scotland accelerating towards independence and others arguing for a United Ireland and a federal United Kingdom as long-term solutions. Regardless of any deal, Brexit will have repercussions for a decade or more ahead, and in the recent UK General Election, the Brexit Party argued that a £200bn programme of regional investment was needed for the North of England to reduce the North/South divide and eradicate some of the long standing inequalities in Northern cities.

Many local leaders are focussed on trying to elaborate how the UK Shared Prosperity Fund can deliver for 'left behind' places, in particular those in need of investment, new policies and programmes to shift deep-seated social, economic and environmental problems. Despite recent announcements from the Conservative government on increased public expenditure growth and new commitments to health, education, police and post-Brexit funding via A Stronger Towns Fund, many of the new funds alone will not tackle these deep-seated and fundamental problems, and the Brexit dividend may fail to materialise.

There is still a tendency for national governments to regard the private sector as a key source of jobs but the danger of ignoring the role of the public and voluntary sectors has been evident for some time since the Coalition government of 2010 abandoned Prime Minister Cameron's mantra of Localism. Moreover, in the field of policing, security and criminal justice, the strain on services and in some cases, the retreat of the state from delivering services to vulnerable individuals and groups has left gaps in coverage that are increasingly being filled by voluntary, third sector, charities and faith groups. There are endless examples of criminal justice agencies and social work agencies incapable of dealing with escalating 'vulnerability' problems, and working in closer collaboration with some of the mental health charities; third and voluntary sector agencies dealing with alcohol and drug abuse; refugee councils dealing with migrants; faith and church groups helping to feed the homeless and rootless members of society. The issues of Vulnerability are no longer the preserve of the public services, in particular the police and social services, instead many other non-state agencies are providing coverage at drop -in centres, all night hostels, foodbank supplies, voluntary transport for elderly, disabled and disadvantaged groups and individuals.

The loss of EU Funds resulting from Brexit will impact more acutely on poor, de-industrialised localities with limited employment opportunities, lower business start-ups and lack of clear discussion or resolution on replacement funds such as UK Shared Prosperity Funds. Numerous programmes within deprived areas were traditionally funded either solely through European Social Funds, or with matched national and local public funding, and aimed at vulnerable groups such as disaffected youth, drug and alcohol dependents, long-term unemployed, female or older potential entrepreneurs, 'hard to reach' young families through Sure Start centres or local young people through probation/police programmes, employment opportunities in training programmes.

The Liberal Democrat Coalition between 2010 and 2016, and the Conservative Government since then have both privileged economic over social priorities with the establishment of Local Enterprise Partnerships, Mayoral and non-Mayoral Combined Authorities and pursuance of an UK Industrial Strategy for economic growth. The creation of a host of deal-making programmes for economic growth, and privileging the economic over the social has been detrimental to many localities, and exacerbated the North/South divide, with many vulnerable groups in de-industrialised and other deprived localities feeling 'left behind'. Brexit has the potential to further divide the North and South of England and exacerbate some of the escalating social problems. It is already regarded by commentators as perhaps the most divisive and cataclysmic event facing politicians and city and regional leaders, both now and after withdrawal from the EU. Undoubtedly on-going austerity and the impacts on localities with less public-sector funding to cope with rising social problems may have catastrophic consequences post Brexit as many hitherto absent issues are arising in the pre-Brexit, and potentially post-Brexit periods. It is arguable also that Brexit has increased the levels of hate crime, racial disharmony, criminal activity, terrorist attacks, people trafficking, cyber-crime, social discord, growth in use of foodbanks, disenfranchised groups and ever more vulnerable and dis-enfranchised individuals and groups.

Discussion and Analysis: Linking the Transnational to the Local

Many of the issues identified in this chapter are crucially important at a transnational level but also have clear links to localities across the United Kingdom. The ways in which policing, security and criminal justice systems have (in the pre-Brexit era) used strong institutional channels to broker cross border connectivity; facilitated communications and information exchange across national borders; as well as developed cross-boundary linkages to connect transnational processes to local processes. The many EU agencies that were created to improve criminal justice across Europe have supported effective cooperation between Member states, and a series of agreements were reached between law enforcement agencies in the 28 EU states. Mutual recognition instruments and measures such as the European Arrest Warrant allowed courts and other authorities to give effect to judgments and orders to similar bodies in EU states, and the harmonisation of criminal law ensured that certain acts such as terrorism would be punishable by appropriate penalties to ensure a common approach to common policing and criminal activities. Agreements on criminal procedures were also harmonised to provide minimum protection for victims of crime or minimum rights for defendants. Mutual recognition of these principles ensured a willingness to enforce foreign judgments and confidence in all legal systems across the EU jurisdictions.

Many long-standing partnerships and networks were created that cross national boundaries, and state and non-state actors continued to interact at different spatial levels within state agencies and across transnational boundaries, but post Brexit many uncertainties remain and numerous senior police, security and criminal justice personnel are voicing concerns on what the future may hold. Obvious downsides to withdrawal from partnerships with EU crime would include an increase in free movement of crime and criminals; lack of mutual recognition deals;

reduction or non-existent police cooperation across national borders, and the need to develop bi-lateral 'inter-governmental' negotiated agreements with individual EU member states and non-EU states. All would be very complex and lengthy processes, as some Police Chiefs suggest, and could jeopardise crime fighting in the future.

Additionally, in the post Brexit period, police, security and criminal justice agencies will need to establish on-going relationships and individually negotiate extradition and other criminal exchanges of data, information and other cross border activities involving crime. A significant impact in this policy domain will be the fact that the United Kingdom will no longer be at to influence policing, security and criminal justice decisions that may still have far reaching impacts at local levels of policing and fighting crime. As criminal activities now reach across national borders with new technology allowing greater scope for criminal activities, the capacity of agencies to detect such activities, renders UK enforcement agencies at a significant disadvantage in solving escalating criminal activities.

The consequences of Brexit for localities are potentially massive, and might prove to have severe, detrimental and long-term repercussions on the levels of Vulnerability in communities. Already there is evidence to suggest an increase in 'wicked' social problems, a rise in stress levels and mental health problems: continuing reduction in public service budgets leading to demoralised and stressed personnel; as well as increased levels of unemployment or fear of unemployment in certain localities. Increased fear of crime, rather than the actual levels of crime are major concerns to citizens, and since the Brexit Referendum, there have been numerous incidences of hate and race crime, Islamophobia; Anti-5Semitism, plus increased incidences of cyber-crime. Homelessness and immigration are also rising, with police and social services under severe strain as a mixture of state and non-state agencies desperately trying to cope with the numbers of vulnerable people. More and more people are experiencing poverty and deprivation and presenting themselves to food bank providers, or charities for the homeless, and refugees and rough sleepers proving difficult for public service agencies to provide effective coverage. This has led to unprecedented levels of non-state and charitable, third and voluntary, and faith and church groups engaging in this policy domain, but without the necessary resources to support the vulnerable people they aim to help.

Conclusions

As has been argued throughout this chapter, policing, security and criminal justice have hitherto, largely been absent from the many political and academic discussions on Brexit, and yet the implications of Brexit in this policy domain may have far reaching and long-term consequences, as well as severe and knock-on ripple effects on a rise in the prevalence of 'wicked' social issues. A consequential rise in the numbers of vulnerable individuals and groups may not be entirely attributed to the fall-out from Brexit, as it is impossible to disentangle the many causal relationships, but in using a transnational-local theoretical framework it is possible to make initial commentaries that evidence is already indicating that continuing instability, uncertainty and ambiguity surrounding protracted Brexit negotiations (and they may continue for decades), will inevitably create greater stress levels, potentially increased crime and disorder, racial discord and social dislocation.

There is a need for even greater levels of research in future in this growing and important field of enquiry, if we are intent on filling gaps in current knowledge and understandings of transnational-local linkages, connections and consequences. Furthermore, we must increase the knowledge base of some of the major, underlying and contested explanations of who the vulnerable individuals and groups in society are; how to interrogate the causes and consequences of a rise in Vulnerability; and, more significantly, how we address these growing problems from both policy and practical perspectives. Despite Party Manifesto promises in the run up to the December 2019 General Election, and more recent positive Prime Ministerial announcements, it is clear that public expenditure cannot keep pace with the levels of demand being placed on UK public services, in particular to deal with a rise in 'wicked issues' such as Vulnerability. Vulnerability is a very complex policy issue, and the causes and effects are difficult to explain in simple terms. Moreover, dealing with Vulnerability may prove to be an uphill task, made more difficult because many of the social and economic issues contributing to Vulnerability lie outside of the direct control of state agencies (including police, security and criminal justice). Without a recognition of the need for 'holistic' approaches to disentangling some of the embedded structural imbalances of past industrial and economic policies and their social consequences, it seems unlikely that any government or state service provider, acting solely or in collaboration with non-state partners, will possess the necessary capacities to address the fundamental and escalating problem of Vulnerability.

References

Amin A (2004) Regions unbound: Towards a new politics of place. *Geografiska Annaler B*, 86 (1), 33–44

Barber S (2017) The Brexit environment demands that deliberative democracy meets inclusive growth, *Local Economy*, 32 (3), 219–239.

Bartlett CA and Ghoshal S (2002) 2nd edition, *Managing across borders: The transnational solution*, Harvard Business School Press, New York.

Conservative Party Manifest (November 2019) Get Brexit done: Unleashing Britain's Talent, UK Conservative and Unionist Party, HQ, London.

Cowling, K and Sugden R (1987) *Transnational monopoly capitalism*, Wheatsheaf Books, Brighton.

Cressida Dick, Metropolitan Police Commissioner (27 November 18), Telegraph interview.

Durrant T, Lloyd L and Jack M T (2018) Institute for Government Report, Negotiating Brexit-Police and Criminal Justice, IFG, London, 2018.

EU Home Affairs Sub-Committee, 'Brexit: future UK-EU security and police cooperation', House of Lords EU Committee, 7th Report of Session 2016–17, 16 December 2016.

Gibney J, Liddle J and Shutt J (forthcoming 2020) It's good to talk: The impact of Brexit disruption on leadership in city and regional transnational working in Europe, Regional Studies.

Harvey D (1982) *The limits to capital*, Blackwell, Oxford.

Her Majesty's Government (2019) House of Commons Housing, Communities and Local Government Committee, Brexit and local government Thirteenth Report of Session 2017–19.

HM Government, (12 July 2000) 'The UK's cooperation with the EU on justice and home affairs, and on foreign policy and security issues', Background Note, 9 May 2016 -European Arrest Warrant, and Under Article 13 of the European Council Act 2000, establishing the Convention on Mutual Assistance in Criminal Matters between Member States of the EU, OJ, 197.

Hudson R (1990) Re-thinking regions: Some preliminary considerations on regions and social change, in Johnston R J, Hoekveld G and Hauer J (Eds) *Regional Geography: Current Developments and Future Prospects*: 67–84. Routledge, London.

Hudson R (2007) Regions and regional uneven development forever? Some reflective comments upon theory and practice, *Regional Studies*, 41 (9), 1149–1160.

Ian Livingston (31 January 2019) Chief Constable of Police Scotland, Policing in Scotland, Wales and Northern Ireland Post Brexit: The Challenges, BBC News, Police Scotland to put 500 officers on Brexit Duty, www.bbc.co.uk/news/uk-scotland-scotland-politics-47061219, downloaded 10 December 2019.

Jackson P, Crang P and Dwyer CM (2004) *Transnational spaces*, Routledge Research in Transnationalism, London, UK.

James Z (2019) Policing Local Communities in England Post-Brexit, Special Edition, Safer Communities, vol 16, issue 4, introduction, Emerald publishing, Bingley.

Kearney V (24 June 2016) Brexit: How will leaving EU impact on border and policing in NI? BBC News Northern Ireland Home Affairs Correspondent.

Keck M E and Sikkink K (2002) Transnational advocacy networks in international and regional politics, *International Social Science Journal*, 51 (159), 89–101.

Kostova T (1999) Transnational transfer of strategic organizational practices: A contextual perspective, *Academy of Management Review*, 24 (2), 308–324.

Levell P, Menon A, Portes J and Sampson T (2018) The Economic Consequences of the Brexit Deal, November 2018, Centre for Economic Performance, LSE. Paper CEPBREXIT12.

Liddle J and Murphy P (2012) Public Administration in an ear of austerity-published, *Public Money and Management*, March, 32 (2), 83–87.

Liddle J and Shutt J (2019) *The NE after Brexit*, Emerald Publishing, Bingley.

Marnoch G (2018) *Brexit and public services in Northern Ireland*, Glasgow University Brexit Briefings, pp. 1–7.

Ministry of Housing, Communities & Local Government (MHCLG), HM UK Government, English Indices of Deprivation (2019) IMD (Index of Multiple Deprivation, (26 September, 2019), www.gov.uk/government/statistics/english-indices-of-deprivation-2019, downloaded 10TH October 2019, London, UK.

North P (2017) Local economies of Brexit, *Local Economy*, 32 (3), 204–218.

Schiller N G, Basch L and Blanc C S (1995) From immigrants to Trans-migrants: Theorising transnational migration, *Anthropological Quarterly*, 68 (1), 48–63.

Shutt J and Liddle J (2019) Are combined authorities in England strategic and fit for purpose? *Local Economy*, Special Edition, 34 (2), 196–207.

Sklair L (2002) Democracy and the transnational capital class, annals, *A A PSS*, 581, 144–150.

Smith M P (2002) *Transnational urbanism: Locating globalization*, Wiley-Blackwell, London.

Spencer J R (2016) 'What would Brexit mean for British criminal justice?', *Archbold Review*, Issue 5, 22 June 2016 [Longer version].

Tarrow S (2001) Transnational politics: Contention and institutions in international politics, *Annual Review of Political Science*, 4, 1–20.

Tannam E (8 June 2018) Northern Ireland Cross-Border Civil Service Cooperation: The Good Friday Agreement and Brexit: 243–262, published online: 08 Jun 2018, downloaded 19 November 2019.

Telford L and Wistow J (2019) Brexit and the working class on Teesside: Moving beyond reductionism, Capital and Class- pages 1–20, doi: 10.1177/0309816819873310.

Thomas Christiansen, Diane Fromage, eds, Brexit and Democracy-The role of Parliaments in the UK and EU, 2019) Danny Dorling and Sally Tomlinson, 2019, Brexit and the End of Empire, Rule Britannia, (introduction).

Van der Pijl K (2005) *Transnational classes and international relations*, Taylor & Francis, London.

Vertovec S (2009) *Transnationalism*, Taylor & Francis, London.

Wainwright R (22 June 2016) 'Europol chief says Brexit would harm UK crime-fighting', The Guardian Newspaper, in Dawson J (2016) Impact of Brexit on policing and criminal justice: A reading list, House of Commons Library, HOC, London.

Williams K (19 November 2018) Quoting Arfon Jones in The secret Brexit policing plan that Crime Tsar claims he's banned from talking about, The Daily Post, North Wales, https://dailypost.co.uk/news/north-wales-news/secret-brexit-policing-plan-crime-15436600, downloaded 13 December 2019.

Williams R (2016) Brexit: The implications for police and criminal justice, www.law.ox.ac.uk/cenres-institutes/centre-criminology/blog/2016/11/brexit, downloaded 2nd December 2019.

Wright O and Cooper C (2016) Brexit-What is it and why are we having an EU Referendum?, *The Independent*, 13 June 2016.

4 Vulnerability a Collective or Individual/Agency Issue?

Has Vulnerability Replaced Community Safety in the UK and Are We Stigmatising the Individual?

Stephen Brookes

Introduction

> A 15-year old high-school student in New York with severe development delay was coaxed into a stairwell at school by seven boys, two of whom forced her to perform oral sex while the other five watched. When the girl reported the assault to the school authorities, she was suspended for engaging in sexual activity on campus.
>
> (Mulkerrins 2019: 2)

This case is one example of many cited by U.S. Lawyer Carrie Goldberg, who specialises in defending victims of sex crimes (Goldberg 2019), herself a victim of such crimes. Goldberg filed a civil lawsuit against the city of New York and won $950,000 for the girl. It is a clear case of a stigmatised vulnerable victim, which, figuratively speaking, is to 'to mark with a sign of disgrace or infamy'.[1] This is a highly distressing, stark but helpful example on which to start this chapter in exploring why and how vulnerable people become stigmatised.

The chapter will illustrate that stigmatisation and vulnerability are two sides of the same coin beginning by defining both of these terms based on the literature and the dilemmas and dichotomies that emerge. Both of these socially undesirable outcomes transcend the criminal justice system specifically and social isolation and/or exclusion more generally. This assertion will be explored through three areas that exploit vulnerability, including two examples of 'wicked problems' which highlight how vulnerability quickly leads to stigmatisation and the resultant impact on the individual; sex work and modern slavery. Both issues will be briefly reviewed and then supported by an outline of research conducted in the North of England (funded and supported by the N8 Policing Research Partnership).[2] A further brief analysis will then explore a contemporary issue that targets vulnerable people, namely youth extremism, in highlighting the opportunities for improving future research and practice. Noting that these examples are not exhaustive, the final part of this chapter will revisit the history and experience of community safety and consider how vulnerability ought to be given centre-stage within community safety strategies, goals and action plans through a collective form of community-based leadership.

Vulnerability and Stigmatisation

The Woeful Dichotomy

The aim of this chapter is to consider vulnerability and the stigmatisation of individuals within the context of community safety. It first describes a woeful dichotomy in examining the role that government agencies play in both deciding on policy and its implementation, often blaming the individual rather than the broader determinants of the policy decision.

Other chapters in this volume have comprehensively considered the meaning and impact of vulnerability within the context of community safety and, as Chapter 1 has observed, from a vulnerable victim's perspective, community safety appears to have been replaced by stigmatisation. It includes victims of sex crimes, immigrants who unwittingly enter the market of modern slavery, young people who are exploited by organised crime groups (OCGs) or alleged terrorist groups. Victims of domestic violence and coercive control will equally be vulnerable as well as people suffering from mental health and those who are socially isolated. For example, the growing number of people who are homeless, many of whom will have been forced into homelessness by being a victim of vulnerability crimes or isolated from society or exploitation by some of its members. It is worrying that the response by statutory agencies has been woeful with the blame for the victim's dilemma often being placed firmly at the feet of themselves rather than engaging in multi-agency approaches. The aim is to tackle the underlying social determinants that create the conditions for predatory offenders to exploit the vulnerable and for apathetic communities and their politicians to ignore these conditions and thus stigmatise the individual. Underlying many of these dilemmas are political, social and economic determinants that deprive these vulnerable victims of life that most of us enjoy, often without gratitude. For example, seeing the homeless on the streets of our cities is viewed as an anathema by many public 'leaders' who want to 'rid' the streets of this undesirable blight on the social and economic regeneration that they seek to supposedly encourage. Victims presenting with mental health conditions may be told to 'pick themselves up', and victims of domestic violence and coercive control often feel as if they are the ones on trial rather than the perpetrators of the violence or controlling behaviour.

The Policy Dilemma or Distortion?

Vulnerability and stigmatisation often exist hand-in-hand and demonstrate the significant impact that pejorative government and agency responses have in promoting and applying the latter as the cause of the former, thus, applying policy distortion rather than facing and responding appropriately to a policy dilemma. Nineteenth-century law is still used to criminalise homeless people in the UK (Kumar 2019) and is one example in which criminalisation drives the activities under-ground thus hiding the symptoms and the real causes. The same applies in relation to the prevalence of sex work which normalises violence; sex workers three times more likely to experience violence from client where trade is criminalised (Boseley 2018).

Other, more specific examples of policy distortion exist in relation to policy discourses; vulnerable females and trafficked migrants in which the UK government aligns aspects of its anti-trafficking plans with ones to enhance extraterritorial immigration and border control. These are two further examples which are tantamount to the construction and manipulation of the idiom of the vulnerable female, intersecting with other (competing) agendas at critical points (FitzGerald 2012). It is further argued that immigration control practices exacerbate the vulnerabilities to the exploitation of modern slavery (Gadd and Broad 2018). The coherence of humanitarian anti-slavery policy and the consistency of its ambitions with a continued prioritisation by governments of security policy and immigration control illustrates the reality that practice is more restricted than the policy rhetoric suggests (Hadjimatheou and Lynch 2018).

The selfish approach of public leaders in which individual leaders and organisations are driven by their individual or institutional ego, respectively, often results in policies that are self-serving rather than driven by a collective vision through selfless leadership that serves the public good (Brookes 2016). This chapter seeks to explore whether this represents a policy dilemma or a distortion. The reality is that policy discourses will lie somewhere between the two, and that context will play a determining role. As a dilemma, it will necessarily involve arguments that involve choices from two (or more) alternatives, either of which is (or appears) equally unfavourable. The Oxford English Dictionary describes dilemmas as arguments between adversaries often resulting in a 'fix' based on a position of doubt or perplexity'.[3] Conversely, if it is a distortion, this suggests a more selfish approach through 'the twisting or perversion of words (or meanings – my emphasis) to give them a different sense; perversion of opinions, facts, history, so as to misapply them'.[4] Such twisting reinforces the need to consider the importance of framing, defined as the 'strategic use of information to define and articulate a negotiating issue or situation' (Singh 2010: 52). It originates from the agenda-setting tradition (Goffman 1974). Framing is a critical element of problem-solving. Leaders will tend to frame a problem around their own perceptions and experiences rather than focussing on the characteristics of the problem that faces them. When responding to what is described as a so-called 'wicked problem' (with undefined characteristics) (Rittel and Webber 1973), they will treat it as a tame problem (one that is easily defined and in which tried-and-tested solutions can be 'taken off the shelf and applied to the problem)' (Brookes 2016). This will often result in 'clumsy solutions' (Grint 2010). Different situations will be evaluated in different ways by different people as a means of making sense of what people perceive the situation to be and to help them in defining that situation in a way that is meaningful to them. Because of this, we each use framing – whether consciously or subconsciously – to make decisions that will help us to act or to avoid acting.

Front-line workers are often those who are in the best position to identify the symptoms, causes and inter-connectedness of vulnerability and to suggest ways in which agencies can respond in tackling the wicked issues that underpin failures to respond to the broader determinants as opposed the attribution of individual blame through stigmatisation. The introduction to this volume and other chapters have considered the concept of street-level bureaucracy. First published in 1980, Street-Level Bureaucracy illustrated how public service workers informally act as policy decision-makers through their considerable discretion in the day-to-day implementation of public programmes (Lipsky 1980). At the time of writing his original seminal work, Lipsky argued that street-level bureaucrats mediated elements of the constitutional relationship of citizens to the state. In brief, he argued, they hold the keys to a dimension of citizenship. However, the context of public leadership in the 1970s/80s was utterly different from that of the last 20 years. New Public Management (NPM) emerged in the early 1980s and has dominated public management for the last 30 years. This has partly led to a crisis of confidence in, and delivery of, public services through an 'audit culture' against a background of apparent decline in trust and confidence in public services and its leaders (Brookes 2011).

Noting Lipsky's work, Ben-Ishai argues 'that attempts to impose measures of accountability within the context of social service delivery have threatened the quality of these services' (Ben-Ishai 2012: 12). Greater accountability, intrusive efficiency and accuracy measures, result in a more mechanistic form of service delivery accompanied by an erosion in workers sense of responsibilities to clients with a less productive and empathetic manner of delivery. Lipsky has not ignored this shift. He revisited his work to reflect on significant policy developments over the last three decades (Lipsky 2010). He describes how street-level bureaucracies can be and regularly are brought into line with public purposes. Street-level bureaucrats continue to interact directly with the public and still represent the frontline of public policy. In comparison with 1980, however, they now have increasingly huge caseloads, ambiguous agency goals and inadequate resources. Their dilemma is significant in balancing their need to help people or make decisions based on individual cases, but within a structural context that makes this impossible. The description mirrors that of Ben-Ishai's mechanistic form of delivery, including the rationing of resources, skewing of priorities based on qualities favoured by the institutions and the mass processing of human responsiveness, thus re-framing the desired outcomes of policy undermining the public value imperatives of effectiveness and equity as well as efficiency. Ad hoc policies in dealing with the dilemmas emerged but also a downright distortion of citizen needs and demands. Stigmatisation, this chapter argues, is one such distortion. However, in Lipsky's 30th-anniversary edition, he expresses optimism in that, despite its challenging nature, street-level work can be made to conform to higher expectations of public service. This chapter will also focus on the optimism at the more senior levels of public leadership in that the challenge is to align the values of public leaders and those of street-level bureaucrats in pursuing the ideals of collective leadership directed towards the creation and demonstration of public value. Stigmatised individuals are critical stakeholders within the authorising environment of public value strategies (Moore 1995). The chapter will now explore some examples in support of this assertion.

Stigmatising the Individual: Opportunities for Service Delivery Reform

Research Conducted through the N8 Policing Research Partnership

The N8 PRP was funded by the HEFCE Catalyst Grant 'Innovation and the Application of Knowledge for More Effective Policing' in 2015 through to 2020. Two key strands of the partnership are relevant to this chapter; the Police Innovation Forum (PIF) and the Small Grants Fund (SGF).[5] The PIF brings together the needs of the police service and the expertise of academics in encouraging innovative approaches to research and practice, and the opportunities for funding, providing a foundation for the launch of each years' SGF. Throughout its five-year programme, vulnerability has been a key feature commencing in 2015 with exploring the vulnerabilities that are exploited through cyber-crime and then progressing through more personal vulnerabilities; Domestic Abuse (2016), Vulnerability and Early Intervention (2017) and Mental Health (2018). The 2019 PIF focussed on knife crime and the vulnerability of those who both engage in knife crime and its victims. The SGF encourages applications that reflect each annual PIF theme and each year, small grants have been allocated to projects that align with the themes. In this section, two examples are briefly described and then considered.

Vulnerability and Sex Work

It is often stated that sex work, more popularly known as prostitution, is the oldest profession in the world (Salmon 2010). Throughout this long history, vulnerability and stigmatisation of sex workers has been evident and is a global phenomenon. Today, stigma affects both public health priorities and the well-being of people living with sexually transmitted disease (STD) such as HIV (Chollier et al. 2016). Women sex workers experience extensive victimisation and criminalisation but experience significant barriers from legal services. A study of 91 women currently trading sex disclosed experiences of community; intimate partner, societal and police abuse; and a history of arrests and incarcerations. Mistrust of the police and the criminal justice system was a significant factor (Sloss and Harper 2010) and illustrated the impact of vulnerability and stigmatisation. Similar evidence of multiple vulnerabilities, including discrimination, criminalisation and violence, were apparent in a study of women sex workers in Johannesburg, the city with the most substantial proportion of South Africa's migrant population (Walker 2017).

Although sex workers are generally viewed as female, male sex workers face the same challenges but with the added stigmatisation and criminalisation of homosexuality. In Zimbabwe, male sex workers (MSWs) are a vulnerable sub-group at risk of violence, abuse, and HIV infection, and, the authors argue, 'the stigmatization and criminalization of homosexuality in Zimbabwe creates an environment where it is difficult for MSWs to protect themselves through consistent condom use and access to basic HIV prevention and care services' (Qiao et al. 2019). Research in India revealed multiple intersecting social and institutional contexts and experiences of stigmatisation, discrimination and violence across police, community, family and health-care systems, with a consequential and negative impact on HIV preventative efforts (Chakrapani et al. 2007). As described earlier, elsewhere, legislation typically outlaws specific types of sexual activity or any sexual activity between persons of the same sex (Bejzyk 2017). Young men are particularly vulnerable and stigmatised, with current explanations of juvenile male prostitution seemingly insufficient to draw out the complex relationships of commercial sex with forms of power, for example older men, as opposed to the stigmatisation of the vulnerable young men, which is predominant (Gonzalez 2010).

More specifically, the prevalence of sexually transmitted disease is often attributed to sex workers and viewed as a public health problem that requires intervention focussed on the particular stereotype even though research has shown that such distortive framing ignores targeted evidence. In Western countries, for example, HIV rates in people involved in commercial sex are low, except in specific groups, such as intravenous drug users. Risks faced by sex workers due to stigmatisation and social, labour and legal vulnerabilities interfere with their health. As a result, the focus should be placed on the strategies used by sex workers to minimise health risks and their discourses of resistance in fighting vulnerabilities (Oliveira and Fernandes 2017). Although this tends to reflect an individual response, the implementation of such preventative programmes is a collective responsibility to prevent the spiral of health and well-being decline, leading to even more supposedly illegal activity thus representing the characteristics of a wicked problem and a vicious cycle. Evidence has also emerged in other studies; the HIV/AIDS epidemic is viewed as a severe public health problem in Mozambique. The research illustrates how gender inequalities increase women's vulnerability to HIV and contribute to their stigmatisation and discrimination. The response is one of the individual's reluctance to disclose their plight in contrast to seeking informal support from others living with HIV. The authors suggest that public policies should focus on women's empowerment and the reduction of HIV/AIDS-related stigma (Andrade and Iriart 2015). Returning to the examples of commercial sex by men (often younger) with other men, in Africa, such men have received little attention in HIV/AIDS programming and service delivery because of the widespread denial and stigmatisation of male homosexual behaviour (Ibrahima Niang et al. 2003: 499).

Prevention is, thus, a key strategy. However, putting in place such a strategy is not of itself sufficient. Appropriate framing, based on intelligence, is critical in order to gain a better understanding of sex workers' risk environments (Bandewar et al. 2016). Stigma and vulnerability in relation to psychosocial health of sexual minorities and the impact of gender-based differences and resilience (Chamberland and Saewyc 2011), multiple socio-structural barriers and lack of access to appropriate HIV prevention, diagnosis and treatment services (Duby et al. 2018) are further challenges. In summary, the preventative approaches associated with the risks of sex work are multi-faceted and require a collective and collaborative approach by public leaders. Individual stories can reveal much. A Swedish longitudinal research study over 10 years investigated the means to enhance health equality for male sex workers despite the discrimination and stigmatisation they face, by following one young Swedish male sex worker at different venues. A key finding is that there is a reciprocal connection between contexts, including 'the structure of the external sex working activity and the internal experience of ownership (capacity of agency) by the young man' (Knutagård 2015: 249). The individual consciousness of and ability to cope with vulnerability was variable, and a clear need for preventative education was apparent (especially the use of the Internet, depending on the sex-working activities). The study concluded that there is a need to gain a deeper understanding of the complex and contradictory nature of male sex work in the light of a 10-year trajectory.

Policing Vulnerability: An Evaluation of the Sex Work Liaison Officer Role in West Yorkshire Police

Sex workers are one of the most vulnerable groups in contact with the police and involve significant amounts of police time, having a profound effect on sex workers' lives, as well as on the local community where sex work takes place. Stigmatisation of sex workers is often evident, and their status as victims often ignored; classified as offenders due to their soliciting sex publicly, sex workers are also often victims of serious physical and sexual violence, which they are reluctant to report for fear of prosecution for soliciting (Kinnell 2010; O'Neill and Jobe 2016; Sanders 2016 cited within the research proposal; N8 PRP 2019).

West Yorkshire Police (WYP), in responding to these concerns, has been at the forefront of national sex work policing innovation with their introduction of a designated Sex Work Liaison Officer (SWLO). SWLO duties include first response to violent attacks on sex workers, assisting investigations of serious crimes and sensitive community liaison work in close partnership with neighbourhood policing units, playing a crucial role in Leeds' 'managed approach' to street sex work. This will be the first detailed study of the value and effectiveness of an SWLO role. It seeks to provide an analysis of the work undertaken by the SWLO, detailing the challenges faced and benefits to accrue and to evaluate the role within a national context, providing a best practice tool for broader dissemination. This project is still underway but demonstrates promise in highlighting how the role of specialist workers can play a part in both the identification of and response to vulnerability and to demonstrate how stigmatisation can be prevented.

Vulnerability and Modern Slavery

Modern slavery is now a significant source for the exploitation of vulnerable people, particularly young children (Gadd et al. 2017) and vulnerable adults. Vulnerability is a common feature of most definitions. For example, the Care Act 2014 (which accompanies the Modern Slavery Act 2015), defines it as a new form of risk within adult social care, identifying different forms of abuse and vulnerability (Craig and Clay 2017). A charity (Hope for Justice, 2018) takes this further; modern slavery is

> where one person controls another by exploiting a vulnerability. It is often linked with human trafficking, where a person is forced into a service against their will – usually forced work or prostitution. The control can be physical, financial or psychological.
>
> (HopeforJustice n.d.)

Exploring the social determinants that underpin this vulnerability is critical to the strategies that are necessary for tackling human trafficking and other exploitation that occurs. Poverty and disadvantaged neighbourhoods are common factors. The presence of such conditions is also a global phenomenon. Almost 16 years ago, an estimated 27 million women, children, and men were then enslaved around the world (Bales 1999) cited in (Herzfeld 2002: 50). Poverty and lack of parental support render children more vulnerable to being trafficked in Nigeria (Adesina 2014). Findings from this African study highlight that the root causes of child trafficking and the vulnerability include acute poverty, unemployment, ignorance and ineffectiveness of the legal framework for tackling trafficking. Domestic workers in Europe and elsewhere may live and work in appalling conditions and are thus vulnerable to abuse (Mantouvalou 2006). Research in this area is often limited and it has been noted that in the United States it has been retricted to the nature and scope of human trafficking (Logan et al. 2009).

The responses to modern-day slavery have also been the subject of criticism. The legislation does not provide adequate remedies to victims and criminal law and regulation of severe labour exploitation often fails the victim. Often the broader political and legislative context suggests that there is no political will to address structural factors, including legal structures that create vulnerability to exploitation (Mantouvalou 2018). There is also an opportunity to engage other agencies other than the police and border agencies. Modern-day slavery is an abuse of vulnerability targeting exploitation; it has significant negative physical and mental health consequences although these may be addressed by victims who present to healthcare professionals (Metcalf and Selous 2020). On this point, we will now explore the opportunities for the police and other agencies in responding to modern-day slavery alongside other vulnerability and stigmatisation examples based on research influenced (and funded) by the N8 Policing Research Partnership and the importance of framing based on meaningful data.

Mapping the Contours of Modern Slavery in Greater Manchester

Gadd et al. (2017, earlier cited) argue that offenders of modern slavery prey on the vulnerability of the populace residing in poor neighbourhoods but with an intense concentration in the city centre and two northern districts. There is a pressing need to understand these place-based indicators better. This research project sought to map the contours of modern slavery as they appeared in 2015 data recorded for the Greater Manchester Policing area by Greater Manchester Police (GMP) and the Modern Slavery Human Trafficking Unit (MSHTU). Almost a quarter of victims known to GMP were children; many more were young adults.

There were differences between the two datasets, although some common trends were identified. Most victims were predominantly Eastern European. The perpetrators of these crimes were almost always adults (one third were male and two-thirds female) and generally at least ten years older than the victims. The extent of positive outcomes differed, and only one in three of offenders charged with offences were convicted. Facilitating travel for exploitation emerged strongly within the intelligence which highlights a significant connection with organised crime groups, although loosely organised forms of exploitation are a vital feature of the crimes that get counted as modern slavery. This finding suggests that slavery is also organised through communities and in response to economic circumstances as much as through organised crime. The research raises new questions abut the importance of intelligence; the success of police action, attrition rate from charge and, importantly, acquiring more extensive intelligence from the public, the VCS/Non-Governmental Agencies (NGOs) and the criminal justice system.

Opportunities for Tackling Vulnerability and Youth Extremism

Framing plays a crucial role in both the identification of vulnerability, and responses to, **youth extremism**. For example, 'extremism and other radical ideologies are often assumed to be a harbinger of terrorism' (van de Weert and Eijkman 2019: 191). An increasing regularity of actual and attempted attacks perpetrated by a tiny minority of young British-born or British-based Muslims in the United Kingdom has seen the wholesale stigmatisation of young Muslims. As a result, young Muslims have become a focal point in the 'so-called War on Terror', identified both by state security and those seeking to recruit vulnerable prey as new terrorists through violent radicalisation (McDonald 2011). The focus has orientated itself to the process of radicalisation and, the authors suggest, a lack of consensus has emerged about the definition and understanding of this process.

The literature tends to focus on terrorism rather than radicalisation, although the impact of the vulnerability is very scant indeed in both cases. 'Grassroots' youth workers operate at the intersection of providing social care and detecting violent extremism and are often confronted with the task of detecting early signs of extremism and radicalisation. Van de Weert and Eijkman (ibid) question whether youth workers are sufficiently equipped to assess potential risks in youth who show no concrete plans for criminal action. The authors suggest that prevention should target ideas rather than violent behaviour. The role of education, as a form of preventative response, has emerged and provided some promise in the emergence of vulnerability as a trigger for responses. McDonald (ibid: 176) highlights the prominence of 'identity', which 'becomes a symbolic battleground co-opted through three recurring narratives: belonging, loyalty and duty.' This is reflected in the role of specialist Muslim youth workers in the provision of coherent, grassroots-orientated challenge to these narratives, working with the most vulnerable young people to create alternative articulations of identity.

The purpose of McDonald's systematic review was to examine the scholarly literature on the process(es) of radicalisation, particularly among young people, and the availability of interventions to prevent extremism. The review found that the evidence base for effective prevention of violent extremism interventions is minimal. Despite much research, few studies contained empirical data or systematic data analysis and are viewed through the lens of terrorism rather than radicalisation. As such, the evidence is concerned with that smaller cohort of individuals who, once radicalised, go on to commit acts of violence in the pursuit of political or religious aims and objectives. The authors argue that this introduces a systematic bias in the literature, away from the radicalisation process that precedes terrorism, including radicalisation that does not lead to violence. Both radicalisation and terrorism originate from a heterogeneous population that varies hugely in terms of education, family background, socio-economic status and income and additionally, responding to political grievances. Based on two UK studies, McDonald drew attention to the need to adopt capacity building and empowering young people, and interventions that challenge ideologies that focus on theology and use education/training.

In summary, a common denominator of these non-exclusive examples is that of the need for prevention to be prioritised over stigmatisation through the identification of vulnerability indicators and the role that street-level bureaucrats can play in preventing vulnerable members of society becoming embroiled in criminal activity whether through sex work, radicalisation or other forms of responses to social isolation. The chapter will now consider the role of community safety and community leadership in the important task of identifying, framing and responding to vulnerability in its various forms.

Revisiting Community Safety and Community Leadership

The Role of Community Safety

The first sections of this chapter have explored the importance of vulnerability and stigmatisation within the context of community safety, suggesting that governments are likely to face a policy dilemma. In response, they will either attempt to make decisions based on a balanced approach or will distort the policy to align to the governments' preferred agenda, apparently pulling into line the street-level bureaucrats who are in a strong position to frame the wicked problems. A discussion then followed exploring three examples of wicked problems; sex work, modern-day slavery drawing on examples from research commissioned by the N8 PRP and the prevention of radical extremism. A common denominator of these non-exclusive examples argued that the need for prevention should be prioritised over stigmatisation through the identification of vulnerability indicators. We explore the relative importance of vulnerability within the context of community safety and then suggests an enhanced role for building capacity and capability for a collective form of community leadership.

Common denominators to the challenges presented in the earlier sections suggest that there is an opportunity to place the response to vulnerability at the heart of community safety strategies and to avoid the stigmatisation that often follows actively. In this final section, the chapter will explore the background, challenges and offers a new approach to community safety more generally and a role for community safety partnerships (CSPs) more specifically. CSPs have become too focussed on crime control models since their introduction 20 years ago and appear to have lost their way somewhat following the cessation of direct funding and political priorities in more recent years.

Community safety appeared to first emerge in the last two decades of the preceding millennium initially as a form of crime prevention (Crawford 1998b) but expanding to broader social aspects as its attractiveness increased. Popularised by New Labours' 'Tough on crime; tough on the causes of crime' from 1998, it was still strongly influenced more by the 'tough on crime' mantra courting the 'zero tolerance' debates of the 1990s as opposed to the more preventative problem-oriented approach (Brookes 1996) and in micromanaging and dictating the action of the local partnerships (Menichelli 2020). This view is supported by Daniel who describes Labour's approach to subject CSPs to a centrally imposed performance management regime, based on an active neighbourhood's agenda, utilising a mostly enforcement-oriented attack on anti-social behaviour (Gilling 2013). As a former founding Regional Home Office Director at that time, this author can also support this description through personal experience as a senior member of that performance management regime. Although the approach was viewed as a more holistic preventative model than its predecessor Conservative government (Blyth and Solomon 2008), Menichelli suggests that the micromanagement is 'in stark contrast with the official discourse on autonomy and flexibility to be found in the CDA (Crime and Disorder Act)' (ibid: 4) ... but to what extent is this more distortion as opposed to dilemma?

A brief exploration of the history of community safety and CSPs are helpful. As Crawford argued, neither crime prevention nor community safety represented a definable set of techniques or established strategies as, he argued, they were still very much in their infancy (ibid: 5).

Community safety was undoubtedly in its infancy, but it is somewhat worrying that crime prevention is described as such, given the top priority afforded to prevention by Sir Robert Peel. Peel's first (of nine) principles was that 'the basic mission for which the police exist is to prevent crime and disorder' (Williams 2003). The first commissioners of the Metropolitan Police in 1829 followed this mantra in their instructions to the new Police, although it is argued that the police only paid lip service to the prevention principle 'while largely channelling their energies into a form of professionalisation'. Gilling (2017: 264).

The role of community safety partnerships (CSPs) was enacted through the Crime and Disorder Act 1998 (CDA) against a strong tide of rising crime. At the time of its introduction, the Act was viewed as a dichotomy between centralism and localism, together with interaction within a common law legal system (Houghton 2000). Moreover, it was considered inextricably aligned to political and moral contestations about the nature of the relationship of the state, public authorities, the citizenry and communities (Hughes 2002), lacking effective accountability (Loveday 2004) and a shallow public profile (Loveday 2006).

While the introduction of CSPs was considered as 'auspicious for improved, evidence-based policy and practice' it was argued that they nevertheless 'face substantial obstacles' (Tilley 2005). From this time onward, the role of CSPs has been criticised heavily as well as applauded. The positive aims provide decision-makers with assistance in identifying strategic priorities for reducing crime, disorder, antisocial behaviour (ASB) and the harm caused by the misuse of drugs and alcohol (Chainey 2013). The further aim of CSPs which is to help improve community safety, including the reassurance of communities and in building confidence that concerns and fears are being addressed, less so. Residential communities were increasingly encouraged to play a part in both the maintenance and restoration of order (Evans 2002).

There is a need to target the multi-faceted nature of community safety often characterised by 'wicked' problems. Responses need to be based on a multi-agency approach and include stakeholders such as social housing providers (Safer 2007), local councils, fire and rescue service, health, probation services and others (such as education, e.g., relating to the vulnerability of school premises (Wastell et al. 2004). From the perspective of this paper, however, the early history of CSP activity has not been conducive to the targeting of vulnerable people. This is despite it being stated at the outset of the partnerships that victimisation amongst minority groups was a priority along with the need to plan effectively to combat harassment based on ethnicity or sexuality. Instead, it focussed on crime reflected in government targets, which are easily measurable, rather than the harder-to-measure more socially oriented outcomes of community safety. Explanations for this have been attributed to the withdrawal of central government guidance, an average reduction in funding amounting to 60 percent and a rearrangement of relationships between localities and the centre including the introduction of Police and Crime Commissioners and the increasing devolution agenda (Menichelli 2020). There was some early promise as Blyth and Solomon (earlier cited) describe, in suggesting a transition from the early focus on situational crime prevention towards a much stronger focus on early intervention and initiatives to target particular individuals.

More widely, Chainey argues, strategic intelligence assessment (SIA) plays a vital role in contemporary intelligence-led policing by helping to identify strategic priorities for policing activity, crime reduction and improvements in community safety. In an analysis of 100 SIAs, Chainey describes two main weaknesses; an inability to generate strategic intelligence products that are fit for the purpose for effective decision making, and in particular, in helping to harness support from local government partners to address persistent and causal factors. He advocates an alternative, which is the introduction of a problem-oriented approach in producing strategic intelligence and assessment based on place (locations and temporal features), offending and offender management, and victimisation and vulnerability.

Interestingly, a literature review search using the terms 'community safety partnerships' and 'vulnerability'[6] revealed only one paper. The one identified paper, cited earlier, describes community safety as 'being centrally directed, situational in nature, focussed on anti-social behaviour and incivilities and not concerned with measures of social crime prevention' (Menichelli 2020: 1). Menichelli further suggests that punitive and exclusionary measures are reserved for those who do not conform to the rules of conduct of their community; therefore, it could be argued, stigmatising the individual rather than tackling the causes of vulnerability. This builds on the argument of Tonry (2010: 389 – cited in Meichelli) in that legal instruments (to reduce anti-social behaviour) 'have short-circuited criminal justice processes, been misapplied, stigmatized young people and sought to blame individual miscreants for effects of social changes that are disturbing to many people'.

Reflections on the Past and Promises for the Future of Community Safety

When the CDA was implemented, Crawford (Crawford 1998a) identified three principal dynamics that were likely to come into play, the first two of which were appeals to community, and managerialism and inter-organisational partnerships. Within and between these dynamics lie the third, which he described as deep ambiguities and conflicts, which may encourage, rather than hold back, the dynamics of social exclusion. This was quite prophetic given the contemporary debates on vulnerability and stigmatisation. Menichelli (2020) described Crawford's three dynamics as the 'unholy trinity' of managerialism, as attempts were made to import management styles and strategies from the private sector into the public sector. Communitarianism, with an emphasis on informal mechanisms of social control and people's responsibilities to their community was a vital component of this unholy trinity and partnership working was viewed as a mechanism to support the prevailing view premised that crime prevention should not be the responsibility of one sole agency – typically the police (Crawford 1998: 242). However, the police remained dominant with formal control traditionally viewed as their responsibility (Corcoran and Thomson 2005).

The final section of this chapter addresses the existence of tensions between the managerialism of policy and the rhetoric of 'partnerships', which pervade community safety (akin to the difficulties now being faced by street-level bureaucrats) and the role that community leadership can play in providing a nexus for effective collaboration. In 2008, Gilling, in describing the first 10 years of CSPs argued that New Labour was to be congratulated for bringing about a radical reform in the landscape of local crime control. However, he was also critical of the central government's high level of control over CSPs and local police business (Gilling 2008). Although during the next 10 years this high level of control appears to have dissipated, what has emerged is the second decades' legacy which is a lack of focus and strategic vision. Stigmatisation continues to take place and vulnerability is not comprehensively addressed as a 'wicked problem' that requires strong community leadership through a collective vision.

Community Leadership

We can view the challenges presented to community safety within the broader lens of community leadership (Brookes 2010) and a comprehensive model and framework for collective public leadership (Brookes 2016) based on a New Public Leadership challenge (Brookes and Grint 2010). Part of the problem is that the CDA did not stipulate which agency should lead the CSPs; hence, the police took a dominant role (Menichelli 2020: 4) and, this chapter argues, without 'ownership', the role of other agencies will be less active. The later development of Health and Well Being boards (HWBs)[7] which fulfil a similar cross-agency strategic partnership are more promisingly led by elected leaders, but face challenges concerning lack of statutory guidance and clarity over roles. There are tensions between their role in overseeing commissioning and promoting integration, between high-level strategic planning. This is opposed to involvement in the operational management of pooled budgets or integrated services, and between tackling population-level health issues and driving forward service changes (Humphries and Galea 2013). There are some HWBs that encouragingly establish and make a link between safer communities as a critical part of the health and well-being agenda (North Yorkshire County Council 2020).

A wider government focus on devolution, shared priorities and local area agreements failed to deliver on their promises in terms of coordination and greater integration between public agencies (Brookes 2010). A 'COMPASS[360]' collective leadership framework may be helpful in this regard (Brookes 2016) which encompasses 'collective vision', 'outcome focus', 'multi-level leadership', 'partnership working', 'action oriented', 'systems and structures' and 'skills and behaviours' thus representing the mnemonic of 'COMPASS'. This chapter has already aligned the first four elements and will focus now on the final three which, combined, could provide a framework for the future development of CSPs and the role that the partnerships can play in promoting community safety with vulnerability at the core.

Building Capacity and Capability in Taking Action to Identify and Respond to Vulnerability: Revisiting a Dilemma or Distortion?

The more recent activities of CSPs have been categorised as 'evidence of talk and possibly decisions, but not of actions' (Menichelli 2020: 3). In this respect, policy distortion, as opposed to policy dilemmas, reside more at the centre-stage rather than a side-show with decisions and actions going in opposite directions (to that of 'talk'). If the CSPs represent 'talk', then the supposed collective vision of community leadership efforts become less appropriate against a distorted approach to action-oriented so-called community leadership although, Menichelli argues, community safety practitioners in England and Wales suggest that a shift towards safeguarding has indeed taken place in community safety work. This presents a useful concept to explore further within the context of CSPs alongside resilience.

Aligning safeguarding and resilience has resonance for the main challenges presented in this chapter. The concept of safeguarding within the context of children has become the gold-standard albeit some vulnerable children are still tragically murdered and abused (News 2015). It is less so ensconced in other areas of vulnerability, although – even where safeguarding is a priority – this in itself can lead to direct stigmatisation: for example with female genital mutilation (FGM). In some safeguarding authorities' pressure is placed on certain families to comply with demands which are stigmatising, unjustified and contrary to their rights as British citizens. One example, is where disempowered Somali community members in a British city were compelled to sign a travel form in the face of implicit and explicit threats by the authorities which prevented travel and exposing children to medical examination when travelling to an FGM-affected country (Karlsen et al. 2019).

Government policy by virtue of the Safeguarding Children Act 2018 acknowledges that children may be vulnerable to neglect and abuse or exploitation from within their family and from individuals they come across in their day-to-day lives. It builds on earlier legislation such as the Safeguarding Vulnerable Groups Act 2006. As a result, safeguarding has become an essential aim in the community to ensure the welfare and safety of children and to give them the very best start in life. The policy appears to respond to the challenges of a dilemma in providing statutory agencies with the right guidance in protecting children from maltreatment and preventing impairment of children's health or development. Other aims include ensuring that children grow up in the circumstances consistent with the provision of safe and effective care and taking action to enable all children to have the best outcomes. In summary, it is a child-centred approach to safeguarding and promoting the welfare of every child (HMSO 2018).

Similarly, the Counter-Terrorism and Security Act of 2015 among other provisions, places the 'Prevent' programme on a statutory footing, providing 'prevent duty' guidance and expectations for local authorities. The establishment or use of existing local multi-agency groups to agree on risk and co-ordinate prevent activity, through local authorities, is required to monitor the impact of prevent work effectively (HMSO 2015). There is a clear role here for CSPs.

Safeguarding and resilience go hand-in-hand. In recent years, resilience has become the favoured solution for a range of contemporary policy problems including natural disasters, mental health issues and terrorism. However, the concept is understood far less in criminology and counter-terrorism than in other fields (Hardy 2014).

A Collective Leadership Framework

If the overall outcome of effective public leadership is the creation and demonstration of public value, we can consider Mark Moore's concept of public value (Moore 1995) and Heifetz approach to adaptive leadership which seeks to achieve socially desirable outcomes (Heifetz 1994). The safety of communities must always represent public value and a socially desirable outcome. Who could argue with this? This suggests a need to better understand the context of community safety. The importance of vulnerability as a wider trigger for action as opposed to the stigmatisation of the individual victim, which will often characterise a crime-control approach, provides a promise for a collective vision that extends well beyond the individualist nature of the community safety enforcement approach that has been so evident over the last 20 years. The community and voluntary sector (CVS) can play an important role but evidence suggests that the CVS is often engaged through 'tokenism' (Arnstein 1969) and perceived as a secondary partner rather than full engagement as a key stakeholder (or, as Moore would argue, part of the public value 'authorising environment').

Organisational efforts to embed problem-oriented work as a routine way of working (such as improving training and interagency problem solving) have been suggested as one way of improving the role of CSPs (Bullock et al. 2014). We can consider Heifetz's seven principles of adaptive leadership as an approach for the work of CSPs generally and to focus on vulnerability specifically.

Heifetz terms an 'adaptive' problem or challenge as:

> Adaptive work consists of the learning required to address conflicts in the values people hold, or to diminish the gap between the values people stand for and the reality they face.
>
> (Heifetz 1994: 22)

Heifetz distinguishes between technical and adaptive work in which the former concerns routine problem solving, whereas adaptive work is about exercising wisdom through intelligence in much the same way as a wicked problem is distinguished from its opposite, a tame problem. Let us now consider this with the practice of leadership in achieving public interest outcomes in relation to community leadership and community safety.

The seven principles are illustrated in Figure 4.1. See Brookes (2016) for a full description but, in essence, principles 1 and 7 encompass principles 2 to 6 inclusively. Figure 4.1 requires leaders to 'get on the balcony' to view the bigger picture, whilst moving between the balcony and the 'dance-floor' to protect the voices from below (the full engagement of all stakeholders). The next stage is to identify the adaptive challenges (thus framing the leadership problem) and then create a holding environment to bring all stakeholders together.

Figure 4.1 Seven Principles for adaptive work, adapted from Heifetz 1994 in Brookes (2016) and reproduced with permission.

Conclusion

As the US lawyer Goldberg counsels, 'There's help if you need it and an army of warriors ready to stand by your side. You matter and you don't have to fight this battle alone. You are nobody's victim' (Goldberg 2019: 211).

Do victims need to rely on an army of warriors, or should they be supported by statutory agencies? An interesting analogy is presented in which CSPs are considered as 'more of a collection of loosely affiliated agencies, that is, a flotilla rather than an armada' (Skinns 2006: 169).

This chapter has highlighted the stressful impact of stigmatisation and the woeful responses that are often exhibited by public agencies who have a duty of care to these victims, focussing more on policy distortion rather than an appropriate, balanced response when faced with policy dilemmas.

There are three key areas that this chapter has suggested in moving more towards a coactive approach towards responding appropriately to a policy dilemma rather than a policy distortion. First, it requires collaborative leadership at all levels of all public agencies. Despite its challenging nature, street-level work can be made to conform to higher expectations of public service, but only if this is supported by the top-level of leadership. Second is the need to align the values of public leaders and those of street-level bureaucrats in pursuing the ideals of collective leadership directed towards the creation and demonstration of public value. The third and, arguably, the most important is that of evidence-based framing of the problem profile and preventative strategies to address the underlying causes of vulnerability.

After 20 years of formal community safety strategies, surely it is now time to take stock and move the focus towards truly socially desirable outcomes in which vulnerability is centre-stage and not just sitting in the side-show. We need to confront the brutal facts of the reality and then engage positively in the conflicts that emerge and move towards a consensus based on the public interest.

Notes

1 'stigmatize, v.' *OED Online*. Oxford University Press, June 2019. Web. 15 August 2019.
2 N8 Policing Research Partnership (N8 PRP) was funded by the award of a HEFCE Catalyst Grant 'Innovation and the Application of Knowledge for More Effective Policing: N8 Policing Research Partnership' for the period April 2015–2020.
3 'dilemma, n.' *OED Online*. Oxford University Press, June 2019. Web. 18 August 2019.
4 'distortion, n.' *OED Online*. Oxford University Press, June 2019. Web. 18 August 2019.
5 https://n8prp.org.uk.
6 Undertaking a scopus.com search on 18th August 2019.

7 Health and well-being boards were established under the Health and Social Care Act 2012 to act as a forum in which key leaders from the local health and care system could work together to improve the health and well-being of their local population Kings, Fund (2016). 'Health and wellbeing boards (HWBs) explained'.

References

Abrahima Niang, C., P. Tapsoba, E. Weiss, M. Diagne, Y. Niang, A. M. Moreau, D. Gomis, A. Sidbé Wade, K. Seck, and C. Castle (2003). "'It's raining stones': Stigma, violence and HIV vulnerability among men who have sex with men in Dakar, Senegal," *Culture, Health and Sexuality*, Vol. 5, No. 6, pp. 499–512.

Adesina, O. S. (2014). "Modern day slavery: Poverty and child trafficking in Nigeria," *African Identities*, Vol. 12, No. 2, pp. 165–179.

Andrade, R. G. and J. A. B. Iriart (2015). "Stigma and discrimination: The experiences of HIV-positive women in poor neighborhoods of Maputo, Mozambique," *Cadernos de Saude Publica*, Vol. 31, No. 3, pp. 565–574.

Arnstein, S. R. (1969). A Ladder of Citizen Participation. *Journal of the American Institute of Planners*, Vol. 35, No. 4, pp. 216–224. doi: 10.1080/01944366908977225.

Bandewar, S. V. S., S. Bharat, A. Kongelf, H. Pisal, and M. Collumbien (2016). "Considering risk contexts in explaining the paradoxical HIV increase among female sex workers in Mumbai and Thane, India," *BMC Public Health*, Vol. 16, No. 1. doi: 10.1186/s12889-016-2737-/NO.

Bejzyk, M. (2017). "Criminalization on the basis of sexual orientation and gender identity: Reframing the dominant human rights discourse to include freedom from torture and inhuman and degrading treatment," *Canadian Journal of Women and the Law*, Vol. 29, No. 2, pp. 375–400.

Ben-Ishai, E. (2012). Fostering autonomy: A theory of citizenship, the state, and social service delivery. USA, Penn State Press.

Blyth, M. and E. Solomon (2008). "Introduction," in M. Blyth and E. Solomon (eds), *Prevention and Youth Crime: Is Early Intervention Working?* Bristol, Centre for Crime and Justice Studies, Policy Press, University of Bristol, pp. 1–8.

Boseley, S. (2018). "Criminalisation of sex work normalises violence, review finds," London, Guardian Newspaper.

Brookes, S. (1996). "Debate on 'Zero Tolerance' –v- 'Problem Oriented Policing'," *Police Superintendents Association of England and Wales National Conference*, Bristol, England.

——— (2011). "Crisis, confidence and collectivity: Responding to the new public leadership challenge," *Leadership*, Vol. 7, No. 2, pp. 175–195.

——— (2010). "Telling the story of place: The role of community leadership," in S. Brookes and K. Grint (eds), *The New Public Leadership Challenge*, Basingstoke, Palgrave Macmillan, pp. 1. online resource.

——— (2016). *The Selfless Leader: A Compass for Collective Leaders*. London, Palgrave Macmillan.

Brookes, S. and K. Grint (2010). *The New Public Leadership Challenge*. Basingstoke, Palgrave Macmillan.

Bullock, K., R. Erol, and N. Tilley (2014). "Problem-oriented policing and partnerships: Implementing an evidence based approach to crime reduction", in J. M. Brown (ed), *The Future of Policing*. Abingdon, Routledge.

Chainey, S. (2013). "A problem-oriented approach to the production of strategic intelligence assessments," *Policing: An International Journal of Police Strategies & Management*, Vol. 36, No. 3, pp. 474–490.

Chakrapani, V., P. A. Newman, M. Shunmugam, A. McLuckie, and F. Melwin (2007). "Structural violence against Kothi-identified men who have sex with men in Chennai, India: A qualitative investigation," *AIDS Education and Prevention*, Vol. 19, No. 4, pp. 346–364.

Chamberland, L. and E. Saewyc (2011). "Stigma, vulnerability and resilience: The psychosocial health of sexual minorities and gender in," *Canadian Journal of Community Mental Health*, Vol. 30, No. 2, pp. 7–11.

Chollier, M., C. Tomkinson, and P. Philibert (2016). "STIs/HIV Stigma and health: A short review," *Sexologies*, Vol. 25, No. 4, pp. 179–183.

Corcoran, J. and B. B. Thomson (2005). "A geographical approach to community safety: A U.K. perspective," in M. Campagna (ed), *GIS for Sustainable Development*, Boca Raton, FL, Taylor and Francis, pp. 385–401.

Craig, G. and S. Clay (2017). "Who is vulnerable? Adult social care and modern slavery," *Journal of Adult Protection*, Vol. 19, No. 1, pp. 21–32.

Crawford, A. (1998a). "Community safety and the quest for security: Holding back the dynamics of social exclusion," *Policy Studies*, Vol. 19, No. 3–4, pp. 237–253.

——— (1998b). *Crime prevention and community safety: Politics, policies and practices*. Harlow, Longman.

Duby, Z., B. Nkosi, A. Scheibe, B. Brown, and L. G. Bekker (2018). "'Scared of going to the clinic': Contextualising healthcare access for men who have sex with men, female sex workers and people who use drugs in two South African cities," *Southern African Journal of HIV Medicine*, Vol. 19, No. 1. doi: doi.org/10.4102/ sajhivmed.v19i1.701.

Evans, K. (2002). "Crime control partnerships: Who do we trust?," *Criminal Justice Matters*, Vol. 50, No. 1, pp. 12–13.

FitzGerald, S. A. (2012). "Vulnerable bodies, vulnerable borders: Extraterritoriality and human trafficking," *Feminist Legal Studies*, Vol. 20, No. 3, pp. 227–244.

Gadd, D. and R. Broad (2018). "Troubling recognitions in British responses to modern slavery," *British Journal of Criminology*, Vol. 58, No. 6, pp. 1440–1461.

Gadd, D., R. Broad, J. Craven, C. Lightowlers, and E. Bellotti (2017). *Mapping the contours of modern slavery in greater manchester*. Manchester, University of Manchester and the N8 Policing Research Partnership.

Gilling, D. (2008). "Celebrating a decade of the crime and disorder act? A personal view," *Safer Communities*, Vol. 7, No. 3, pp. 39–45.

Gilling, D. (2013). "Crime reduction and community safety: Labour and the politics of local crime control," in J. Muncrie J and D. Wilson (eds), *Student Handbook of Criminal Justice and Criminology*. London, Cavendish Publishers.

Goffman, E. (1974). *Frame Analysis: An Essay on the Organization of Experience*. Cambridge, MA, Harvard University Press.

Goldberg, C. (2019). Nobody's Victim – Fighting Psychos, Stalkers, Pervs and Trolls. United States, Great Britain, Little, Brown Book Group. Kindle Edition.

Gonzalez, C. (2010). "Selling youthful sex: An anthropological approach to juvenile male prostitution," *Advances in Sociology Research*, Vol. 6, pp. 257–269.

Grint, K. (2010). "Wicked problems and clumsy solutions: The role of leadership," in S. Brookes and K. Grint (eds), *The New Public Leadership Challenge*, Basingstoke, Palgrave Macmillan.

Hadjimatheou, K. and D. J. Lynch (2018). "UK anti-slavery policy at the border: Humanitarian opportunism and the challenge of victim consent to assistance," *European Journal of Criminology*. doi: 10.1177/1477370818820645.

Hardy, K. (2014). "Resilience in UK counter-terrorism," *Theoretical Criminology*, Vol. 19, No. 1, pp. 77–94.

Heifetz, R. A. (1994). *Leadership without easy answers*. Cambridge, MA, Belknap Press of Harvard University Press.

Herzfeld, B. (2002). "Slavery and gender: Women's double exploitation," *Gender and Development*, Vol. 10, No. 1, pp. 50–55.

HMSO. (2015). "Counter-terrorism and security act 2015," in Home Office (ed), *Part 6-Amendments of, or relating to the Terrorism Act, 2000, UK Government,*, London, HMSO.

——— (2018). "Working Together to Safeguard Children: A guide to inter-agency working to safeguard and promote the welfare of children," in Department of Education (ed), *Working Together to Safeguard Children, UK Government*. London, HMSO.

Hope for Justice (2018). "Modern Slavery." UK Office, Hope for Justice, P.O. BOX 5527, Manchester, UK, https://hopeforjustice.org.

Houghton, J. (2000). "The wheel turns for policing and local government," *Local Government Studies*, Vol. 26, No. 2, pp. 117–130.

Hughes, G. (2002). "The audit culture and crime and disorder reduction partnerships: Exorcising the wicked issue of community safety?" *Crime Prevention and Community Safety*, Vol. 4, No. 2, pp. 9–18.

Humphries, R. and A. Galea (2013). "Health and wellbeing boards: One year on," Kings Fund.

Karlsen, S., N. Carver, M. Mogilnicka, and C. Pantazis (2019). "'Stigmatising' and 'traumatising' approaches to FGM-safeguarding need urgent review". Policy Press, University of Bristol, Bristol, UK, Policy Briefing, www.bristol.ac.uk/policybristol/policy-briefings/fgm-safeguarding/

The Kings Fund (2016). "Health and wellbeing boards (HWBs) explained." London, The Kings Fund.

Knutagård, H. (2015). "The story of a male sex worker," in D. E. Friedman and J. Merrick (eds), *Public Health, Social Work and Health Inequalities*, New York, Nova Science Publishers, Inc., Kristianstad University, School of Health and Society, pp. 249–264.

Kumar, A. (2019). Fellow of the RSA, "End the criminalisation of homelessness," Royal Society of Arts (RSA) Policy Paper, RSA London, 13 February.

Lipsky, M. (1980). *Street-level bureaucracy: Dilemmas of the individual in public services*. New York, Russell Sage Foundation.

——— (2010). *Street-level bureaucracy: Dilemmas of the individual in public services* (30th anniversary expanded ed.). New York, Russell Sage Foundation.

Logan, T. K., R. Walker, and G. Hunt (2009). "Understanding human trafficking in the United States," *Trauma, Violence, and Abuse*, Vol. 10, No. 1, pp. 3–30.

Loveday, B. (2004). "Police reform and local government: New opportunities for improving local community safety arrangements in England and Wales," *Crime Prevention and Community Safety*, Vol. 6, No. 2, pp. 7–19.

——— (2006). "Learning from the 2004 crime audit. An evaluation of the national community safety plan 2006–2008 and current impediments to the effective delivery of community safety strategy by local crime reduction partnerships," *Crime Prevention and Community Safety*, Vol. 8, No. 3, pp. 188–201.

Mantouvalou, V. (2006). "Servitude and forced labour in the 21st century: The Human Rights of domestic workers," *Industrial Law Journal*, Vol. 35, No. 4, pp. 395–414.

——— (2018). "The UK modern slavery act 2015 three years on," *Modern Law Review*, Vol. 81, No. 6, pp. 1017–1045.

McDonald, L. Z. (2011). "Securing identities, resisting terror: Muslim youth work in the UK and its implications for security," *Religion, State and Society*, Vol. 39, No. 2–3, pp. 176–189.

Menichelli, F. (2018). "Transforming the English model of community safety: From crime and disorder to the safeguarding of vulnerable people," *Criminology and Criminal Justice*, Vol. 20, No. 1, pp. 39–56.

Metcalf, E. P. and C. Selous (2020). "Modern slavery response and recognition training," *Clinical Teacher*, Vol. 17, No. 1, pp. 47–51.

Moore, M. H. (1995). *Creating public value: Strategic management in government*. Cambridge, MA, London, Harvard University Press.

Mulkerrins, J. (2019). "Weinstein and my revenge porn battle," *The Times*, London, The Times Newspaper Group, p. 2.

News, BBC (2nd June 2015). 'Oliver Sargent death: Safeguarding opportunities missed', *BBC News*. https://www.bbc.co.uk/news/uk-england-shropshire-32963741.

Oliveira, A. and L. Fernandes (2017). "Sex workers and public health: Intersections, vulnerabilities and resistance," *Salud Colectiva*, Vol. 13, No. 2, pp. 199–210.

North Yorkshire County Council (2020). Partnerships, North Yorkshire "North Yorkshire partnerships working together: Health and well-being partnership." NYCC, Northallerton, Yorkshire, UK.

Qiao, S., E. Yuk-ha Tsang, J. S. Wilkinson, F. Lipeleke, and X. Li (2019). "'In Zimbabwe there is nothing for us': Sex work and vulnerability of HIV infection among male sex workers in Zimbabwe," *AIDS Care – Psychological and Socio-Medical Aspects of AIDS/HIV*, Vol. 31, No. 9, pp. 1124–1130.

Rittel, H. W. J. and M. M. Webber (1973). "Dilemmas in a general theory of planning," *Policy Sciences*, Vol. 4, pp. 155–169.

Safer, C. (2007). "Safe as some houses: Crime, social tenure and community safety a case study based on a CDRP in northern England," *Safer Communities*, Vol. 6, No. 4, pp. 16–24.

Salmon, C. (2010). "The world's oldest profession: Evolutionary insights into prostitution," in J. D. Duntley and T. K. Shackelford (eds), *Evolutionary Forensic Psychology: Darwinian Foundations of Crime and Law*, New York, Oxford University Press, pp. 121–135.

Singh, B. D. (2010). *Negotiation & counselling: Text and cases*. New Delhi, Excel Books.

Skinns, L. (2006). "Flotilla or armada? Interpreting the practices and politics of three community safety partnerships," *Crime Prevention and Community Safety*, Vol. 8, No. 3, pp. 169–187.

Sloss, C. M. and G. W. Harper (2010). "Legal service needs and utilization of women who trade sex," *Sexuality Research and Social Policy*, Vol. 7, No. 3, pp. 229–241.

Tilley, N. (2005). "Crime reduction: A quarter century review," *Public Money and Management*, Vol. 25, No. 5, pp. 267–274.

van de Weert, A. and Q. A. M. Eijkman (2019). "Subjectivity in detection of radicalisation and violent extremism: A youth worker's perspective," *Behavioral Sciences of Terrorism and Political Aggression*, Vol. 11, No. 3, pp. 191–214.

Walker, R. (2017). "Selling sex, mothering and 'keeping well' in the city: Reflecting on the everyday experiences of cross-border migrant women who sell sex in Johannesburg," *Urban Forum*, Vol. 28, No. 1, pp. 59–73.

Wastell, D., P. Kawalek, P. Langmead-Jones, and R. Ormerod (2004). "Information systems and partnership in multi-agency networks: An action research project in crime reduction," *Information and Organization*, Vol. 14, No. 3, pp. 189–210.

Williams, K. L. (2003). "Peel's principles and their acceptance by American police: Ending 175 years of reinvention," *The Police Journal: Theory, Practice and Principles*, Vol. 76, No. 2, pp. 97–120.

5 Responding to Vulnerability in Practice – Ambulance, Police and Fire and Rescue Services

Jonathan Knox, Stephen Down, Helen McMillan and Peter Murphy

Introduction

This chapter contains three separate professional and practice contributions from senior personnel. The first two contributions are written by officers occupying strategic positions in Emergency and Blue Light services, who are also familiar with front-line service provision (Knox and Downs, Ambulance and McMillan, Police), together with a contribution from Murphy, an academic who provides consultancy for Fire and Rescue Services, and draws on his long experience as the Chief Civil Servant and first responder in dealing with Emergencies and other Crises across the East Midlands region of England. They all provide a different dimension on the role of front-line professionals in day-to-day dealings with vulnerable groups and individuals, but each addresses the European and national policy imperatives on how Blue Light and Emergency service agencies prioritise and operationalise their responses to this 'wicked issue' within given statutory requirements and available resources.

North East Ambulance Service NHS Foundation Trust (NEAS)

Dr Jonathan Knox and Mr Stephen Downs

All human beings have a right to live their lives free from the fear of harm and abuse. The NHS definition of vulnerability is where an individual, be they an adult or child, is at risk of harm, whether through direct abuse, or neglect. The North East Ambulance Service NHS Foundation Trust (NEAS) applies this definition, often dealing with situations where patients have been physically or emotionally harmed. We must make decisions about the best means of supporting everyone to ensure prevention of harm, whether by a safeguarding referral or raising welfare concerns.

In this section, we discuss how we are uniquely placed to discuss the practical issues and categories of vulnerability in the region. Often, we are working in conjunction with other emergency services to mitigate situations that may cause vulnerability. For example, operational crews are very good at identifying an adult who may need additional care and support, and act in a safeguarding role when issues of vulnerability are identified.

This section addresses the operational responsibilities of prioritising safeguarding and welfare for an ambulance service. Areas of vulnerability are identified through attendance at 999 call outs and include common circumstances such as adults living alone, predominantly the frail elderly, who may be struggling to take medication correctly, attend to their own personal or domestic hygiene and are at risk of falls. The section also refers to selected situational examples identified across the region, such as addiction, victims of violence, human trafficking, sexual exploitation, Domestic Abuse, Mental Health and Mental Capacity issues.

NEAS Safeguarding Processes

Under international law, all states have a duty to uphold the basic human rights of their citizens. NEAS has a legal duty to protect children, young people and adults at risk. We exercise this duty through a variety of measures, which include, identifying, reporting and investigating allegations of abuse and raising welfare concerns where adults at risk stand in need of greater care and support. NEAS is committed to operate within agreed Safeguarding Policies and procedures developed in partnership with local authorities.

There are legal definitions, such as in the Care Act 2014, of what constitutes an adult at risk. Adults at risk must be aged 18 years old, in receipt of or eligible for care and support, at risk of or experiencing harm or abuse and unable to protect themselves from harm or abuse. 'Working Together to Safeguarding Children' (Great Britain 2018) defines safeguarding as; safeguarding and promoting the welfare of children by; protecting children from maltreatment, preventing impairment of children's health or development, ensuring that children grow up in circumstances consistent with the provision of safe and effective care and taking action to enable all children to have the best outcomes.

The biggest category of abuse identified by our staff is neglect/acts of omission, which fits with the national picture of all Section 42 enquiries. A Section 42 enquiry refers to Section 42 of the Care Act 2014, specifically where there is 'a reasonable belief that an adult in its area (a) with care and support needs (b) is experiencing, or at risk of experiencing abuse and neglect (c) and is unable to safeguard themselves' (TSO 2014). The North-East has more Section 42 Enquiries than any other part of England. Although there is no definite explanation as to why this is the case, one explanation is that Local Authorities across the North-East have tended to provide more free safeguarding training to provider organisations than other regions across the UK. As a result, training in the ambulance service has focussed on ensuring that we do not miss identifying vulnerability or potential vulnerability. Through the assessment of a call handler or clinician on the 999 call, we may advise patients to see their GP or attend a walk-in-centre. There are, however, limitations in the ability of NEAS to follow up these referrals, to check if patients have followed the care advice.

Traditional safeguarding services run by the local authority are based on a casework system. For example, alerts that may be raised about an individual child in a family setting. Management of these cases may pose some limitations. For example, for many older children the abuse often takes place outside the family home setting and therefore may not be appropriately managed by using traditional service models. A 'Contextual Safeguarding' (Firmin 2015) approach means that instead of assessing a child in a family setting, they assess the risk based on the location of abuse. For example, abuse such as sexual exploitation may take place around a bus stop, shopping centre, stair well or burger bar. This flexible model involves working with groups of friends/peers to offer advice and support to victims. The next section addresses issues of vulnerability across, but not exclusive to the North-East region.

Regional Issues of Vulnerability

This section addresses the most common areas of vulnerability identified by NEAS and how NEAS responds to these issues. The practical challenges raised for service model delivery and paramedic staff in their role on the ground are also discussed. In terms of process, ambulance services triage every call, whether 999 or NHS111, based on the information presented by the caller. This can lead to complexity caused by language and cultural barriers. For example, NEAS has a very low ratio of staff from black and minority ethnic (BAME) backgrounds, especially when compared with the population distribution across the North-East region.

In contrast, the recent recruitment of Polish paramedics has increased the diversity of our staff team. Traditionally, there are not many safeguarding referrals from these communities and there is limited understanding of how well our services are received in those areas. In contrast, there has been some excellent work done by our in-house Equality and Diversity teams to create a 'communication passport', supporting those with a learning disability to request an ambulance and understand the processes and types of questions they will be asked. Equally, there is improved awareness of hate crime and the challenges faced by the Lesbian, Gay, Bisexual and Trans (LGBT) community.

Focussing on issues identified in the North-East, Northumbria Police opened 'Operation Sanctuary' which highlighted a significant problem with both children and young adults with disabilities being criminally exploited for sex. There was found to be a criminal network of drug trafficking, whereby children and young adults were being trapped through fear, addiction and violence and forced to sell drugs. Often the vulnerable person is removed from their home under threat of harm to themselves or their families, plied with alcohol and drugs and groomed to be abused. The primary role for such removals is provided by social services, with police involvement to ensure the safety of all involved, and ambulance crews in place to respond to physical health concerns.

One of the greatest challenges in identifying vulnerability are the changing patterns of abuse and the methods used for exploitation. For example, modern technology can be very useful but can also be misused to abuse and exploit the vulnerable. Additionally, in these cases, there is often a misconception that the children and young adults are runaways and criminals, rather than victims.

NEAS crews are ideally placed to identify young people at risk of sexual and other forms of exploitation. Many victims are too afraid to inform the Police as they fear they won't be believed or are too afraid to press ahead with a prosecution. NEAS crews are in a position of trust and victims may be more willing to disclose. Similarly, entering homes, crews can often pick up of tensions and unusual dynamics within a home that could indicate cuckooing or other forms of exploitation.

Loneliness exposes people to issues that may involve them becoming vulnerable. For example, elderly people struggling to cope, those at risk of neglect/self-neglect or at risk of experiencing domestic violence and/or exploitation. Despite trying to better support these patients through collaborative working with external agencies, there are some individuals that will call more frequently than is necessary, attempting to mitigate loneliness. Ambulance crews work well with lonely vulnerable adults, but they often don't identify that they are in a vital position in their role to alert social service providers.

Training is currently undertaken for front-line paramedics to recognise signs of vulnerability in all types of call outs. For example, following a training presentation from Newcastle Council on Human Trafficking and Sexual Exploitation, a crew member contacted their manager to say they were called to a job in a takeaway where there were ten mattresses on the floor of the back room. They had recognised that this was a strong indicator of potential illegal labour or other forms of exploitation.

Mental Health Risk Assessment and Triage

There is a challenge in terms of legal literacy for our staff regarding terms such as Mental Capacity and Mental Health, which are often confused as meaning the same thing. Mental Health refers to a state of emotional health and includes a plethora of conditions including, Anxiety, depression, Psychotic disorders, Bipolar disorder, eating disorders and personality disorders. Mental Capacity refers to a patient's legal right and practicable ability to make their own care and treatment decisions.

There is limited robust knowledge of Mental Health services, particularly when seeking alternatives to hospital admission. For example, patients diagnosed with a personality disorder can be particularly challenging to front-line crews who are afraid to leave them at home, due to a fear the patient will harm or kill themselves and also that this would be seen as negligent practice for which they could lose their professional certification.

Crews often believe that the Mental Capacity of the patient is the primary issue. For example, if the patient is suffering from a significant mental illness which is leading to them trying to kill/harm themselves, then the Mental Health Act (TSO 2007) may be the most effective tool to empower the crew to ensure the patient gets the care and treatment they need.

NEAS staff must take at face value any threats of self-harm or suicide; compounding this situation is that they are not traditionally trained in suicide risk assessment. A challenge for all ambulance services is how to quickly and effectively conduct a robust risk assessment of the patient's vulnerability to the Mental Health service, whilst on-scene in a potentially volatile situation. This can lead to a risk averse response whereby the patient is taken to hospital unnecessarily.

We are a caring and compassionate organisation. It is, however, this very compassion that often leaves crews afraid to leave the patient on-scene having provided medical care for their physical presentation of need. Some trusts have dedicated Mental Health response services, such as London Ambulance Service (LAS), and this has greatly reduced their inappropriate transfers to hospital, provided a better experience for patients, and upskilled ambulance staff working alongside Mental Health professionals.

Adopting these mechanisms alongside improved training, procedures and enhanced vigilance approaches supports crews to act as early identifiers of vulnerability when they are called out, and to enable appropriate referrals for safeguarding and welfare issues. The next section addresses the ambulance service as a safeguarding service and the process of welfare and referral.

Safeguarding Teams and Welfare Referrals

Almost three out of every four safeguarding adult referrals are welfare concerns rather than safeguarding issues. The NEAS safeguarding team has prioritised updating the training to operational crews to help identify the difference. A safeguarding concern is where an adult or child is at risk of significant harm or abuse. A welfare concern or early help referral refers to individuals who are struggling to cope and may need additional formal care and support to be able to live as independent life as possible.

For example, if a person is able to ring NHS111 for advice suggesting a loved one is struggling to cope, the call handler will often make a safeguarding referral, when perhaps a better route would be to support the adult to contact their local social services or primary care service. This way people can request their own needs assessment, which adult social care services can respond to.

If our call handlers and operational crews refer using the safeguarding rather than welfare route, depending how that Local Authority triages referrals, the referral may be deemed as not meeting the Care Act (TSO 2014) definition of an adult at risk. This can lead them to take no further action. An example of where a safeguarding referral is a caller to 999 saying they are feeling suicidal; of which at least half of the cases tend to be teenagers. We need to ensure improved quality of referrals and relationships with receiving Local Authority teams to ensure no cases fall through the net.

There are challenges for the ambulance service regarding where the vulnerable person is referred but there is no receiving service open. For example, if a 999-call received is a suicidal teenager at 8 pm on a Friday night, it will not be triaged by the Local Authority until Monday morning, when their service re-opens. In these situations, Local Authorities should have Emergency Duty Teams (EDT), but even then, there can be delays in referral. This is often because alongside the potential social or Mental Health issue, there is often a physical care presentation which the ambulance service needs to respond to. Coordinating the services to achieve timely physical and social care is often challenging.

Findings from 'Domestic Homicide Reviews', which are a 'multi-agency review of the circumstances in which the death of a person aged 16 or over has, or appears to have, resulted from violence, abuse or neglect' (Home Office 2016), there are challenges to making a safeguarding referral for the victims of, or those vulnerable, to domestic violence and abuse.

What is not clear are the reasons why. This may partly be due to the challenges of cross-agency working. Often it is the police attend the incident first, and who request NEAS attendance if the victim has suffered a physical injury. Domestic violence may not be understood as the cause of the physical injury, making it difficult to refer on this basis. This is prevalent, particularly if the alleged perpetrator is on scene, and the victim cannot fully disclose events. This situation can lead to issues of gaining consent for referral. For example, if the patient is still in a high-risk situation and to do so could leave them more vulnerable.

Finally, it is important to note that making a referral for a vulnerable person can cause significant distress to family or the patient. Welfare referrals made as a safeguarding referral can sometimes lead to cares feeling they are being accused of abusing their loved one. These referrals can form a permanent record once received by the local authority. This record could for example, create problems if that person then wants to be a foster carers or train to work in health and social care. It also causes untold mental anguish as they feel that in some way they have been falsely accused or that they have let down their loved ones in not protecting them from harm and abuse.

Northumbria Police Helen McMillan, Assistant Chief Constable

It is a universal truth that the measure of any society can be found in how it treats its most vulnerable members and in recent years mission statements and visions of Chief Constables in Police forces throughout the United Kingdom have pledged to prioritise resource allocation to ensure that those who are the most vulnerable, those at greatest risk of harm, receive a timely response and are the focus of preventative and protective efforts. Post 2010 when the resources available to Policing diminished, the service was forced to think about how it prioritised its resources against ever increasing demand. Policing no longer had the ability to deal with everything and it had to turn its attention to how it rationed its resources. This was something that began with the Crime and Disorder Act (CDA) in 1998 with need for partnership working and police no longer having the monopoly for crime control, which is important from a demand and needs assessment. What followed has been a concerted effort to focus resource upon those most vulnerable and to think more broadly about who is vulnerable and when. The Equality Act 2010 requires all public agencies, including police services, to have regard to socio-economic inequalities, and protect individuals on the basis of age, disability, gender re-assignment, marriage and civil partnership, pregnancy and maternity, race, religion and sexual orientation. The College of Policing also offers standards on safeguarding vulnerable groups, in line with the Safeguarding Vulnerable Groups Act, 2016. These include the vulnerable and at-risk individuals, who have become (or are at risk of becoming) victims of crime. This also encompasses the care and welfare of those detained in custody, dealing with individuals who suffer from mental ill-health and the management of sexual and violent offenders.

It is a universal truth that the measure of any society can be found in how it treats its most vulnerable members and in recent years mission statements and visions of Chief Constables in Police forces throughout the United Kingdom have pledged to prioritise resource allocation to ensure that those who are the most vulnerable, those at greatest risk of harm, receive a timely response and are the focus of preventative and protective efforts. Post 2010 when the resources available to Policing diminished, the service was forced to think about how it prioritised its resources against ever increasing demand. Policing no longer had the ability to deal with everything and it had to turn its attention to how it rationed its resources. This was something that began with the Crime and Disorder Act (CDA) 1998 with need for partnership working and police no longer having the monopoly for crime control – important point perhaps for demand and needs assessment What followed has been a concerted effort to focus resource upon those most vulnerable and to think more broadly about who is vulnerable and when.

I will now attempt to explore from a practitioner's view what this means to officers and how forces at first point of contact identify vulnerability in order to ensure an appropriate response. I will go on to explore how the demand on forces has changed significantly and how they are expected to understand and deliver services for a society with complex needs.

The starting point for forces is to understand and apply the definition of vulnerability as it applies to policing. The College of Policing defines vulnerability as

> A person is vulnerable if as a result of their situation or circumstances, they are unable to take care of, or protect themselves or others from harm or exploitation.

> (College of Policing, UK)

The following equation assists

$$\text{Personal factors} \times \text{situational factors} = \text{harm/risk of harm}$$

Personal factors can include age, Mental Health, gender, sexual orientation, ethnicity, religion, difference and physical ability/disability.

Situational factors can include location, time of day, temperature, lack of power, language barriers, poverty, adverse family, community or cultural circumstances. The presence of an abuser and grooming.

The College of Policing also identifies 13 strands of vulnerability, which are:

- Domestic Abuse
- Adult sexual exploitation
- Stalking and harassment
- Missing and absent
- Female genital mutilation (FGM)
- Managing of sex and violent offenders
- Adults at risk
- Child abuse
- Honour based abuse (HBA)
- Modern slavery and trafficking
- Forced marriage
- Serious sexual offences
- Child sexual exploitation

The first contact for the public with any Police service is via the force control room, where operators assess the level/speed of response to reported incidents based upon threat, harm, risk, immediacy, vulnerability and engagement also known as THRIVE. (Threat, Harm, Risk, Investigation Opportunities, Vulnerability of the victim and the Engagement level required to resolve the issue). Applying THRIVE to the circumstances of an incident allows the operator to prioritise the service response. Threat risk and harm are obvious indicators upon which to predicate response time; vulnerability adds a further dimension which means that those most in need of assistance can be prioritised over those able to take care of themselves and who can therefore wait longer for a police response without suffering a detriment.

Those victims, witnesses and on occasion offenders, who fall neatly into those strands of vulnerability or who possess the personal vulnerability features are relatively straight forward to identify. Call handlers are easily able to identify a 93-year-old victim of a distraction burglary, or a child victim of sexual abuse as vulnerable. Society would recognise what could be considered as obvious vulnerability factors and expect an enhanced and swift response to calls for service.

When thinking more broadly and applying the situational factors and the strands it becomes apparent that it is highly likely that every one of us could be considered vulnerable at certain times in our lives and in certain circumstances.

It is challenging for policing to correctly identify those who are temporarily vulnerable due to situational factors. Situational vulnerability is much more subtle and complex. A mixture of factors can affect individuals in a unique way resulting in a flawed response if not properly probed/investigated and their impact understood.

Vulnerability can change over time, not just in terms of age but in other ways. For example, the longer a person is without the basics to sustain life, water, food, shelter, the more vulnerable they become. Exposure to elements and the drop in temperature between night and day can affect vulnerability. The presence of a predator, or proximity to a known danger or presence at a dangerous location can result in a person who would otherwise not be so, becoming vulnerable. A member of the public making a call for service may not initially be classed as vulnerable, however, this must be monitored, for as the situation evolves they may become more vulnerable. For example, they may need access to medication, their Mental Health may decline, they can become exposed to those who would seek to exploit them, needed or do them harm.

It is therefore important that the vulnerable status or otherwise of a caller is kept under review as their situation improves or deteriorates. In terms of recognising vulnerability within the context of initial contact, forces have invested heavily in training their teams to recognise vulnerability and respond appropriately to it. For those answering calls it is imperative that they do so not just quickly but also thoroughly so the vulnerability or otherwise of a caller is probed and understood.

Early identification of vulnerability and reducing the exposure to harm of the vulnerable can have a significant impact upon the quality of life of individuals and upon the future demand they place upon services. Police forces are not always the best service to deal with vulnerable people, particularly those in Mental Health crisis and there is a growing and active consideration, awareness and knowledge within policing of how to protect and support people in a Mental Health crisis. Some Mental Health trusts have practitioners located in police control rooms to assist in ensuring that there is a partnership approach to improving patient care, informed by professionals.

Beyond the initial response, the police have a duty to prevent and detect crime. Understanding who is vulnerable to becoming a victim of crime in order to best protect the public is an important part of policing. It's always better to prevent a crime from occurring than to respond after the fact. Understanding vulnerability is hugely important in the problem-solving work carried out by police and partners to protect the public. As society changes, we are recognising that with change comes new threats and risks which can offer criminals new ways to identify vulnerabilities to exploit. Perhaps the most obvious example of this is the explosion of the use of the internet, with the rise of cyber space which has inadvertently created a whole new sphere for criminals to exploit. Those who are vulnerable in cyberspace are a further group to be identified and protected. Cybercrime and cyber-enabled crime and those vulnerable to it are complex to identify and victims, in particular corporations, do not always want to report crimes or admit to being vulnerable to cyber-attack for fear of adverse business consequences. Adults who would not have previously been thought of by themselves or services as vulnerable and likely to become victims of crime, have found themselves targeted on-line by unscrupulous fraudsters. New scams or sophisticated attacks are constantly being developed and institutions struggle to keep up with the differing types of fraud. Fraudsters, sometimes operating from a different country, who often never have personal contact with their victims, posing as would-be lovers in in danger due to financial difficulties, tax inspectors, banks and so on, have gone on to relieve victims of their life savings. It seems that we can all be very vulnerable whilst on-line.

Isolated individuals who have previously been thought to be safe have now been identified as being vulnerable to a multitude of cyber-enabled crimes and this vulnerability is exploited in the closed space in the privacy of victims' bedrooms where they can be groomed, exploited and radicalised to become victims or perpetrators, often without the knowledge of even those closest to them.

The technological advances of the World Wide Web have been numerous and speedy and will continue apace. Policing is constantly changing and adapting to keep up, usually one step behind and often operating within a legislative framework which requires updating to allow law enforcement and partners to deal with the threat and identify and protect those vulnerable to it.

Crimes committed or enabled on-line are 'hidden' crimes. The absence on-line of a parent or other capable guardian who can step in to protect victims or deter offenders makes it an attractive arena for those who would wish to target the vulnerable. Many victims of grooming, CSE, and stalking and harassment have been targeted on-line.

Police forces across the UK work with multi agency partnerships such as Local Safeguarding boards and Community Safety Partnerships to have a holistic approach to protecting the vulnerable across the services (on the back of legislative partnership arrangements mentioned previously re: CDA 1998). Social media platforms and providers of on-line services are also under increasing pressure to play their part to protect users on-line and this is an area of constant change with law enforcement often taking some time to catch up.

Immigrant and refugee communities are very vulnerable to being exploited. Society can see them as problematic and be hostile on occasion to their presence. The language barrier creates a vulnerability and some communities have a fear and distrust of public services, particularly policing which makes them very vulnerable to exploitation. In these communities, hidden crimes such as modern slavery, trafficking, FGM, and HBV (Hepatitis B Virus) are all very difficult for services to identify, tackle and prevent. Forces over time have become smarter and more effective at working with partners to identify and tackle these types of crimes which target very vulnerable people and are often conducted out of sight, needed or within very close groups.

The vulnerable may often be in positions where no exploitation offences have yet been committed, but they are being significantly taken advantage of by people whose motivation is to exploit that vulnerability for their own gain. It is difficult for policing and other services to deal with this type of crime as those who are exploited will often not perceive themselves to be victims. This is particularly the case with victims of Child Sexual Exploitation, trafficked individuals, those involved in modern slavery and those who have been targeted by fraudsters using false personal/romantic relationships. They can be unwilling to trust the authorities, needed or may consider that their life in an exploited situation is better to the alternative, which may be returning to another country or no relationship at all.

Perhaps where it becomes even more difficult for society, and by extension for policing and wider law enforcement to recognise and deal with vulnerability effectively, is when the vulnerable are both perpetrator and victim. Vulnerable victims who are drug users, sex workers, whose immigration status is unclear for example, are all more vulnerable to exploitation and less likely to seek assistance from services and law enforcement. Historically policing and other services have dealt with individuals as either a victim or an offender but not as both. Drug addicts and sex workers were treated as criminals, not as vulnerable exploited victims, as policing and society weren't nuanced enough to recognise and deal with them as both. They tended to be dealt with as criminals, and their safeguarding was not routinely considered; fortunately attitudes have changed, and forces are recognising that they need to ensure that their staff looks beyond the crime or incident itself. Vulnerable people can also be offenders and the criminal justice partners must work together to ensure appropriate sanctions which deter recidivism and also seek to put in place appropriate interventions and support.

Attitudes towards young people, in particular have changed over time. In the wake of sexual exploitation investigations in cities such as Rotherham and Bradford, authorities and the public have begun to recognise that young girls are vulnerable to grooming and sexual exploitation, which is a crime. Rather than street wise, the actions of difficult girls who chose to be sexually active with much older men and constantly ran away were viewed as a problematic demand on stretched services rather than a cry for help or an attempt to escape from impossible circumstances. Greater knowledge and understanding on the part of all public services means that authorities and parents are much more likely to identify these young people as vulnerable potentially exploited victims in need of protection and assistance.

The Police Service is now routinely dealing with serious and complex offences and incidents involving vulnerable people. Perhaps this is because more members of communities we serve are becoming vulnerable to clever fraudsters, perhaps it is because those preventative services offered to young people have dwindled in an age of austerity resulting in them being more likely to become a victim or an offender. Moreover, it may be because as a society we have shone a light into dark places and created new offences, such as modern day slavery, stalking and FGM, to deal with the problems that have always been there but not been recognised as unlawful by the criminal justice system.

Whatever the reason, identifying and protecting the vulnerable has never been more complex or more important. The focus upon properly identifying and dealing with vulnerable people as a priority is well and truly embedded in policing and must remain at the heart of our mission and that of society so we that can measure up to public expectations and be a service worthy of the public we serve.

The Fire and Rescue Service

Professor Peter Murphy

The fire service exists to protect the public, keep them safe from fires and rescue them from actual or potentially harm. It also has a responsibility to prevent harm to the public. As with the police and ambulance services, it is constantly operating in conjunction with the other two blue light services, and with a wide range of other public and non-profit services, such as the local authorities, health, social care and housing providers as well as a range of welfare organisations, both public and non-profit. Efficient and effective multi-agency working and emergency planning is vital to its success.

Although all of the services mentioned above have to take risks and potential risks into account in all of their activities, and some have very sophisticated risk assessments and procedures, unlike the other two services, the fire service is fundamentally configured and operationalised on the basis of risk rather than the basis of demand or need.

For many years up to the start of the 21st century, this configuration was on the basis of risks to buildings and premises with prioritisation given to high-risk buildings or uses of premises, such as chemical, biological and nuclear plants or places where hazardous materials are used or stored for use in industrial processes, or manufacturing or extractive industries. Having to deal with incidents caused by arson or deliberate fire setting; faulty electrics, smoking (particularly smoking in bed), chip pans and in multiply occupied domestic and non-domestic buildings made the service very aware of vulnerable individuals and groups within communities. Nevertheless, stations, appliances and the key resources at the services' disposal were located and configured on the basis of the risk to buildings and premises and the time taken for fire engines to attend incidents following calls to their control rooms.

The 2003 White Paper 'Our fire and rescue services' (ODPM 2003) proposed that each Fire and Rescue Authority produce an Integrated Risk Management Plan (IRMP), including targets and objectives for reducing risks, balancing prevention and intervention and determining response standards and resource allocation. Crucially, they were to focus on risks to people and communities and not just buildings and premises. The subsequent Act also mandated authorities to concentrate more heavily on fire prevention. It gave Fire and Rescue Authorities greater freedom to allocate resources to local concerns, to be more proactive, to engage in dealing with environmental hazards (such as flooding), and to work more closely with others. Since 2004, all national frameworks for fire and rescue services and all local fire service strategies have been predicated on IRMPs while the response to major emergencies and disasters has been based on national and regional risk registers and emergency planning as a result of the 2004 Civil Contingencies Act.

IRMPs have to reflect up to date risk analyses including an assessment of all foreseeable fire and rescue-related risks that could affect the area of the authority. They cover at least a three-year time span and must be reviewed and revised as often as it is necessary. A recent appraisal from Her Majesty's Inspectorate of Constabulary and Fire & Rescue Services (HMICFRS) confirmed that all services had IRMPs in place (HMICFRS

2018, 2019), while another study confirmed that the vast majority covered between three and five years (Murphy *et al.* 2019). There is however, growing concern that their scope and content have not been systematically and comprehensively reviewed since they were first introduced, and the recent inspections demonstrate that protection and prevention activity has been disproportionately de-prioritised in response to reductions in financial support from the government (Murphy *et al.* 2019).

IRMPs must demonstrate how prevention, protection and response activities will best be used to prevent fires and other incidents and mitigate the impact of identified risks on communities, through authorities working either individually or collectively, in a way that makes best use of available resources (Home Office 2018). As with the police and the ambulance services, fire and rescue services are members of community safety partnerships, children and adult safeguarding boards, and local health and well-being boards. They have to have a sophisticated knowledge and understanding of vulnerable groups and individuals in their local communities and they draw heavily on their partners (particularly public health, the NHS and local authorities) for this information. They are not quite as dependent on data from control rooms, call-outs or incidents, as the other two emergency services, as they are required to be pro-active in identifying and mitigating risk. The latest national framework for fire and rescue services is explicit and worth quoting

> Wherever appropriate, we expect fire and rescue services to develop partnerships to support risk reduction services to those identified as vulnerable, including from exploitation or abuse, and wherever possible to share intelligence and relevant risk data. In many cases, fire and rescue staff may be in a position to identify individuals' wider vulnerabilities and exposure to risks beyond fire. By working closely and collaboratively with other public and voluntary sector organisations"......"we recognise fire and rescue authorities can make an important contribution to increasing the effectiveness and efficiency of public services and alleviating pressures on local response resources. However, this should not be at the expense of effective delivery of their statutory core fire functions.
>
> (Home Office 2018, p. 6)

The government and the fire community therefore publish a wide range of leaflets and advice notes both on-line and in hard copy for different audiences such as vulnerable groups. Some examples include, Fire Safety for Parents and Carers, Fire Safety for Gypsies and Travellers, Frances the Firefly for Children and Fire Safety for Students.

One particularly useful service introduced in recent years has been what is commonly known as a 'Safe and Well' visit (although some fire and rescue services may still call these Home Fire Risk Assessments or

Home Fire Safety Checks). These consist of members of the fire and rescue service carrying out an inspection of an individual dwelling at the individuals request. It may be undertaken by operational officers or a dedicated fire safety team, and it includes the facility for those carrying out the visit to ask the occupant(s) some health and well-being questions. The visits focus on three key areas:

- Identification of the potential fire risks within the dwelling
- Knowing what to do in order to reduce or prevent these risks
- Ensuring smoke alarms are present and working with an escape plan in case a fire does break out.

More recently, in practice, services have added a fourth with a clear increase in the identification of risks for signposting to other services. The number of referrals between the services has continually increased, although the greatest proportion are lower risk referrals when services need to increasingly prioritise higher risk referrals.

Thus, theoretically fire and rescue services appear to comprehensively address vulnerability and vulnerable groups, in their mandatory and enabling legislation, albeit naturally focussing on vulnerability to fire risks. However, there is considerable doubt about the reality in practice being as reassuring as the guidance would suggest (Murphy *et al.* 2019).

Recent inspection evidence shows that Safe and Well visits are being reduced, although those that are being undertaken are becoming more focussed on 'vulnerable' groups (HMICFRS 2018, 2019). The inspections also show that despite consistent exhortations to the contrary over the last ten years, prevention and protection activity has been significantly and disproportionally reduced across the services.

The IRMPs are clearly the place where the operationalisation of risk and protection for vulnerable groups should be articulated and kept up to date. We know from the inspections that fire and rescue services in configuring their services reflect the risks in their IRMPs, but we do not know whether they are all fit for purpose and whether they reflect the scope, nature and pattern of risks that was evident in 2003/04 or is evident today.

We know the nature, extent and pattern of risks has changed significantly in this time, as evidenced by the Grenfell Inquiry (Moore-Blick 2019) and Dame Judith Hackitts's review of the regulations for high-rise buildings demonstrates (Hackitt 2018). Similarly, our knowledge of the nature and extent of vulnerabilities and vulnerable groups has changed in the same period, but we do not know how well these changes are reflected in Fire and Rescue Services or in their IRMPs. The 'Operational Assessments' which were part of the former Fire Peer Challenge process between 2011 and 2016, investigated whether an authority's risk strategy reflected the diverse nature of its community, and whether they prioritised those most at risk through the IRMP, but the Fire Challenge process has been superseded by HMICFRS inspections.

In practice, an assessment of the extent and pattern of risk in an area underpins all IRMPs, but this assessment (as opposed to the updating of the IRMP itself) is only required to be reviewed every five years. The Inspectorate found IRMPs 'vary widely in content, size, style and even name', and 'assess risk in very different ways' (HMICFRS 2019, p. 12). In reality IRMPs are not underpinning either strategic or operational decision making, they are currently window dressing or 'sitting on the shelf'.

The National Fire Chief's Council (NFCC) has a strategic commitment to consistent risk-based approaches to IRMPs. This should, in time, enable services to focus resources on activities where they will have the greatest impact on 'reducing risk and vulnerability within their communities', but developing and operationalising this is proving to be a challenge and will not be quick. As a result, there is growing concern that the scope and content of IRMPs has not been systematically reviewed on a consistent national basis since they were first established in 2003. As the sectors most prominent professional publication recently commented 'it is clear that a comprehensive review of the IRMPs process and outcome is long overdue' (FIRE 2019, p. 13).

Fire and rescue services have a very low ratio of staff from black and minority ethnic backgrounds, and from the LGBT communities who are severely under-represented in senior staff, control rooms and in fire-fighting teams. This can lead to services underestimating language and cultural issues. This under-representation is not helped by the recent historically low recruitment activity or by cuts to training budgets. The Local Government Association (LGA) offered an Equality Peer Challenge based on the Fire and Rescue Service Equality Framework, following the Equality Act 2010 and the introduction of the Public Sector Equality Duty. It had disappointingly low take up and the LGA and the NFCC produced an updated Fire and Rescue Service Equality Framework in 2017 as part of the LGA portfolio of improvement toolkits.

In February 2017, the Minister for Policing and the Fire Service, Brandon Lewis announced that the issues he wanted HMICFRS to focus on in their first 'thematic' inspections included diversity. However, the first themed inspections are not due to begin until the Inspectorate have carried out their second round of service inspections for all services which are scheduled for completion in October 2021.

In practice, the EU General Data Protection Regulation of 2016 has facilitated the process of sharing data. Emergency services are also encouraged to share data and information as a result of the policing and Crime Act 2017. The fire services' knowledge and understanding of vulnerabilities has been greatly helped by access to the 'Exeter' data on vulnerability from the NHS and from the 'ECINS' data platform from the Police. The latter being a people centred database rather than a property-based information platform which has also helped facilitate the general move to a people centred service.

Overall, in terms of its understanding of vulnerable groups and vulnerable people, it appears that Fire and Rescue Services are moving from being the most conceptually limited and definitionally imprecise of the three emergency services to being the most conceptually pluralist while (at the very least) acknowledging the need for more definitional precision. They are acutely aware that they need to improve their approach to vulnerability both strategically and operationally and at national and local levels of the service.

References

Crime and Disorder Act (CDA) 1998.

Equality Act 2010.

Fire Knowledge Briefing (2019) Fire Risk Dilemma: postcode lottery or national standards? *FIRE* Vol 115 (1420) pp. 13–15.

Firmin, C. (2015) *Peer on Peer Abuse: Safeguarding Implications of Contextualising Abuse between Young People within Social Fields.* Luton: University of Bedfordshire.

Great Britain (2014) *Care Act 2014.* London: The Stationery Office.

Great Britain (2007) *Mental Health Act 2014.* London: The Stationery Office.

Great Britain (2018) *Working Together to Safeguard Children.* Retrieved from: https://assets.publishing.service.gov.uk/government/uploads/system/uploads/attachment_data/file/779401/Working_Together_to_Safeguard-Children.pdf.

Hackitt, J. (2018) *Building a Safer Future - Independent Review of Building Regulations and Fire Safety: Final Report.* London: Ministry of Housing, Communities and Local Government.

HM Inspectorate of Constabulary and Fire & Rescue Services (2018) *Fire and Rescue Service Inspections 2018/19: Summary of findings from Tranche 1.* London: HMICFRS.

HM Inspectorate of Constabulary and Fire & Rescue Services (2019) *Fire and Rescue Service Inspections 2018/19: Summary of findings from Tranche 2.* London: HMICFRS.

Home Office (2016) *Multi-agency Statutory Guidance for the Conduct of Domestic Homicide Reviews.* Retrieved from: https://assets.publishing.service.gov.uk/government/uploads/system/uploads/attachment_data/file/575273/DHR-Statutory-Guidance-161206.pdf.

Home Office (2018) *Fire and Rescue National Framework for England.* London: TSO.

Moore-Blick, M. (2019) *The Grenfell Tower Inquiry.* Retrieved from: https://www.grenfelltowerinquiry.org.uk/.

Murphy, P., Lakoma, K. and Toothill, A. (2019) Do we need to review IRMPs? *FIRE*, June 2019 pp. 13–16.

Office of the Deputy Prime Minister (2003) Our Fire and rescue service. *White Paper CM 5808.* London: TSO.

6 Professional Vulnerability in the UK Public Sector

The Social Work Operational Environment

Brian Brown and David Cook

Introduction

United Kingdom (UK) citizens and politicians expect that public-sector service, front-line professional groups are well functioning and capable of delivering services to members of the public, to the high standards set by government (Dunleavy, 2017). There is some evidence that people are generally satisfied with services: for example, Evans and Wellings (2017) noted that 77 percent of people polled viewed the National Health Service (NHS) as crucial to British society, with 63 percent stating that the professional services they receive are very or fairly realistic. However, the reality of service delivery exposes a number of professional groups to a range of vulnerabilities. Research by Gibb et al. (2010) noted that higher rates of stress-related illness were more prevalent among health-care professionals in comparison with those in other sectors. Sickness absenteeism was correlated with professionals experiencing increased clinical demand, working excessive hours, low staffing levels and poor support from colleagues and management. Sickness absence costs the NHS 31.7 billion annually. A 2017 survey of 487,000 health service staff (Stephenson, 2018) had a key finding that 34.4 percent of staff had suffered from work-related stress over the past 12 months, with 56.7 percent reporting attending work despite feeling unwell in the past three months. A similar situation is highlighted in a survey undertaken across the UK education sector, referred to as a 'stress epidemic' (Teachers Wellbeing Index, 2018). The survey covered 1,502 professional teachers working in the education sector. Some 67 percent of teachers describe themselves as 'stressed', with 29 percent reporting having to work more than 51 hours per week. More alarmingly 74 percent indicate that an inability to 'switch off' is a major contributing factor to experiencing a negative work/life balance. Some 45 percent of teaching professionals view family and friends to be their main source of help and support when experiencing mental health difficulties.

The Assaults on Emergency Workers (Offences) Act, 2018 is a further example of the UK government acknowledging and acting to protect vulnerable frontline staff. Justice Minister, Rory Stewart, noted:

> Every day these public servants do extraordinary work on our behalf, and they must be able to do it without being assaulted.
> (Ministry of Justice, Press Release, published 13, Sept. 2018)

The need for legislation was based on a significant escalation in assaults on emergency workers, with 26,000 assaults on police officers and over 17,000 assaults on NHS staff in 2017. Prison officers experienced a 70 percent rise in assaults in the three years up to 2017 and fire-fighters recorded an 18 percent increase in attacks (933 incidents) in 2017/18 (Ministry of Justice Circular, 2018).

The definition of 'emergency worker' is categorised within the Act as, police, prison officers, fire and rescue personnel and certain NHS professionals who have direct interaction with the public. However, there has been significant disquiet expressed about the omission of the social work profession from the legislation to safeguard front-line professionals. Ruth Allen, Chief Executive of the British Association of Social Workers (BASW) has challenged this apparent omission, stating that social workers undertaking daily operations are exposed to risky, often dangerous situations so why are they viewed differently to other emergency service personnel (Allen, 2018)? A 2014 Community Care survey of 446 social workers revealed that 85 percent stated they had been physically assaulted, verbally abused or harassed in the past year (Schraer, 2014). A further Community Care survey in 2015 showed that 80 percent of the 2,000 frontline staff surveyed reported that stress levels were affecting job performance, with 17 percent of respondents using prescription drugs and a third using alcohol to cope with stress. According to Beer and Asthana (2016) there is little public debate around the stressful status of the social work profession. It is acknowledged that social workers practice within a progressively complex operational environment characterised by escalating service demand, diminishing resources, high levels of management compliance auditing and negative media scrutiny (Munro, 2011, ibid., 2016). Social workers engage with the most marginalised, desperate, angry and neglected individuals and groups in society, as a consequence they regularly encounter hostile, risky and dangerous situations (Allen, 2018) and are often faced with situations where both time and resources are pressured (Tupper et al., 2016).

This chapter will focus on presenting the case for the social work profession to be identified and acknowledged as one of the most vulnerable professional groups in the UK public sector. The discussion will highlight the interplay of the dynamics that create high levels of vulnerability for social workers in their everyday duties.

Understanding the Vulnerabilities in Social Work Practice

Defining social work has proved a complex and controversial issue as the profession is located in the broader social care sphere (Horner, 2003). The International Association of Schools of Social Work (IASSW) and the International Federation of Social Workers (IFSW) developed a global definition of social work as:

> Social work is a practice-based profession and an academic discipline that promotes social change and development, social cohesion, and the empowerment and liberation of people. Principles of social justice, human rights, collective responsibility and respect for diversities are central to social work. Underpinned by theories of social work, social sciences, humanities and indigenous knowledge, social work engages people and structures to address life challenges and enhance wellbeing.
>
> (IASSW/IFSW, 2014, pp. 1–2)

From this definition it would seem there is a high expectation placed on social workers to perform to the highest standards of service delivery to promote positive development within society. But it is important to bear in mind that this is a global definition; therefore, the social work function and remit may differ across countries and continents. In the UK public-sector social work is governed by a legislative framework and regulated by professional bodies.

There are around 91,000 social workers registered with the Health and Care Professions Council (HCPC, 2014 – cited Moriarty et al., 2015) which constitutes a comparatively small number when compared with the teaching and nursing professions, yet as noted by Moriarty et al. (2015) it is highly regulated and the largest professional group regulated by the HCPC. Social work professionals are required to be educated to degree level and qualified to practice by demonstrating a level of competence to meet agreed practice standards (BASW, 2014). Professional standards for social workers in England, for example, are governed by the HCPC and documented in the 'Standards of Proficiency – Social Workers in England' (HCPC, 2017 – note: responsibility will transfer to a new regulatory body 'Social Work England' –10th Dec. 2019). In general, social work in the UK is organised around the delivery of children and families' services and adults' services with social work professionals employed in Local Government statutory services (e.g., Local Councils) and Voluntary non statutory organisations (e.g., Charities).

The UK social work profession has been blighted over the post war decades by failures in service delivery and a series of child abuse tragedies leading to public inquiries which culminated in the social work profession being one of the most maligned and criticised of all UK public servants (BASW, 2013). The profession has been placed under increasing government, public and media scrutiny. One of the most notable child death cases was that of 17-month-old 'baby P' in 2007, which attracted extensive media coverage and government ministerial intervention. This ministerial intervention led to an external inquiry being ordered to examine the role of the local authority, primarily Haringey Borough Council Children's Services. The inquiry report was presented to ministers on 1st December 2008. In the aftermath of the report findings the then responsible minister, Ed Balls, used special powers to dismiss the Director of Haringey London Borough Council Children's Services, Sharon Shoesmith, from her post. Following internal inquiries by Haringey council it was announced in April, 2009, that the deputy director of children's services, two other managers and a social worker, all previously suspended while enquiries were conducted, had been dismissed from their posts as a consequence of failings in the 'baby P' case (Beckford, 2009). This example highlights the parlous position of social work professionals in the context of being very vulnerable to blame and sanction when things go wrong. This example is one of many thus making it important to explore the nature and context of this inherent vulnerability to provide an insight to its causality.

The authors have utilised their extensive knowledge and expertise in social work practice, development and management to construct a model to explore vulnerability in social work practice, see Figure 6.1

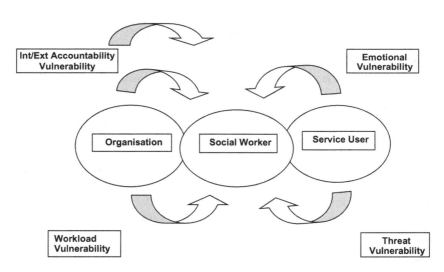

Figure 6.1 The vulnerability map.

THE VULNERABILITY MAP. The scope of this model is limited to social workers employed in statutory organisations, primarily local authorities, governed by Acts of Parliament, government department operational guidance/circulars and the professional regulatory bodies.

The vulnerability map shows the unique position of the social work practitioner acting as the interface that links the organisation's legislative function and the needs of the service user. The vulnerability map has identified four key vulnerability dynamics which will be discussed in the following sections of this chapter: accountability vulnerability, workload vulnerability, emotional vulnerability and threat vulnerability. Finally, conclusions will be drawn including recommendations to suggest how the high levels of vulnerability in social work might be ameliorated.

Key:

Internal Accountability Vulnerability: Organisational – Public Sector Governance* regimes & External Audit framework (EA) – 'bullying' – performance driven – 'blame culture' – organisation vs professional value base creates practitioner/professional dilemma, performance audit, Ofsted inspection**, resource allocation, leadership, accountability dilemmas/tensions, emotional intelligence deficit'.

Note: *Public Sector Governance includes: New Public Management (NPM) New Public Governance (NPG) & Public Value Management (PVM) also External Audit regime – are discussed in the main body of this chapter.

**Ofsted – Office for Standards in Education, Children's Services and Skills – is a non-ministerial department of the UK government reporting to Parliament. Ofsted is responsible for inspecting a range of educational institutions, also childcare, adoption and fostering agencies and initial teacher training, and regulates a range of early years and children's social care services (www.gov.uk/government/organisations/ofsted).

External Accountability Vulnerability: Regulatory Agency, Professional body, media, service users.

Workload Vulnerability: Case work overload, long working hours, professional supervision deficit (lack of reflection and emotional intelligence), impact on physical and mental health.

Emotional Vulnerability: Impact of working with – abject poverty, child abuse, alcohol and substance misuse, self-harm, suicide, failing to meet service user needs and expectations due to resource limitations.

Threat Vulnerability: Risk of verbal and physical attack, car damage, stalking, malicious/vexatious complaint, impact on mental health.

Accountability Vulnerability

Activities in the UK public sector are governed by a framework of ethical standards developed by the Committee on Standards in Public Life, 1995. The committee developed seven principles also referred to as the 'Nolan Principles' after the Committee Chair, Lord Nolan. One of the key principles is 'accountability' which requires an individual in public office to be accountable for their decisions and actions to the public and must be open to scrutiny of their activities (Standards in Public Life, 1995).

The social work profession has developed around a core knowledge base leading to the adoption of core skills, values and characteristics that define activities acknowledged and recognised by society as contributing to the public utility or well-being (Worsley et al., 2013). When practitioners undertake social work duties and activities the interaction is often in the context of people's private environments and with some of the most disadvantaged groups in society who are often the least likely to hold service providers to account (Cameron et al., 2010). It is in the public interest therefore, that a defined 'accountability framework' is in place, that requires social workers to take responsibility for their actions. Therefore, social work roles and responsibilities are a key strand of accountability and governance, thus, require clarification through defined role descriptors, practice expectations and employment/professional standards (Worsley, 2013). Cameron et al. (2010) cites Braye and Preston-Shoot (2001, p. 67) definition of accountability which articulates 'the twin concepts of "accountability to" – to those on whose authority professionals act – and "accountability for" – the range of activities that is open to scrutiny'.

Whilst this notion of professional accountability may appear straightforward and simple to apply, this is not the case. Social workers are subject to a multi-dimensional network of accountability that encompasses the employing organisation and statutory functions, professional and regulatory bodies, service users, self and even held to account by the mainstream media as demonstrated in the previous section and introduction to this chapter. There are inherent tensions between the competing demands of these accountability dimensions that can 'muddy' the lines of accountability in social work practice. Accountability in social work is complex and complicated to apply; hence, the subtlety of the intrinsic vulnerability for the social worker in attempting to meet their accountability obligations (Cameron et al., 2010). For example, social workers often encounter conflicts of interest when working with children and their families leading to the practitioner having to navigate between their duty to the employing agency and their professional and personal values.

It may be useful to provide an actual example of how this accountability conflict might emerge in case work.

James is an 8 year old child living at home with parents. The school make a referral to Children's Services that James presented in school today with a bruise beneath his left eye which may be non-accidental. A social worker is charged with making enquiries as to the safety of the child including assessing potential future risk. When interviewed by the social worker the child discloses that the bruising was a result of being hit by dad for being naughty. This disclosure and the initial risk assessment indicate that it is not safe for James to stay in the care of parents. Parents identify an aunt who will care for James while a more detailed risk assessment is undertaken. The necessary checks of the aunt are undertaken which are positive, so James is placed in the aunt's care pending further risk assessment and the convening of a multi-agency Initial Child Protection Conference to consider the assessed information and potential risk. The social worker takes the view that the aunt is entitled to financial payment from the local authority on the basis that James is unable to stay at home due to a potential risk of harm. Regulation 24 of The Care Planning, Placement and Case Review Regulations, 2010 details how this kinship care arrangement should be set up. The social worker puts the case for payment to her manager who takes a different view stating it is a 'family arrangement' where parents have agreed voluntarily to place James with the aunt therefore no payment is due.

The dilemma for the social worker is that accountability to the employing agency (local authority) obliges the worker to accept the view of the manager but her accountability to profession (HCPC and BASW codes of conduct/standards of practice) and self (personal value base) indicates the manager's decision is incorrect and based on cost limitation. The social worker acts as agent for their employer when undertaking work in the agency's name and is obliged to follow the policies of the organisation. The social worker has to make a choice to either accept the management decision or to follow her professional judgment by advising the aunt to challenge the local authority decision via the complaints policy or a legal route. In essence, this represents an unequal balance of power between the worker and the organisation on the basis that if the worker follows her professional judgement it could lead to disciplinary action on the grounds of not following a management instruction thus placing the practitioner in a very vulnerable position. If the social worker accepts the manager's decision and the aunt unilaterally seeks legal advice leading to a successful claim against the local authority for payment, then the social worker may come under criticism for not undertaking a proper assessment of the circumstances and advocating for payment, so again placed in a vulnerable situation. Any dissent or complaint by the social worker about the manner, in which the employing agency resources have been organised and allocated, may be viewed as the worker's reluctance to accept the authority of the organisation.

Some commentators have observed that this power or authority imbalance has worsened with the advent of New Public Management (NPM) being introduced to the public sector in the UK (See: Hood, C. 1990, 1991, Clark, D. 1996 and Diefenbach, 2009). Diefenbach (2009) argues that NPM emphasises the primacy of the management function, the elevated status of managers and espouses the supremacy of managerial concepts over once valued concepts like professional competencies and credentials. Kirkpatrick et al. (2005) view this erosion of long-established values and concepts as the colonisation of the professional domain by an NPM ideology that promotes top down control and surveillance. NPM introduces performance management and measurement systems to monitor organisational and individual performance, in essence the ability to hold individuals to account and reduce 'illegitimate privileges' (Dienfenbach, 2009). Butterfield et al. (2005) argue that the performance framework or 'measure mania' associated with NPM places constraints on desirable aspects of professional practice with far reaching negative implications for public-sector employees and the services delivered. NPM emphasises the capture of the 'measurable outputs' of service delivery or the quantitative aspects of efficiency, productivity, performance and accountability that facilitate management control (Dienfenbach, 2009). This shift to NPM quantitative performance management has consigned the less measurable qualitative aspects of organisational performance to having little or no value. Thus, NPM structures ignore the core public-sector concepts of professional ethics and erodes professional values such as 'care', 'duty' and 'self-management/autonomy' (Kirkpatrick et al., 2005).

Liddle (2018) argues that the emergence of New Public Governance (NPG) and Public Value Management (PVM) in the UK public sector resulted from a long-standing debate on the role and size of government. NPM focussed on efficiency but did not address other challenges such as diminishing government resources, the increased size of government agencies, and, the intricate linkages developing between state, non-state and civic institutions in the delivery of public goods and services.

NPG is concerned with promoting the optimum utility for the public in the delivery of public-sector activities based on a public management style requiring cooperation between government departments and state/non-state agencies (Osborne, 2006). The foundation and appeal of NPG included less government involvement based on the belief that the private and non-profit sector could provide public services more efficiently with less funds (Morgan and Shinn, 2014 – cited in Liddle, 2018).

PVM centres on the needs of the public that requires the creation of added value to the community rather than simply achieving targets as with NPM. In essence public agencies, in addition to the provision of good quality services, have a duty to promote broader value – added benefits to the community which are measurable (Moore, 1995). PVM is viewed as a replacement for NPM in the reform of the public sector (Benington and Moore, 2010). However, PVM still requires a performance framework but with more comprehensive performance indicators, for example, evidence of the citizens' preferences being identified and met to create value added.

It is evident that the UK public sector has undergone a series of reforms over recent decades, but the central tenet of governance developments remains to improve performance in public services (Liddle, 2018). Skelcher et al. (2013) argue that successive governance reforms leave markers that produce a governance hybrid adopting a combination of governance modes. This argument is supported by Crouch (2005) who states hybrid governance is the norm in advanced capitalist societies. Some commentators argue that these governance reforms obscure the influence of governments, making it look like less involvement but in fact governments still set the rules for public-sector interactions within the 'shadow of hierarchy' (Scharf, 1997; Jessop, 2000, 2003 – cited in Dickinson, 2016).

The emergent argument is that irrespective of the governance regime there remains an undercurrent of control and accountability manifest in performance regimes based on efficiency, effectiveness and economy. Jakobsen et al. (2017. P1.) refer to this as the 'ubiquitous presence of public sector performance regimes' which the authors term the external accountability (EA) regime, which is a manifestation of the need to provide accountability to the political overseers. The EA regime remains very evident in local authority social work departments leading to a loss of professional value base and autonomy, also to the power imbalance discussed above. An example of this EA is evidenced in the 'Working Together to Safeguard Children' (WTSG) framework issued by the UK government, 1999 (previously 'Working Together Under the Children Act), the most recent version issued in 2018. The WTSC sets out the statutory framework for compliance with duties, standards and timescales for Local Authority Children's Services and partner agencies (HM Government, 2018). Also, provides the basis for social work service performance management and quality assurance. Further discussion on the impact of the EA regime on social workers will be discussed in the next section.

Social work practice has almost routinely been held to account by the Main-Stream Media (MSM) or open to 'trial by media'. In 2014 Sir

James Munby, President of the Family Courts (England & Wales) issued two pieces of practice guidance – *Transparency in the Family Courts, Publication of Judgements* and *Transparency in the Court of Protection, Publication of Judgements*. This guidance facilitated the publication of court judgements in family law cases and the naming of key expert witnesses providing evidence in the case, unless there were compelling reasons not to make public such information. According to the Public Sector Union, UNISON, the impact of this guidance has exposed social workers to selective media coverage resulting in a backlash of public hostility and hounding by the media (UNISON, 2015). It is often the least senior staff in the decision-making process who are named, primarily the case social worker moreover, the least able to defend themselves by making comment because of their accountability to governance and confidentiality obligations. Critical scrutiny and key decisions approval in these cases are often made by senior managers and legal experts but the social worker has to present the case in court leaving them open to criticism and naming by the MSM. Unison maintain that this skewed accountability system leaves staff vulnerable to scapegoating for decisions where the actual burden of responsibility should be owned by the local authority.

According to Legood et al. (2016) the increasing media coverage of social services case activity in recent years, particularly the negative narratives presented, has been a major driver in creating a climate of fear and blame within the social work profession, also for generating public mistrust of the profession. A concerning finding in research undertaken by Legood et al. (ibid) found that the threat of media exposure was being 'weaponised' by some service users to intimidate the case social worker, for example, threatening the worker with going to the press. The research participants expressed their anxiety and fear of doing something wrong leading to a serious case review and being publicly shamed. This ongoing sense of vulnerability was captured by a Unison survey (2015) of 1028 social workers. Some 97 percent of respondents stated they were worried about being named in the media coverage of a court case. Only 28 percent believed their employer would offer support in the event of them being named in media coverage and 80 percent expressed concern about the risk of being 'scapegoated' for decisions made by their local authority decision makers. Alarmingly 79 percent agreed or strongly agreed that being negatively portrayed by the media in court proceedings would lead them consider leaving the profession.

The above discussion provides a lens through which to observe that social workers are a highly vulnerable professional group as a consequence of the applied external accountability regime. Often being exposed to a power imbalance in their employing agency, moreover, unmitigated media scrutiny and negative narrative without a right to reply and seemingly little or no support from their employing agency.

Workload Vulnerability

Research produced by Community Care and UNISON (Stevenson, 2016) looked at a working day experience of 2032 front-line social workers. This research revealed that 56 percent said their caseload size was determined by staff shortages, with 48 percent stating they felt overwhelmed by the work generated by their caseload size which was a notable increase from 43 percent in 2014. Perhaps most revealing was that 67 percent of those surveyed indicated that they had not taken a lunch break that day with 64 percent stating they never took a break at work. A study of working conditions and well-being of 3,241 social workers found that an increasing number are seeking to leave the profession as a result of excessive workload and 'chronically poor' working conditions (Ravalier and Boichat, 2018). A key finding of the study showed that on average social workers were forced to work an additional 64 unpaid days per year. On average social workers worked 9.5 hours per day, but were paid for their contracted 7.5 hours, with one in ten workers reporting having to work 12 hours or more (Cooper, 2017). Working conditions were identified as a major contributory factor to ill health, for example, data showed that stress levels among social workers were worse than 90–95 percent of other UK employees in both the public and private sector. The survey identified the main stressors as high caseloads and excessive bureaucratic tasks (Ravalier and Boichant, 2018).

Some commentators (Powers, 1997, Munro, 2004) have argued that the growth of New Public Management (NPM) has dramatically increased bureaucracy and had an adverse effect on organisational performance. For example, Diefenbach (2009) states there is now evidence to show that instead of reducing the bureaucratic tasks, NPM has actually increased the time spent by staff on administrative activities. Butterfield et al. (2005) point out that NPM organisational regimes actually increase the workload placed on staff through addition requirements on administrative task, monitoring and collecting performance data and communication. Kirkpatrick et al. (2005) provide empirical evidence of rising stress levels among staff as the NPM working environments became more challenging and demanding. Somewhat paradoxically a cohort of stressed, de-motivated, de-moralised, unable and/or unwilling employees provides greater credence for management to move toward a more robust application of the managerial doctrine inherent to NPM. In essence a harder governance approach characterised by more policies and operational procedures, more systematic performance management and appraisal, more monitoring and oversight, more leadership and motivational techniques (Diefenbach, 2009).

As discussed in the last section an external accountability (EA) regime remains irrespective of a change in governance structure or as a result of a hybrid governance arrangement (Dickenson, 2016, Jakobsen et al., 2017) much of which requires bureaucratic time that reduces the available time social workers have with children and their families. Ferguson (2014) cites the research by Broadhurst et al. (2010) that showed Children's Services social workers were spending a disproportionate amount of their working time in front of a computer completing administrative tasks in order to comply with performance management requisites and processes, consequently reducing the time spent with children and families. Further research by Ferguson (2014) drew a similar conclusion that social workers were not spending enough time with children at risk due to the requirements of an organisational bureaucratic compliance culture. As a consequence, children were considered not to be properly safeguarded, and hence placed at higher risk of harm.

This tension between undertaking more direct work with children and their families and having to complete administrative tasks was revealed in some detail in a local authority children's services case study undertaken by Gibson (2016). The local authority had adopted a policy of having no unallocated cases as this would attract a negative evaluation by Ofsted if the authority was inspected. Consequently, all cases were allocated to social workers who were already overloaded. Once allocated the social workers were assigned timescales to complete the designated case work. Failure to complete the work was considered to be under-performance resulting in criticism and possible disciplinary action against the worker. Evidence of work undertaken had to be presented in compliance with the authorities recording systems increasing time spent on administrative tasks. All case administrative activity by the social workers had to be read and signed off as meeting required standards by the team manager. Consequently, managers were unable to observe any direct work with children undertaken by the social worker. The outcome was that social worker case administration was perceived as the main priority and utilised by managers to analyse case work progress and direct social worker case activities. Social workers prioritised their time around administrative tasks to ensure completion within timescales and avoid being criticised and blamed for poor performance. Social workers interviewed during the study estimated they spent between 70 and 90 percent of their working time on bureaucratic activities, which was borne out by the researcher's observations. Incredibly, the case administrative tasks became embedded as the worker's primary task not the direct work with children. As study participant stated:

> I'd like to spend a lot more time actually doing social work rather than typing minutes, typing reports, writing case notes, especially the direct work with the children ... [but] we don't have indicators or targets to do that.
>
> (Gibson, 2016, p. 1191)

The conflict between what social workers are trained to undertake (i.e., direct work with service users) and what employing organisations expect of social workers (i.e., administrative case oversight and compliance) creates a vulnerable workload environment for social workers. Ferguson (2014) draws the distinction between '*automated/dead social work*' and '*alive social work*' while Forrester (2016) refers to the emergence of '*Zombie social work*'. Gibson (2016) noted that social workers expressed a sense of disillusionment and feelings of being constrained in how their social work knowledge, skills and expertise were being undermined by the rigid case procedural governance required by the employing organisation. This clash between professional expectations and organisation expectations results in a sense of frustration and vulnerability being felt by workers, these emotions were captured in comments made by two social workers:

> So why do the academics teach us to communicate with children, teach us child development, because you're teaching us and it's not exercised ... I'm scared for the profession.
> I think it's a bit hypocritical. I think you're saying this needs to be done but I can't do it cos I've got ten thousand other things to do, and I think that's not what social work is about, isn't it? Social work is about social work, you know, going into people's houses, supporting them with this, supporting them with that and you don't do it so the role's very different.
>
> (Gibson, 2016, p. 1192)

It would seem the social work profession is exposed to extreme pressures within their working environment as a consequence of unacceptable workloads and a pressurised working environment. Beer and Asthana (2016) acknowledge how vulnerable workers are to both short-term and long-term health risks associated with stress, depression and burnout. The researchers examined responses to a stress survey by 427 social workers employed across 88 local authorities in England. The findings revealed significant levels of chronic stress among respondents with 63 percent having sleep problems, 56 percent reporting being emotionally exhausted and 75 percent being concerned about burnout.

Emotional Vulnerability

Like a number of public-sector professional groups (e.g., nurses, police officers, fire officers) social workers engage in emotionally challenging work. But how vulnerable are social workers, in the context of their health and well-being, as an outcome of being exposed to highly charged emotional situations? The authors can testify that some feelings remain engrained in their personal emotional history from their time of being front-line social workers. Memories such as having to tell a looked after child her parents won't have her home for Christmas, and she would be left alone in the children's home with staff. Joint research undertaken by Community Care and UNISON (Cooper, 2016) explored the typical day of 2032 social workers and found that 80 percent of respondents had experienced emotional distress during that day. One example of the emotional trauma a social worker might encounter was a practitioner having to deal with a nine-year-old child self-harming and attempting to commit suicide. Many respondents mentioned being unable to switch off, feeling anxious and emotionally exhausted, leading to difficulties with engaging with partners and family members.

According to Ingram (2015) there is a paucity of literature dealing specifically with managing emotions in social work, but there is evidence of the centrality of emotional resilience and reflection in social work practice subsumed in other wider social work research topics, for example, reflection, skills, stress identification and management, also in practice directives and guidance. For example, Professional Capabilities Framework (PCF; College of Social Work, 2012) explicitly requires social workers to consider emotional resilience and the need to consider emotions in their practice and their personal well-being. The Munro Report (2011) advocates that social workers should be supported and afforded space to explore the emotional aspects of their practice.

According to Gilbey (2017) emotions are an essential and inescapable aspect of child safeguarding work. Yet the concept of emotions as an important practice dynamic is not clearly included in Western notions of professionalism, which may create tensions for social work professionals who are trained to use emotions as a reflective process and diagnostic tool. Ingram (2015) argues that reflecting and understanding emotions is pivotal in how social workers interpret and make sense of the myriad of contexts and situations they encounter on a daily basis. As child safeguarding practice came under greater scrutiny, criticism and blame for a number of high profile child abuse tragedies (Maria Colwell, 1973, Tyra Henry, 1984, Baby 'P', 2007) the system transitioned to increased proceduralism and quantifiable data collection with little room for direct work and the emotional relationship building elements of professional practice. Gilbey (2017) argues that this sterile bureaucratic system makes practitioners vulnerable to being labelled as 'too involved' or 'at risk of bias' if they display emotion within their case work. Moreover, an emotional reaction to the plight of a child may be considered as the practitioner being 'unable to cope' with the job. In essence social work has become a proceduralised and administrative driven profession void of reflective emotional space where factual evidence-based decisions are the norm. Ingram (2015) offers a plausible explanation as to why emotions have been relegated in the current bureaucratic social work system. People are familiar with quotes like 'I think they were just too emotional to thinks straight' or 'don't let your heart rule your head' which suggests that emotions might be contaminating a person's situational clarity and rational thought processes, thus, emotions should be controlled and marginalised. Munro (2011) postulates that relationship building between social worker and service user based on interpersonal dynamics and face to face encounters can generate vital information about a service user's situation, but this crucial process has been made subordinate to the new imperatives of following procedures and data collection. This sanitised system is designed to ignore the emotional subtleties that social workers are trained to identify and reflect upon. For example, a social worker may 'feel' strongly that is child is being sexually abused by observing interactions within the family but there is no concrete evidence to prove this is happening. From the discussion so far it is appears that social workers have little outlet to share their feelings, reflections and concerns so potentially left vulnerable in an emotional limbo?

So, following on from the above discussion, if emotional resilience and emotional reflection in social work practice is acknowledged as a central tenet in education and training then how are front-line social workers '....supported and afforded the space to explore the emotional aspects of their practice' (Munro, 2011). Ingram (2015) argues that traditionally social workers have utilised professional supervision as a process designed to explore practice issues in an effort to become more effective, accountable and feel supported in their role, it has also been a safe space to reflect, explore and make sense of emotions. However, as noted by Moriarty et al. (2015) there are identified tensions between the management functions of supervision (organisational aims, policies, and resource management and efficiency) and the supportive elements of supervision (reflective practice and emotional support). Davys and Beddoe (2010) contend the supervision process often translate into a surveillance system for monitoring vulnerable and dangerous populations. This position was supported by a survey undertaken by Community Care where over half of the 601 participants reported they would not view their supervision as offering space for reflective practice (McGregor, 2013). An Ofsted Inspection report of the Wirral MBC Children's Services noted that there was limited evidence of reflective supervision as prescribed by the organisation's supervision policy (Ofsted, 2016). These findings are supported by Moriarty et al. (2015) which suggests that tensions over the function and purpose of supervision are apparent in the practice arena. Yet the significant benefits of providing positive reflective supervision to practitioners is broadly acknowledged (Carpenter et al., 2012, Beddoe et al., 2014). Moriarty et al. (2015) point out that the risk of stress, depression, alcohol and substance misuse is strong in the social work profession. The authors conclude that the existence of a supportive organisational culture, attention to workloads and cultivating job satisfaction can counteract the occurrence of stress and burnout among social work practitioners. A report produced by Sidebotham et al. (2016) that analysed the emergent themes from serious case reviews during the period 2011–2014 noted a number of structural and systemic failings not least the absence of adequate supervision. A report (Casey, 2015) commissioned to consider improvement levels made by Rotherham council's children services found that supervision remained inadequate in spite of this serious deficit being identified in a series of inspections (2002, 2009, 2010, 2011, and 2014) and noted in a serious case review (2012).

Given the paucity of current research on the quality of supervision in social work practice in the UK (Carpenter et al., 2012) and scant attention to weaknesses in supervision in serious case review reports (Revell and Burton, 2017), the authors conducted a review of recent Ofsted Inspection Reports. To avoid an allegation of confirmation bias (seeking data to confirm occurrence) the reports were randomly selected from published inspections of Children's Services across 12 local authorities in England completed in the period 2015–2016 (Calderdale, 2015, Cheshire East Unitary Authority, 2015, Middlesbrough, 2015, Norfolk, 2015, Peterborough, 2015, Birmingham, 2016, Dorset, 2016, Durham, 2016, Hackney, 2016, Telford and Wrekin, 2016, Tameside, 2016, Wirral, 2016). In all the reports inspectors raised concerns about management oversight and quality and frequency of professional supervision. Two emergent themes common to all the reports is the lack of 'reflection' in the supervision process and the inconsistency in frequency of supervision occurrence. In addition, there were concerns expressed by inspectors about poor supervision records and a lack of continuity in monitoring and reviewing agreed case actions which lead to drift and delay in case work and children not properly safeguarded from risk of harm (Ofsted, 2015, 2016). The evidence reviewed indicated that supervision was task focussed, lacked reflection and did not sufficiently challenge inertia in implementing and completing recommendations to progress children's plans.

It would appear that social work professionals are subject to enormous levels of emotional vulnerability in their everyday practice, yet the evidence suggests that the one process that could mitigate a significant degree of this vulnerability, professional supervision, either lack focus or is missing. This raises a question as to why professional supervision is much vaunted in social work literature (see: Morrison, 2005, Beddoe, 2010, Carpenter et al., 2012, Kadushin and Harkness, 2014, Moriarty, 2015) yet, the actuality of professional supervision delivery, in terms of meeting the prescribed level of quality, appears to be questionable. Indeed, Rose (2018) found that in order for social workers to thrive in the profession it is essential to acknowledge and support emotional resilience building; however, the failures in the system, as discussed above, meant workers were only surviving with professional development virtually non-existent. The recommendations made by Eileen Munro (2010) and followed up by the Social Work Reform Board, particularly the provision of reflection practice, have not been met. This failure has left a legacy of unmet need creating an emotionally vulnerable social work profession leading to high levels of anxiety and stress, high staff turnover and potential burnout.

Threat Vulnerability

As mentioned in the introduction to this chapter social work professionals are subject to a range of threats from verbal abuse to physical assault while undertaking their operational duties. This is notwithstanding the fact that social workers face organisational threat of sanction and dismissal for any failure to meet compliance requirements. At least eight social workers have died at the hands of service users since 1980 (Littlechild, 2005).

BASW, Northern Ireland, produced a report (2018) that looked at the impact of intimidation, threats and violence against social workers employing both qualitative and quantitative data from a survey of 220 social workers from across the service delivery spectrum. The key findings showed that 86 percent of respondents reported they had experienced intimidating behaviour while undertaking their social work role causing anxiety and fear of personal harm. A range of examples of intimidating behaviour were provided by respondents ranging across areas like: a growth of abuse posted on social media platforms; misuse of the complaints procedure by vexatious service users (highlighted as a significant factor in undermining practitioner confidence); verbal abuse (often severe, causing the worker to feel 'mentally battered'); service users deliberately blocking entry to a home or from exiting the home even blocking vehicles to prevent the social worker from leaving. A small number of respondents reported feeling harassed and intimidated by their manager and noted feeling under threat because of the power imbalance in the relationship. Some 75 percent of respondents recorded that they or a family member or colleague were the subject of a threat of violence. The report noted the nature of the threats were 'deeply shocking' with examples provided of death threats, threats to torture and threats to rape, with some threats directed at the social worker's partner and children. The report highlighted that 59 percent of respondent had actually experienced physical violence. An overall finding showed that the consequence of experiencing intimidation and threats is a detrimental impact on social worker health and sense of well-being, leaving social workers feeling vulnerable and at times unsupported by their employing agency (ibid., 2018). Schraer (2014) noted that respondents to an online survey stated that while employers had formal policies covering violence against staff some 70 percent said no steps were taken to investigate reported incidents. The survey revealed that violence against social workers is still viewed through the lens of 'just part of the job'. The Institute of Occupational Safety and Health Magazine (IOSH, 2017) reported that Serious head injuries to two social workers at the hands of a service user in 2015 resulted in the employing local authority, London Borough of Brent, appearing in court and being fined £100,000. The authority pleaded guilty to failing to follow its corporate lone working policy and guidance on violence and aggression at work. After the hearing, the Health and Safety Executive (HSE) commented that injuries from violence and aggression within the social care sector are the third largest reported to the HSE. Chief Social Worker, Sean Holland, chair of a Department of Health taskforce established to tackle the serious level of intimidation and violence against social workers in Northern Ireland stated that

> When it comes to intimidation, threats and violence, employers need to understand how to meet their responsibilities to employees to fulfil their duty of care and to do that they have to understand particular issues associated with social work.
> DoH, (2018) - New Taskforce set up to help protect social workers from violence and abuse. P1.

The British Association of Social Workers (BASW) criticised two national newspapers for naming social workers in cases of child fatality as this led to the workers receiving death threats and a tirade of threatening abuse on social media (Stevenson, 2017). A Community Care's online survey (2014) of 446 social workers, reported that 85 percent stated they had been physically assaulted, verbally abused or harassed in the past year. In most cases the abuse was carried out by a service user or service user's relative. Social workers reported being threatened with weapons, verbally abused, stabbed, held hostage, harassed in the street and having hot drinks thrown on them. Some had to move house or leave their jobs due to persistent abuse. The evidence indicates that there can be little doubt of the scale and severity of the threat vulnerability encountered by social workers; moreover, the magnitude of the impact on social worker health. According to Winstanley and Hales (2015) the correlation between increased workplace aggression and increased social worker stress is well documented.

Having established that social workers are exposed to intimidation and threat of physical harm on a regular basis when undertaking their social work duties, it seems inconceivable that the Department of Health has established a taskforce to address intimidation and violence against social workers in Northern Ireland in apparent isolation. It seems that the threat vulnerability of social workers in England and Wales are not being considered as evidenced by their exclusion from The Assaults on Emergency Workers (Offences) Act, 2018. Yet in contrast social workers in Scotland working in children's services and mental health are protected under the Emergency Workers (Scotland) Act, 2005 Allen, 2018. Little wonder that Ruth Allen, Chief Executive BASW, refers to social work as the 'forgotten profession' (Allen, 2018).

Conclusion

This chapter has introduced the notion of 'vulnerability mapping' to enable an overview, insight and understanding of the interplay of the dynamics that make the social work profession a highly vulnerable group when undertaking their operational duties. This mapping model has facilitated a framework through which to explore how social workers are affected by a number of context elements; organisational context, workload context, emotional context and threat context. By exploring the available research and literature associated with each context it has been possible to demonstrate how vulnerable social workers are to stress, anxiety, poor mental health and ultimately burnout. Research by Ravalier and Boichat (2018) concluded that social workers were subject to poor working conditions which resulted in high levels of stress, presenteeism (attending work while ill), job dissatisfaction, and expressed intentions to leave the current employer and, the social work profession. This research indicates a number of problems around workforce retention and social workers leaving the profession. A Community Care article (2019) captured this problem in a commentary made by a social worker qualified for just eight months. The social worker stated:

> Eight months in, I feel pessimistic and tired, I wonder if social work will be the career for me.
>
> Community Care, May 2019. P1

This social worker reported feeling overwhelmed by excessive caseload and being made to feel guilty by managers when expressing fears and anxieties. Stevenson (2019) points to a survey of 640 newly qualified social workers where 82 percent stated they had a commitment from their employer for a protected caseload (reduced workload) but 49 percent reported their employer reneged on the commitment. In the same survey 74 percent of social workers said they had three hours or less of professional supervision a month. It would seem getting the standards right for newly qualified social workers is too variable which does not bode well for worker development and staff retention. As discussed earlier in this chapter workload vulnerability was a significant contributory factor to social worker stress levels. Ravalier and Boichant (2018) found that the workload demand placed on social workers was the most influential factor to stress development. This is compounded by the fact that local authority's ability to recruit and retain high quality social work staff is a high-risk factor associated with the future delivery of Children's Services (Stevenson, 2017). Research by the Department of Education (2017) indicated that only 12 percent of the 69 local authorities surveyed were 'very confident' of having sufficient trained social workers over the next 12 months, while 25 percent were 'not very confident' or 'not confident at all' (Lepanjuuri et al., 2018).

A further context factor was the exposure of social workers to negative interactions with service users and their families. Ravalier and Boichant (2018) found that of the 3221 survey respondents over 25 percent experienced negative comments from service users and their families via social media at least once a month. Around 40 percent of respondents were exposed to negative behaviours from service users and their families. The discussion around the organisational and emotional contexts also demonstrated how social workers felt the impact of feeling unsupported on their stress levels and overall mental health. Poor management support was identified as a factor contributing to social worker stress levels and job dissatisfaction (ibid., 2018).

The discussion in this chapter has revealed the vulnerability of the social work profession, as a consequence of exposure to contextual factors, and shown this leads to debilitating health conditions, both mental and physical, which is worrying for the overall health and safety of the UK's social workers. High stress levels not only affect the individual worker but their employing organisations, for example, over 11 million working days were lost in 2016 due to stress related conditions (ibid., 2018). As shown in the discussion stress and anxiety among social workers is an emergent common theme resulting in a negative influence on job satisfaction, intentions to leave the job and profession, and increased presenteeism.

The question is 'what can be done to alleviate social worker stress and anxiety'?

Golightley and Holloway (2019) argue that the impact on the mental health and well-being of social workers in the operational environment is a key issue for the future of social work in the UK. Ravalier (2019) explores the context and conditions within which the social work profession will develop by investigating the influence of the psychosocial working conditions on stress levels and related outcomes for social workers. The study findings suggest that if employers are to reverse growing staff turnover and retain an effective and quality workforce then greater emphasis is required in establishing a more supportive working environment by addressing root cause factors.

One of the root cause factors may well be associated with the devaluation of the social work profession in favour of the managerial and performance approach to service delivery inherent to the governance models discussed earlier. Social work professionals become passive and marginalised resulting in 'automated/dead social work' (Ferguson, 2014). Munro (2011) argued for social workers to reclaim the profession where workers are freed from the constraints of arbitrary timescales and target driven services. Professor Sue White (2011) commenting on the Munro report argues for less bureaucracy in social work stating there is no magic database, IT system or inspection system capable of safeguarding children and supporting vulnerable families. Social work emphasises the application of human factors, for example, professional judgement with its understanding of cognitive and emotional complexities. Social work professionals need to be involved in systemic thinking that enables the design of safer organisations.

Jakobsen et al. (2017) argue that EA regimes exclude purposeful professional engagement so does not deliver the anticipated performance gains. The authors offer an alternative governance regime based on 'internal learning' which involves extensive professional involvement in the identification, development and interpretation of performance goals. The internal learning regime not only informs the design of the performance framework, but also offers a prospective research agenda to reveal and address how performance regimes affect important aspects of performance like professional motivation and behaviour also, public-sector outcomes. This new regime does not advocate for the exclusion of the EA performance approach but that it is moderated to allow greater professional autonomy where learning contributes to improved service performance and professional well-being.

If the inherent vulnerabilities of social work practice discussed in this chapter are to be moderated to an acceptable level, then new thinking must occur around inclusive governance for public-sector organisations involved in complex task service delivery. What is clear is that the various manifestations of the NPM movement and other governance regimes over the last four decades have not delivered cheaper or improved services for the UK government and service users.

References

Allen, R. (2018) – Why are Social Workers Excluded from New Bill to Protect Emergency Staff? *Social Care Network*, 13th June, 2018.

BASW (2013) – All Party Parliamentary Group on Social Work - Inquiry into the State of Social Work Report. Published by BASW.

BASW (2014) – Roles and Functions of Social Workers in England: Advice Note. Published: The College of Social Work.

Beckford, M. (2009) – Baby P: Haringey Council Sacks Three Managers and a Social Worker. *The Telegraph*, 29th Apr. 2009.

Beer, O. & Asthana, S. (2016) – How Stress Impacts Social Workers _ and How They're Trying to Cope. *Community Care*, 28th Sept. 2016.

Benington, J. & Moore, M. H. (eds) (2010) – *Public Value: Theory and Practice.* Basingstoke: Palgrave Macmillan.

Cameron, K., Long, L., Roche, J., & Stringer, D. (2010) – Accountability in Social Work Practice. In *The Law and Social Work*. Basingstoke: Palgrave McMillan.

Community Care (2019) – Eight Months In. I Feel Pessimistic and Tired, I wonder If Social Work will be the Career for Me. *Community Care*, May, 2019.

Cooper, J. (2017) – Social Workers Face More Emotional Distress and Abuse Each Day. *Community Care*, Mar. 2017.

Dienfenbach, T. (2009) – New Public Management in the Public Sector: The Dark Sides of Managerialistic 'Enlightenment'. *Public Administration*, Vol. 87, No. 4, pp. 892–909.

Department of Health (2018) – New Taskforce Set Up to Help Protect Social Workers from Violence and Abuse. *DoH*, Nov. 2018.

Dunleavy, P. (2017) – Audit 2017: How Representative and Effective are the Civil Service and the Wider Public Services Management Systems? – Democratic Audit UK.

Education Support Partnership (2018) Teachers Wellbeing Index, (2018) – www.educationsupportpartnership.org.uk

Evans, H. & Wellings, D. (2017) – What Does the Public Think About the NHS? – The King's Fund.

Ferguson, H. (2014a) – What Social Workers do in Performing Child Protection Work: Evidence from Research into Face-To-Face Practice. *Child and Family Social Work*, Feb. 2014.

Ferguson, H. (2014b) – Envisioning Social Work by Putting the Life Back into It: Learning about What Social Workers Do and How They Do It (Well). In Joint Social Work Education and Research Conference: Social Work Making Connections, London, 23–25 July 2014. London: JSWEC.

Forrester, D. (2016) – What, When, Why and How: Zombie Social Work and the Need for a New Narrative. In Solomon, E. (ed.) *Rethinking Children's Services Fit for the Future?* London: Catch22 and NCB. pp. 8–35.

Gibb, J., Cameron, I. M., Hamilton, R., Murphy, E., & Naji, S. (2010) – Mental Health Nurses' and Allied Health Professionals' Perceptions of the Role of the Occupational Health Service in the Management of Work-Related Stress: How Do they Self-Care? *Journal of Psychiatric and Mental Health Nursing*, Vol. 17, No. 9, pp. 838–845.

Gibson, M. (2016) – Social Worker or Social Administrator? Findings from a Qualitative Case Study of a Child Protection Social Work Team. *Child and Family Social Work 2017*, Vol. 22, pp. 1187–1196. John Wiley & Son Ltd.

Gilbey, B. (2017) – 'Too Involved' or 'Unable to Cope': How Can we Bring Emotions Back into Social Work. *Community Care*, Aug. 2017.

Golightley, M. & Holloway, M. (2019) – Editorial: Social Work in the Eye of the Storm: Politics and Prejudice. *The British Journal Social Work*, Vol. 49, No. 2, Mar., pp. 277–281.

Horner, N. (2003) – *What is Social Work? Context and Perspectives* (Transforming Social Work Practice) 2003 Edition. Exeter: Learning Matters Ltd.

Ingram, R. (2015) – *Understanding Emotions in Social Work: Theory, Practice and Reflection*. Milton Keynes: Open University Press.

Institute of Occupational Safety and Health (2017) – Council Fined for Violent Mother's Assault on Social Workers. *IOSH Magazine*, 1st Dec. 2017.

Legood, A., McGrath, M., Searle, R. & Lee, A. (2016) – Exploring. How Social Workers Experience and Cope with Public Perception of Their Profession. *The British Journal of Social Work*, Vol. 46, No. 7, pp. 1872–1889.

Lepanjuuri, K., Cornick, P. & Leach, T. (2018) – Children's Services Omnibus – Wave 3 Research Report. NatCen Social Research May, 2018. Department of Education.

Liddle, J. (2018) – Public Value Management and New Public Governance: Key Traits, Issues and Developments. In E. Ongaro and S. van Thiel (eds.), *The Palgrave Handbook of Public Administration and Management in Europe*, doi:10.1057/978-1-137-55269-3_49

Littlechild, B. (2005) – "The Stresses Arising from Violence, Threats and Aggression against Child Protection Social Workers". *Journal of Social Work*, Vol. 5, pp. 61–82.

Ministry of Justice (2018) – Circular 2018/0. Assaults on Emergency Workers (Offences) Act 2018.

Ministry of Justice (2018) – Jail Time to Double for Assaulting and Emergency Worker (Press Release, 13th Sept. 2018). Ministry of Justice.

Moore, M. (1995) – *Creating Public Value: Strategic Management in Government*. Cambridge, MA: Harvard University Press.

Moriarty, J., Baginsky, M. & Manthorpe, J. (2015) – Literature Review of Roles and Issues within the Social Work Profession in England. Kings College London. Social Care Workforce Research Unit, 35 London.

Munro, E. R. (2011) – *The Munro Review of Child Protection: Final Report – A Child Centred System*. London: DFE.

Ongaro, E. & van Thiel, S. (eds.) (2018) – *The Palgrave Handbook of Public Administration and Management in Europe*. doi:10.1057/978-1-137-55269-3_49

Ravalier, J. & Boichat, G. (2018) – UK Social Workers: Working Conditions and Wellbeing. Bath: Bath Spa University.

Schraer, R. (2014) – 85% of Social Workers Were Assaulted, Harassed or Verbally Abused in the Past Year. *Community Care*, 16th Sept. 2014.

Schraer, R. (2015) – Social Workers Too Stressed to their Job Survey. *Community Care*, 7th Jan. 2015.

Standards in Public Life (1995) – *First Report of the Committee on Standards in Public Life*. London: HMSO.

Stevenson, L. (2017) – Social Worker Recruitment and Retention among Biggest Risks Facing Children's Services, Say Leaders. *Community Care*, Aug. 2017.

Stevenson, L. (2018) – 49% of ASYE Social Workers Promised a Protected Caseload Don't Have One, Survey Finds. *Community Care*, June, 2018.

Unison (2015) – Social Workers in the Courts and the Consequences of Transparency. *Report of a UNISON Survey of Social Work Practitioners*, UNISON, June 2015, Unison HQ, London.

White, S. (2011) – Munro Review: We Need Less Bureaucracy, More Social Work. *Guardian Article*, 7th Feb. 2011.

Winstanley, S. & Hales, L. (2015) – A Preliminary Study of Burnout in Residential Social Workers Experiencing Workplace Aggression: Might It Be Cyclical? *The British Journal of Social Work*, Vol. 45, No. 1, Jan., pp. 24–33.

Worsley, A., Mann, T., Olsen, A. & Mason-Whitehead, E. (2013) – *Key Concepts in Social Work Practice*. SAGE Publications. www.gov.uk/government/organisations/ofsted

7   Virtually Vulnerable
Why Digital Technology Challenges the Fundamental Concepts of Vulnerability and Risk

Andy Phippen and Emma Bond

Introduction

The digital environment redefines the concept of vulnerability by challenging conventional theories of place, identity and situation. This is something that Yar (2013) refers to as the problem of 'who' and the problem of 'where'. In the digital world traditional boundaries to vulnerability are removed – traditional understandings of geography cease to exist, and, therefore, abuse can occur from anywhere in the world. While abuse in the more traditional context might have occurred face-to-face or in a written form, digital environments explode the volume, and audiences for abuse and abusers can hide from view through anonymity, pseudonymity or even multiple online personas. By removing geographical boundaries, providing far more complex opportunity for anonymity and presenting the potential abuser with the opportunity to access potentially millions of victims, the online world challenges criminological norms. In this chapter, we argue that the online environment presents the potential for anyone to be vulnerable and that stakeholders – those with responsibility for safeguarding from practice to policy – routinely fail victims because their solutions fail to understand the wider social context.

According to Ofcom[1] (2018) nearly 90 percent of adults in the United Kingdom (UK) are online, and this increases to 96 percent amongst 45–54s and to 98 percent amongst 16–24 year olds. Given that smartphones are more popular than a computer or tablet for going online (a continuing a trend first seen in 2016), Ling (2012) suggests that mobile internet technologies have become taken for granted in everyday life. As such our everyday lives, our identities, communities and relationships between the self and other are interwoven, increasingly seamlessly, with mobile internet technologies. Mobile technologies in the form of smartphones and tables, WIFI and 4G networks have transformed how we access online spaces enabling us to get online anywhere and at any time and the previously private, 'safe' space of the home can be open to the outside world through mobile devices. People are contacted 24 hours a day, sent abusive messages, hateful content and images, viruses and scams and online privacy concerns are high on both public and policy agendas (Ofcom, 2019). Rapidly changing technological landscapes have blurred the boundaries between public and private spheres and dramatically altered the contours of risk in relation to self-identity in late modern society (Bond, 2014). Yet as Stokes (2010, p. 321) observes 'conceiving of the 'web' as a dimension of reality rather than a separate space frees us from the traditional false dichotomies found in social science and the false analogy of 'virtual' and 'real'. As such, 'given the ubiquity of digital technology and connectively in contemporary society, an honest, empirically driven, and sociologically grounded discussion of these dynamics is long overdue' (Barnard, 2017, p. 199).

The concern for safety in 'virtual' space is a very real one for those experiencing abuse, victimisation and online crimes. It is the 'desire for safety and security has become one of the ways we justify ownership of the [mobile] device' (Ling, 2012, p. 116) yet arguably in ameliorating risk and uncertainly they also simultaneously facilitate risk and risk anxiety in people's everyday lives. Thus risk-profiling, a central part of modernity (Giddens, 1991), involves both human and non-human entities (Bond, 2014) and dominates both public discourse and private behaviours. The concept of risk is, according to Beck (1992) directly bound to reflexive modernisation and we suggest that online risks are a prime example of his risk society thesis. In late modernity, self-identity has become, according to Giddens (1991) a reflexively organised behaviour in which individuals make life choices about lifestyle and life plans. Concerns over identity theft, online scams, image-based abuse, fear of being stalked and harassed online or downloading a virus influence how we use the internet, how we behave online, what we post and share and why we invest in software to protect ourselves.

Beck (1992) and Giddens (1990, 1991) and their research on *risk society* provide a useful theoretical framework for examining the contemporary world, its hazards and social change which shape and influence political comment, policy direction and the lives and futures of individuals. The concept of risk has changed in late modern society from natural hazards to be understood as the unintended consequences of modernisation itself. Anxieties and uncertainly related to the internet and the associated technological developments in the form of mobile devices appear as consequences of technological advances. The concept of risk has dominated media discourses on mobile technologies and whilst much of the reporting reflects determinist approaches, it is important to remember that the relationship between risk and vulnerability in virtual environments is actually a highly complex one. Risk is helpfully defined by Beck as:

> A systematic way of dealing with hazards and insecurities induced and introduced by modernisation itself. Risks, as opposed to older dangers, are consequences which relate to the threatening force of modernization and to its globalisation of doubt.
>
> (Beck, 1992, p. 21)

As outlined above, the landscapes of risk have also changed as boundaries, for example, between public and private are increasingly blurred with the home remaining the main context of internet use. The affordances (see Hutchby, 2001) of mobile technologies have blurred the boundaries between time and space, public and private, human and non-human (Bond, 2010, 2014) and the internet, a media-based public sphere (Devereux, 2007) has become a ubiquitous technology – a taken-for-granted source of information, social interaction and community in everyday life.

Risk is, therefore, a social construction and:

> an idea in its own right relatively independent of the hazard to which it relates. Risk is thus understood in relation to perception that is generated by social processes – such as representation and definition – as much as it is by actual experience of harm.
>
> (Burgess et al., 2017, p. 2)

Actor network theory (ANT) offers a useful approach to our understanding here. In conceptualising society as produced by and through networks of heterogenous material, it is made up through a variety of human and non-human entities (Prout, 1996). 'ANT is committed to demonstrating that the elements are bound together in a network (including the people) are constituted and shaped by their involvement with each other' (Lee and Brown, 1994, p. 774). ANT as interdisciplinary can overcome the unhelpful dualisms proposed by modernist social theory to approximate an 'ecological sociology' (Murdoch, 2001) in order to understand the 'intricate and mutually constitutive character of the human and the technological' (Prout, 1996, p. 198) and, we suggest, the socially constructed nature of risk and vulnerability. Using ANT to conceptualise online risk and vulnerability helps to tease out the complexity of the relationships between the *actants* (see Latour, 1997) in the networks. ANT attempts to explain and interpret social and technological evolution using neither technical -material nor social reductionism, but rather it incorporates a 'principle of generalized symmetry', that what is human and non-human should be integrated into the same conceptual framework.

In overcoming vulnerability in responding to online harms and developing resilience the importance of adopting a holistic approach through a multi-stakeholder perspective is essential if we are to avoid the technological determinism of recent policy approached to online harms. Law (1991) distinguishes between previous approaches to society and technology as technological determinism (technical acts as explanation) or social reductionism (expression of social relations) and argues that it is a mistake to ignore the networks of heterogeneous materials that constitute the social. Our everyday lives, our identities, communities and relationships are interwoven with people and technology, with offline and online an, as such, we need to better understand the dynamic and multifarious nature on everyday life in late modernity.

Such an understanding needs to include a wider rights-based underpinning of the philosophical foundations of legal approaches to the constructions of abuse and harm online. We have argued elsewhere (Bond, 2014 and Phippen, 2017) for adopting a theoretical pluralism which constructing a conceptual framework in an attempt to understand the multifarious and complex network of hybridity and the wider, political and economic environment.

The model below (Figure 7.1) is adopted from Bronfenbrenner (1979) and is a development of our own stakeholder model for online child safeguarding (Bond and Phippen, 2019), and illustrates the broad range of influences, and the interactions between them when considering any adult who might become vulnerable to, or a victim of, online abuse.

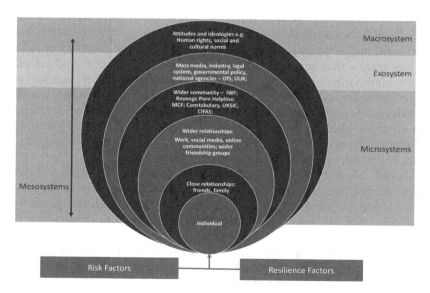

Figure 7.1 Understanding vulnerability adapted from Bronfennbrener's (1979) Ecology of human development.

While the policy focus, as discussed below, tends to centre on technology providers and the role of mass media, as we can see from the model, there are many stakeholders who have closer influence over the individuals. Policy drivers also fail to acknowledge the importance of the meso-systems in interacting between different stakeholder layers.

Cybersecurity and online safety have become pressing concerns for policy makers, industry (including internet service providers and technology manufacturers), law enforcement and the general public. It is the notion of vulnerability to risk and potential harm that underpins the drive for protection, and importantly as perceptions of risk change, so do responses to risk management. Furthermore, as awareness increases with the dynamic nature of knowledge, the notion of risk becomes central to society and to individuals as they reflexively construct their own life biographies (Giddens, 1991). Thus, risk management has become part of everyday life and this includes managing risk online and with and through mobile devices. As risk is a social construction, perceptions of risk are underpinned by cultural, social and historical factors and just as risk is understood as a social construction, it is important to remember that the factors that lead to online abuse and internet-related crimes are complex and intertwined. For example, as children whose parents lack education or internet experience tend to lack digital safety skills which leaves them more vulnerable to online risk and teenage girls with sexual abuse history and depressive feelings are more at risk of internet-related sexual abuse (Göran Svedin, 2011). Awareness raising and educational initiatives to increase online safety and protection are based on motivating people to change their behaviours online as the most widely acknowledged factor associated with online vulnerability is risk-taking behaviour. However, the complexity and diversity of risks online means that such initiatives are not always effective and people can remain vulnerable to certain types of risk. For example, in relation to online abuse, whilst is it well known that those open to online sexual activities especially flirting and having sexual conversations with strangers are more likely to become victims of sexual harassment, solicitation or grooming, many victims of online sexual abuse have not engaged in such behaviours previously.

Online risk and vulnerability, therefore, affect everyone. Risk and risk management strategies have profound implications for self-identity especially for self-identity online in late modernity through risk-profiling and adopting risk taking behaviours. Online risks and responding to online risks connect the individual and society and the increasingly interventionist role of the state transforms social, legal and cultural constructions of everyday experiences of risk through that Foucault (1977) identifies and 'disciplinary networks' for spatial control.

Many of the discourses on risk and online protection have to date been dominated by child protection concerns and by constructions of childhood in late modernity based on notions of innocence, naivety and dependence. Policy initiatives based on protectionist ideals derived from adultist perspectives have defined public space and adult space where children's participation is controlled and limited through formal and often legal restrictions. Jenks (2005) develops Foucault's ideas of spatial control to suggest that the exercise and manipulation of space is a primary example of adult's controlling children's worlds and he suggests that the postmodern diffusion of authority has not led to a democracy but to an experience of powerlessness, which is not a potential source of identity but a perception of victimisation. However, as Lee (2001, p. 10) argues such 'adult' authority has been called into question:

> So far, then, we have seen that adult authority over children, the ability of adults to speak for children and to make decisions on their behalf, has been supported by the image of the standard adult. We have also briefly noted that there are good reasons to be suspicious of the degree of authority that adults have, and that, in the light of these suspicions, adult authority has become controversial. But beneath this controversy, widespread social changes have been taking place that are bringing those forgotten questions of whether adults match up to the image of the standard adult to the fore. In fact, these changes are eroding standard adulthood. Over the past few decades, changes in working lives and in intimate relationships have cast the stability and completeness of adults into doubt and made it difficult and, often, undesirable for adults to maintain such stability.

Thus, adults and their assumed state of completeness is exposed as a falsehood and we see adulthood as a dynamic state which changes over time and space to include degrees of resilience and also vulnerability. Vulnerability, associated with both natural disasters and terrorists attacks (Misztal, 2011), applies to people's everyday lives online. As the Ofcom report (2018, p. 1) observes,

> although the internet seems ubiquitous, the online experience is not the same for everyone. Our research reveals significant differences, by age and by socio- economic group, in the numbers who are online at all, and in the extent to which those who are online have the critical skills to understand and safely navigate their online world.

People who are more vulnerable 'offline' are also more likely to be vulnerable online especially those experiencing abusive relationships relating to coercion and control. Having low self-confidence/self-esteem and being influenced by alcohol and/or drugs are also influential factors in both risk-taking behaviours and being at risk online. Furthermore, people with mental health issues and psychological difficulties tend to encounter more risk online and be more upset by it but it is important to remember that the absence of vulnerability is not fixed, but is a variable that can change very quickly. An understanding of online vulnerability is particularly important for those working with people who are understood to be more at risk than others (e.g., victims of domestic abuse) as they can specifically benefit from improvements in online self-protection and developing resilience through recognising and understanding how to respond to risk. Although some studies have identified specific characteristics associated with online vulnerability, the relationship between online and offline vulnerability remains a complex one as although some people who appear more vulnerable offline are also likely to be more vulnerable online, some may appear highly resilient offline but can be highly vulnerable online and vice versa. Thus, stereotyping is unhelpful and can even be dangerous in some cases presuming that because an individual does not appear to 'fit' with a risky profile that they are safe. Many victims of online abuse, for example, did not appear vulnerable previously but had strong friendships, good relationships and a high level of educational attainment but their public or professional identity ultimately made them vulnerable to trolling. Thus, online risks often manifest in unexpected ways.

Known individual vulnerability factors include, age, gender, socio-economic status, level of educational attainment, self-efficacy, sexuality, ethnicity, experience of domestic abuse and/or sexual abuse, disability, emotional and/or behavioural difficulties, poor off line relationships, exclusion of access, use of drugs and alcohol. However, while individual risk factors, such as those outlined above, do not independently lead to vulnerability, accumulation of these or in combination are considered to increase a person's vulnerability to online risk and harm. Furthermore, multiple long-term risk factors in day-to-day life interplay with trigger events which can result in the loss of protective factors and online behavioural risks and engaging in risk-taking behaviour. Vulnerable people are not a self-contained or static group and anyone could be vulnerable to some degree some time depending on any one, or a combination of, the risks or challenging life events they face and their resilience.

As the barriers of time and space are blurred, the anonymity of the internet and social media has been attributed to bullying, abuse and trolling behaviours which take advantage of opportunities for deception and disguise. Criminals can masquerade themselves to victims pretending to have a very different identity to fool others into parting with money, information and images and the ease of access which the internet allows results in 100 or 1,000 of victims potentially be reached. Therefore, from a criminological perspective, the affordances of both anonymity and the ability to create and change online identities are powerful mechanisms which facilitate offences being committed and abuse taking place. Whilst increasing numbers of individuals are potentially victims of online crime and abuse, it is the impact on business and the economy, however, which seemingly dominates the debates on cybercrime, as according to the National Cyber Security Centre and NCA (2018, p. 6):

> With attackers able to achieve many of their aims by using techniques that are not particularly advanced, the distinction between nation states and cyber criminals has blurred, making attribution all the more difficult.

Furthermore, it is the blurring of geographical boundaries that make protection through legal control and regulation of the internet and digital content so problematic. 'Although regulators have for years struggled with rising transnationality, in the forms of global trade and transnational corporations, the internet presents an entirely new dimension to the problems of squeezing transnational activity into the national legal straight jacket' (Kohl, 2007, p. 4). As such traditional approaches to law enforcement and criminal justice are challenged as they struggle to remain effective and even relevant to online crimes and are similarly failing to protect victims whether they are individual citizens and or large-scale organisations which further contributes to both risk and risk anxiety in the late modern age.

We can see clear illustration of this in a statutory instrument emerging in the UK to attempt to control what is referred to by the Government as 'online harms'. In April 2019 the UK Government released its 'Online Harms' White Paper (UK Government, 2019, p. 5) to much press coverage and ministerial comment on how it will ensure that the UK is 'the safest place in the world to go online'.

It claimed to set out both the problem domain and solutions that included a regulatory framework, an independent regulator for 'online safety'; the scope of companies within this framework; how enforcement might work; the role of technology and the empowerment of the end user. However, we feel it is more useful as a tool for exploring how, and why, nation states struggle to tackle online vulnerabilities and 'protect' citizens from digital harm and, arguably, result in an environment that will both fail to reach its goal and also introduce cultural normalisation that potential introduces greater risk of harm.

The white paper makes little effort to define what an 'Online Harm' actually is, aside from the following from the Ministerial introduction which states:

> Online harms are widespread and can have serious consequences.

We should also point out that there is neither a clear definition of online safety – therefore, the statutory instrument fails to define either the problem domain or the solution prior to proposing a legislative framework to achieve it. Given that there seem to be two key themes in this paper – the legislative proposal and the 'duty of care' for organisations requiring them to implement technical solutions to these issues – the lack of clarity in the initial definition is concerning. Both law and algorithms (which, as Lessig, 1999 argues, defines the laws of cyberspace) require clear definition if they are to be successfully implemented, and this instrument has neither.

The rhetoric around safety and unacceptability of harmful content is set out from the outset of the paper without actually defining it:

> The government wants the UK to be the safest place in the world to go online, and the best place to start and grow a digital business. Given the prevalence of illegal and harmful content online, and the level of public concern about online harms, not just in the UK but worldwide, we believe that the digital economy urgently needs a new regulatory framework to improve our citizens' safety online.
>
> Illegal and unacceptable content and activity is widespread online, and UK users are concerned about what they see and experience on the internet. The prevalence of the most serious illegal content and activity, which threatens our national security or the physical safety of children, is unacceptable. Online platforms can be a tool for abuse and bullying, and they can be used to undermine our democratic values and debate. The impact of harmful content and activity can be particularly damaging for children, and there are growing concerns about the potential impact on their mental health and wellbeing.
>
> *(p. 5)*

And we might observe that this seems to the starting point for the ambiguity and lack of focus that is to come throughout the document. Digital technology has achieved immeasurable impacts on our everyday lives, but is it possible to address every possible concern in a single legislative intention? There is also a fleeting reference to the intention to tackle both 'illegal' and 'unacceptable' harms and the paper defines a wide range of harms, from those with an apparent clear definition to those that are more ambiguous:

- Harms with a clear definition, including child sexual exploitation and abuse, terrorist content and activity, organised immigration crime, modern slavery, harassment and cyberstalking, encouraging or assisting suicide, incitement of violence, content illegally uploaded from prisons and the sexting of indecent images by under 18s.
- Harms with a less clear definition, including cyberbullying and trolling, extremist content and activity, disinformation, advocacy of self-harm and the promotion of Female Genital Mutilation (FGM).

- Underaged exposure to legal content – children accessing pornography, and children accessing inappropriate material (including under 13s using social media and under 18s using dating apps; excessive screen time).

While we do not wish to dwell upon the debate around legal access to social media platforms, in passing we reiterate once again that the 'law' around young people's access to social media is defined under advertising (Federal Trade Commission, 1998) and data protection (The European Union, 2018) legislation, not harm. The white paper continues to place expectations on technology providers to ensure 'harms' do not happen, without actually defining the clarity needed for code to achieve this. However, more specifically, the state approach to 'protection' resides in the control on information flow and restriction of access, rather than placing a broader social perspective of tackling underlying criminal behaviours. We might argue that this perspective, of itself, negatively impacts upon victims because there is an ideological position that one can control the online world and prevent harm from occurring – one can make oneself 'safe', and therefore if they fail to become safe, the failing lies with them.

While we are bound to explore these issues in a single chapter, and are, therefore, unable to explore multiple examples of harm and vulnerability, an effective exploration of the failures of such prohibitive approaches can be shown through examining victimisation and vulnerability on *revenge pornography*. Within this single example, we can consider how social discourse already fails the vulnerable by way of categorising these behaviours as something other than what they actually are, which is forms of domestic abuse through digital technologies and also how legislative 'solutions' are bound to fail victims.

The term 'revenge pornography' has only emerged in recent times (as can be seen in Figure 7.2).

However, we would also take exception with the term *revenge pornography* in general, given that most acts described as such rarely include a vengeful or pornographic element. If we take definitions of each word in turn:

> Revenge:[2] the action of hurting or harming someone in return for an injury or wrong suffered at their hands.

By using the term 'revenge' to talk about these crimes, we are, in essence, providing some reason or excuse for this behaviour. The perpetrator is taking revenge on the victim, for a slight the victim has performed on them. However, given one of the primary motivations for the non-consensual sharing of indecent images is the breakdown of a relationship, it seems utterly disproportionate to suggest that a fair response to

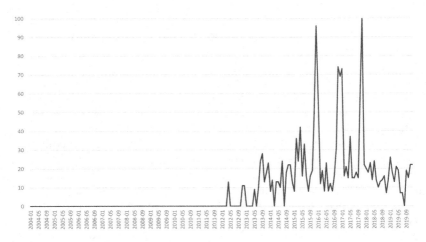

Figure 7.2 Revenge Pornography Google Trend.

someone end a relationship is to publicly share indecent images of the without their consent. This is not revenge, it is abuse.

Pornography:[3] printed or visual material containing the explicit description or display of sexual organs or activity, intended to stimulate sexual excitement.

In the second part of the definition, while we might argue that self-produced sexually explicit material might have been produced to as a form of a gift (see Mauss, 1966) to represent intimacy and/or stimulate sexual excitement, the intention of the individual sharing the images/materials in a non-consensual way is not for sexual excitement, it is to harm, to embarrass, to shame, and to hurt the subject of the images. While sexual excitement might arise for those viewing these images, it is not the intention of the poster.

The early recognition of revenge pornography as a term related to websites that provides the facilities for ex-partners to post up indecent materials of people that had been in relationships with. These 'revenge' websites, such as IsAnyoneUp, IsAnyBodyDown or UGot-Posted, marketed themselves as pornography sites with 'user driven content'. However, much content posted in these sites would invite indecent images of an individual where contributors would linked to people's social media profiles and online identity. While these images were frequently either nude or images of victims engaged in sexual acts, the motivation for the websites were financial for the site owners.

Before being shut down by the FBI (as a result of an investigation that many of the images were obtained by hacking victim's email accounts, rather than having them donated by anonymous contributors) it was estimated that IsAnyoneUp generated $13,000 per month (Gold, 2011) from advertising revenue. IsAnyBodyDown offered a takedown service (FTC, 2015) for victims where, in exchange for payment, the website would offer but then fail to take down images of them shared without consent. Since this high-profile emergence of the concept of mass shaming, the behaviours, as discussed below, have evolved to encompass a wide range of what should more correctly be referred to as image-based abuse or the non-consensual sharing of indecent images. The impact on victims is severe and makes them highly vulnerable to further harm. Moreover, a lack of law enforcement understanding (Bond and Tyrell, 2017) and public opinion related to these acts will, undoubtedly, compound the harm further.

We should acknowledge the power the possession or existence of these images have over the victim. If one is in possession of indecent images of another, it is understandable that they will not wish for those images to be shared. Therefore, the affordances of the technology (Hutchby, 2001) and the threat of sharing these images allows control over the victim, to either coerce them into behaviours they would be unwilling to do without this coercion (for example, sending further images), or to blackmail or further harass the victim. It is perhaps more powerful to hold the images with threat of sharing, rather than actually sharing due to the control the abuser can hold over the victim.

However, impact on the victim can be severe and, by way of illustration, quotations from victims who contacted the Revenge Porn Helpline[4] show the extent of harm and vulnerability:

> I became very depressed and vulnerable. This affected my social life as I rarely went out just in case someone recognised me. It has caused me to have trust issues, the incident happened quite a while ago but I have not been able to stay in a stable relationship since due to my trust issues, it causes a lot of arguments'. I also live in constant fear that there may be another image out there, or that it will happen to me again.
>
> I felt like I had my dignity ripped away from me, this affected my job as I often took time off as a result, I was too scared to leave the house and I did not want people to find out at work. I eventually lost my job due to the time off and paranoia, I felt like every time someone looked at me it was because they had seen the images.

The two above quotes highlight the impact of the non-consensual sharing of indecent images, the humiliation that follows, and the long-term nature of that impact. These quotes reflect a number of issues that are reflected in the literature, which categorises both psychological and professional identity.

Citron and Franks (2014) develop further categorisations on psychological impact, raising concerns around anxiety that can possibly lead to suicidal tendencies, highlighted by the recent tragic suicide of Veronica Rubio (Patel, 2019). The harms that can arise from the non-consensual sharing of images cannot be underestimated and can be as wide ranging as personal safety; body image anxieties; long-term trust issues and, as illustrated in the quotes above, the ongoing anxiety of not known where images have been posted, whether new images will emerge, or to who or how many people have seen them. We need to start referring to 'revenge pornography' for what it is – domestic abuse, exploitation, coercion and harassment.

When considering whether there might be a stereotypical victim of such behaviours, the literature victim profiling, as discussed above, can focus on women as the abused and males as offenders. However, in an analysis the cases brought to the Revenge Porn Helpline one thing that is that there is no 'typical' revenge pornography scenario or client. While they deal with many cases current discourses consider the 'usual' in terms of modus operandi (i.e., an ex-partner non-consensually shares indecent images of the victim either onto a public online space or to targeted private individuals), they deal with as many that do not fit into this category (Bond and Tyrell, 2018).

Analysis of the helpline data highlighted the following key issues:

- people contacted the service because they felt they had nowhere else to turn
- they have exhausted options themselves, which may include pleading with the offender, contacting law enforcement and service and platform providers and talking to friends and family
- the key trigger for them contacting the service was after the images had been shared
- whilst they felt that they could have dealt with the issues when an abuser was threatening to share images, once they had moved from private threat to public online space, the victim felt that they were no longer in control and had no idea how to manage the disclosure
- they turned to the helpline in order to try to get the images removed, because their own efforts were often in vain.

Though further research that we have conducted with the helpline has highlighted very strongly from discussions with the both staff and the exploration of over 2,000 cases that for many victims they were not subject to the sharing of an image but had the anxiety of the threat to share. For example, the offender having received images from the victim and they would then use the threat to share as a means to coerce or exploit the victim further sometimes over considerable periods of time and unless they sent more images, or engaged in sexual acts with the offender, the images would be posted online or shared with people known to the victim (mainly employers or family). Therefore, the threat of sharing is more powerful than the act of sharing itself – once the image has been shared, the offender has reduced their power over the victim because the impact of sharing has been achieved. However, this is not always the case, particularly when a campaign of abuse is conducted by the offender, then the image will be shared multiple times with multiple targets. The helpline talked about repeat callers who had been subjected to sharing and re-sharing of images – in one case the offender would share the images with every new employer the victim had. In these cases, a repeated revictimisation occurs – every time the images are viewed by a new third party, the harm and shame are repeated as the victim experiences these harms again. As one victim said:

it feels like im being raped online every day.

Moreover, there is another seriously distressing impact around not knowing who has seen the images and where they have ended up. And while the images may have been shared once, unless the offender is tackled for their behaviours, there is no guarantee that images will not be shared again. The uncertainty is another aspect of harm that is lacking in a lot of the discussion and literature around revenge pornography. With the focus on the non-consensual act of sharing, there is an assumption these are one off offences. In reality, victims can be subject to abuse many times, and from many difference perspectives. To repeat part of the quotation from the victim of revenge pornography from earlier in the chapter:

I felt like every time someone looked at me it was because they had seen the images.

The online dissemination of images, and the lack of control of the image once on image is either shared with multiple parties or posted in a public online space, means that the audience for viewing is entirely unknown. With digital images sharing once does not prevent further sharing, unless the offender is challenged on their behaviour and taken to task with what they have done. There is a crucial need for legislation to protect victims because, in a lot of instances, offenders feel they can do what they like with no challenge to their behaviour. Once images are in their possession, there is persistent threat to the victim. Once images have been shared once, there is no guarantee the sharing of images can be controlled further or who ends up seeing them.

While legislation to tackle revenge pornography was introduced in 2015, as part of the Criminal Justice and Courts Act 2015 s33 (UK Government, 2015), stating:

1   It is an offence for a person to disclose a private sexual photograph or film if the disclosure is made—

a   without the consent of an individual who appears in the photograph or film, and
b   with the intention of causing that individual distress.

The legislation failed to address issues of threat, victim impact or even, as a result of it being classified as a communication, rather than a sexual crime, anonymity of victim. Therefore, while there was now potential for an abuser to be charged for an abusive act, there was also the risk of revictimisation through a lack of anonymity. The absence of threat in the legislation meant that an abuser had to actually send or post an image before being capable of being charged. Furthermore, the intent to harm focusses upon the motivation of the abuser, rather than the impact upon the victim. Therefore, the abuser need only state the intention was not to cause distress to provide a solid defence against this legislation. And while we would question why anyone would attempt to justify the non-consensual sharing of indecent photographs in order to achieve anything other than distress, the defence exists in the legislation. Moreover, the state view of the crime being communication based, rather than sexual, also highlighted the ideological position that technology is to blame, rather than social practices. And therefore, compounding the expectation that, in some way, without technology, the vulnerability would not exist. Moreover, guidance from within the Criminal Justice System (Crown Prosecution Service, 2017) around coercion and control makes like reference to digital or online elements that might exist, again isolating the act of image sharing from the wider context of domestic abuse.

Recent news reporting from a BBC investigation (BBC News, 2019) further demonstrated that victims, the vulnerable, had little confidence in this legislative, measure, not just because the legislation was not fit for purpose, but because the broader stakeholder community (for example, police, social care, education professionals and employers) did not respond effectively to the abuse. The reporting highlighted concerns raised by our own work with the Revenge Pornography Helpline and working directly with victims (Bond, 2015) that many times victims will go to employers, friends and police (Bond and Tyrell, 2018) and be met with judgement rather than sympathy. Helpline practitioners have recounted stories of how victims have been told 'if you hadn't taken the images, he wouldn't have been able to share them'. The recent coverage has highlighted a very important issue considering how states might address online vulnerability for their citizens; legislation is not enough if stakeholders fail to engage with the wider social conditions.

According to Ofcom (2018) the majority of adults in the UK continue to say that for them the benefits of the internet outweigh the risks. However, they also mentioned that constant connectivity can be overwhelming as nearly half of internet users over the age of 16 reported seeing hateful content online in the past year. In the outer layer, the Macrosystem, it is the wider attitudes and ideologies that can influence online vulnerability as understanding human rights to privacy and to respect for private life, family life, your home and your correspondence. Social and cultural norms also change but influence what it considerable acceptable and appropriate behaviour and content online which impact on constructions of risk. In the exosystem, mass media, the legal frameworks, government policy and national agencies are influential as they offer and provide laws and law enforcement for online crime. Understanding what is legal and illegal online can also help individuals manage and respond to risks. The microsystems cut across many different types of relationships from interactions with the constabulary, for example, and national help and advice lines to friendships and memberships of cultural groups to closer ones with friends and family. The individual's vulnerability online is influence by all these relationships and the interactions between the layers – the mesosystems – and by the risk and resilience factors unique to that person.

Yet legislative solutions will in general focus on the exosystem and fail to understand that the closer to the individual the stakeholder is, the more effective they can be in addressing vulnerability and harm.

Returning to the Online Harms White Paper, we can see an ideology of technological intervention:

> There is currently a range of regulatory and voluntary initiatives aimed at addressing these problems, but these have not gone far or fast enough, or been consistent enough between different companies, to keep UK users safe online...
>
> ...The UK will be the first to do this, leading international efforts by setting a coherent, proportionate and effective approach that reflects our commitment to a free, open and secure internet.
>
> ...We want technology itself to be part of the solution, and we propose measures to boost the tech-safety sector in the UK, as well as measures to help users manage their safety online.
>
> ..Tackling harmful content and activity online is one part of the UK's wider ambition to develop rules and norms for the internet, including protecting personal data, supporting competition in digital markets and promoting responsible digital design.

The position follows a policy direction that can be seen to allegedly take shape in 2012 (Phippen, 2017). That direction focusses upon the use of technology to 'solve' issues related to online protection and safeguarding. The view being that given the online environment provides the access to these harms, the technology must also be able to provide the solution to prevent these things from happening. As we have illustrated in Figure 7.2, technology providers exist far away from the individual, in the exosystem, and will therefore only be able to have limited value to addressing the vulnerabilities of the individual.

These pro-active technological interventions, which began with filtering approaches that would prevent access to harmful content, have already been something of concern to the United Nations, with the 'Report of the Special Rapporteur on the promotion and protection of the right to freedom of opinion and expression' (UN Human Rights Council, 2018) stating that:

> States and intergovernmental organizations should refrain from establishing laws or arrangements that would require the "proactive" monitoring or filtering of content, which is both inconsistent with the right to privacy and likely to amount to pre-publication censorship.

Nevertheless, the UK Government's 2019 position on protection of the victim is an increased focus on pro-active and interceptional content moderation from those businesses within the scope of the proposed regulation. The approach fails to acknowledge the lack of robust empirical evidence relating to "online harms" and therefore, doesn't adequately explain how they intend to prioritise regulatory action to address the harms that have the greatest impact – it would seem, from the paper, that all "online harms" are equal and should be treated as such. The failure to critically consider the conceptual underpinnings of the inclusion of harm versus crime results in a lack of clarity relating to definitions of harm. For example, if we are to consider this ideological position to those made vulnerable through the myriad approaches to image-based abuse, we might question the role of the service/technology provider in reducing harm. While these platforms may provide locations for an image to be posted, or the technology to share them, they have no control over the behaviour of the abuser to threaten, to control, to repost on a different platform, or to harass the victim further.

Each one of the *online harms* defined in the paper are complex issues which require holistic approaches with a deep understanding of the many potential social variables and interfaces that result in an 'online harm' happening, yet throughout the paper this is ignored and 'sticking plaster' solutions put forward which fail to address the fundamental issue that different harms require specific and appropriate responses – responding to 'harmful' content is not the same as tackling gang culture or predatory grooming online.

Throughout the White Paper the discourse on the intention to adopt a 'risk-based approach' is flawed and is based on rhetoric rather than reality. The language and tone treat all individuals as equal and a single, passive entity. For example, it states (p. 85): '*Users want to be empowered to manage their online safety, and that of their children, but there is insufficient support in place and they currently feel vulnerable online*', which completely fails to acknowledge that children are users in their own right and depicts children as 'passive' consumers of internet content rather than 'active' users and contributors to the digital economy.

Perhaps the biggest failing of the white paper is that it has moved beyond Internet Safety to try to encompass anything that might constitute an online harm, then present a single solution to address all of them. Within the introduction to the white paper (p. 6), the Ministers with responsibility stated the paper relates to the:

UK's wider ambition to develop rules and norms for the internet.

Is it really the UK government's place to develop rules and norms for the Internet, a global technological infrastructure, as a whole? We question the motivations of nation states to try to impose their rules upon an environment that transcends geographical and legislative boundaries, particularly when the perspective seems to view online harms as entirely technologically facilitated, and therefore digitally solved. These policy directions demonstrate a failure to understand both the nature of technologically facilitated abuse, and the broader social context in which it takes place. We are reminded of Marcus Ranum's much quoted Law (Cheswick et al., 2003, p. 202):

You can't solve social problems with software.

We would argue that failure to appreciate this results in the vulnerable being failed by policy and legislative solutions. If we are to consider the nature of image-based abuse the technology, and control of technology, will never be able to prevent harm. We absolutely need technology and platform providers to play their part – implementing reporting and take down mechanisms that are effective, providing the means to block abusers on their networks, and working with law enforcement to provide evidence. However, we also need legislation that is fit for purpose and understands the social dimensions in while the harm take place, and those with safeguarding or law enforcement responsibilities to appreciate the impact on victims and not cast judgement on their behaviour.

Conclusions

Digital technology clearly redefines the nature of vulnerability and arguably results in an environment where anyone can be vulnerable. However, digital technology is not the cause of this redefinition of the vulnerable, it is merely the passive conduit through which abuse occurs. Due to the opportunities afforded by technology, the reach of the abuser can be extended, and they have many tools to make use of, such as the perceived anonymity or dispersed presence. However, abuse, and the impact upon victims, are human behaviours and responses. While counter measures can be introduced through code, code cannot make judgements, make inference or understand context. It has to follow rules, and those rules have to be logical and literal. On the 25th anniversary of the World Wide Web in 2014, Tim Berners Lee, its founder, was interviewed about what he thought were the important policy issues facing digital technology in the future (Kiss, 2014). In a wide-ranging interview, among other things, he stated, *'we need our lawyers and our politicians to understand programming, to understand what can be done with a computer'.*

We suggest that five years after this statement was made there is still no evidence that this is the case. It is far easier for a policy maker to point the finger at someone else than to appreciate the role they have in challenging abusive and complex social behaviour. Until we move beyond technological intervention as the solution to protecting victims of online abuse and appreciate the relationships between stakeholders and the roles they play in this protection, as well as challenging abusive behaviours, we would suggest that legislation and the wider criminal justice system will continue to fail the vulnerable, whomever and wherever they may be online.

Notes

1 The UK's communications regulator –www.ofcom.org.uk/.
2 https://en.oxforddictionaries.com/definition/revenge.
3 https://en.oxforddictionaries.com/definition/pornography.
4 https://revengepornhelpline.org.uk/.

References

Barnard, S. (2017). 'Digital Sociology's Vocational Promise'. In Daniels, J. Gregory, K. and McMillan Cottom, T. (Eds.) *Digital Sociologies*, Bristol: Policy Press, pp. 195–210.

BBC News (2019 May 19). 'Revenge Porn Laws "Not Working", Says Victims Group'. www.bbc.co.uk/news/uk-48309752

Beck, U. (1992). *Risk Society towards a New Modernity*. London: Sage.

Bond, E. (2010). 'Managing Mobile Relationships – Children's Perceptions of the Impact of the Mobile Phone on Relationships in their Everyday Lives'. *Childhood*, Vol. 17 (4), pp. 514–529.

Bond, E. (2014). *Childhood, Mobile Technologies and Everyday Experiences*. Basingstoke: Palgrave.

Bond, E. (2015). *Understanding Domestic Abuse in Suffolk: Understanding Survivors experiences*. Ipswich: UCS with Suffolk OPCC.

Bond, E. & Phippen, A. (2019). Why Is Placing the Child at the Centre of Online Safeguarding So Difficult? *Entertainment Law Review*, Vol. 30 (3), pp. 80–84., 3.

Bond, E. & Tyrrell, K. (2018). 'Understanding Revenge Pornography: A National Survey of Police Officers and Staff in England and Wales'. *Journal of Interpersonal Violence*. DOI: 10.1177/0886260518760011

Bronfenbrenner, U. (1979). *The Ecology of Human Development: Experiments by Nature and Design*. Cambridge, MA: Harvard University Press. ISBN 0-674-22457-4.

Burgess, A., Wardman, J. & Mythen, G. (2018). 'Considering Risk: Placing the Work of Ulrich Beck in Context'. *Journal of Risk Research*, Vol. 21 (1), pp. 1–5, DOI: 10.1080/13669877.2017.1383075

Cheswhick, W. R., Bellovin, S. M., and Rubin, A. D. (2003). 'Firewalls and Internet Security: Repelling the Wily Hacker'. *Addison-Wesley Professional*, pp. 202–. ISBN 978-0-201-63466-2.

Citron, D. & Franks, M. (2014). 'Criminalizing Revenge Porn'. *Wake Forest Law Review*, Vol. 49, pp. 345–391.

Crown Prosecution Service (2017). 'Controlling or Coercive Behaviour in an Intimate or Family Relationship'. www.cps.gov.uk/legal-guidance/controlling-or-coercive-behaviour-intimate-or-family-relationship

Devereux, E. (2007). *Understanding the Media (2nd Edn.)*. London: Sage.

The European Union (2018). 'General Data Protection Regulation (GDPR)'. https://gdpr-info.eu/

Federal Trade Commission (1998). 'Children's Online Privacy Protection Rule ("COPPA")'. www.ftc.gov/enforcement/rules/rulemaking-regulatory-reform-proceedings/childrens-online-privacy-protection-rule

Federal Trade Commission (2015). 'Website Operator Banned from the "Revenge Porn" Business after FTC Charges He Unfairly Posted Nude Photos'. www.ftc.gov/news-events/press-releases/2015/01/website-operator-banned-revenge-porn-business-after-ftc-charges

Foucault, M. (1977). *Discipline and Punish: The Birth of the Prison*. London: Penguin.

Giddens, A. (1990). *The Consequences of Modernity*. Cambridge: Polity Press.

Giddens, A. (1991). *Modernity and Self-Identity: Self and Society in the Late Modern Age*. Cambridge: Polity Press.

Gold, D. (2011 November 10). 'The Man Who Makes Money Publishing Your Nude Pics'. www.theawl.com/2011/11/the-man-who-makes-money-publishing-your-nude-pics/

Göran Svedin, C. (2011). 'Research Evidence into Behavioural Patterns Which Lead to becoming a Victim of Sexual Abuse'. In Ainsaar, M. and Lööf, L. (Eds.) *Online Behaviour Related to Child Sexual Abuse. Literature Report: Robert*, 37–49. www.childcentre.info/robert/public/Online_behaviour_related_to_sexual_abuse.pdf

Hutchby, I. (2001). 'Technologies, Texts and Affordances'. *Sociology*, Vol. 35 (2), pp. 441–456.

Kiss, J. (2014). 'An Online Magna Carta: Berners-Lee Calls for Bill of Rights for Web'. www.theguardian.com/technology/2014/mar/12/online-magna-carta-berners-lee-web

Kohl, U. (2007). *Jurisdiction and the Internet*. Cambridge: Cambridge University Press.

Latour, B. (1997). 'The Trouble with the Actor-Network Theory'. *Danish Philosophy Journal*, Vol. 25, pp. 47–64.

Law, J. (1991). 'Introduction: Monsters, Machines and Sociotechnical Relations'. In Law, J. (Ed.) *A Sociology of Monsters: Essays on Power, Technology and Domination*. London: Routledge.

Lee, N. (2001). *Childhood and Society: Growing Up in an Age of Uncertainty*. Buckingham: OUP.

Lee N. & Brown, S. (1994). 'Otherness and the Actor Network: The Undiscovered Continent (Humans and Others: The Concept of "Agency" and Its Attribution)'. *American Behavioural Scientist*, Vol. 37 (6), pp. 772–790.

Lessig, L. (1999). *Code and Other Laws of Cyberspace*. New York, USA: Basic Books, Inc.

Ling, R. (2012). *Taken for Grantedness: The Embedding of Mobile Communication in Society*. London: MIT Press.

Mauss, M. (1966). *The Gift; Forms and Functions of Exchange in Archaic Societies*. London: Cohen & West.

Misztal B.A. (2011). *The Challenges of Vulnerability: In Search of Strategies for a Less Vulnerable Social Life*. London: Palgrave Macmillan.

National Cyber Security Centre and NCA (2018). 'The Cyber Treat to UK Business'. https://nationalcrimeagency.gov.uk/who-we-are/publications/178-the-cyber-threat-to-uk-business-2017-18/file

Ofcom (2018). 'Adults Media Use and Attitudes Report'. www.ofcom.org.uk/__data/assets/pdf_file/0011/113222/Adults-Media-Use-and-Attitudes-Report-2018.pdf

Patel, B. (2019 May 29). 'Mother of Four-Year-Old and Nine-Month-Old Baby Hanged Herself After Jealous Lover Sent their Sex Tape to Her Colleagues'. www.dailymail.co.uk/news/article-7083597/Mother-hanged-jealous-lover-sent-sex-tape-colleagues.html

Phippen, A. (2017). *Children's Online Behaviour and Safety Policy and Rights Challenges*. Basingstoke: Palgrave.

Prout, A. (1996). 'Actor-Network Theory, Technology and Medical Sociology: An Illustrative Analysis of the Metered Dose Inhaler'. *Sociology of Health and Illness*, Vol. 18 (2), pp. 198–209.

Stokes, P. (2010). 'Young People as Digital Natives: Protection, Perpetration and Regulation'. *Children's Geographies*, Vol. 8 (3), pp. 319–323.

UK Government (2015). 'Criminal Justice and Courts Act 2015'. www.legislation.gov.uk/ukpga/2015/2/section/33/enacted

UK Government (2017). 'The Digital Economy Act 2017'. www.legislation.gov.uk/ukpga/2017/30/contents/enacted

UK Government (2019). 'Online Harms White Paper'. https://assets.publishing.service.gov.uk/government/uploads/system/uploads/attachment_data/file/793360/Online_Harms_White_Paper.pdf

UN Human Rights Council (2018). 'Report of the Special Rapporteur on the Promotion and Protection of the Right to Freedom of Opinion and Expression'. http://daccess-ods.un.org/access.nsf/Get?Open&DS=A/HRC/38/35&Lang=E

8 Relational Pressure and Policing Vulnerable Populations in China

Xiaojian Wu

Introduction

Street-Level Bureaucrats (SLBs) like the police interact directly with citizens of all statuses and situations over the course of their line duties, and in doing so they use substantial personal discretion in executing public responsibilities (Lipsky, 1980, 2010). Police officers do this either by routinizing procedures and assessing contextual priorities or adopting approaches tailored for specific cases. In other words, they develop discretionary practices that permit them, in some ways, to process or even reformulate the work itself. Such personal discretions are often entangled in various social, legal or ethical quagmires, and are also conditioned by certain deeply embedded cultural and political factors, especially when dealing with vulnerable populations in a society. As Lipsky (2011: 188) noted, the broader social environment 'significantly affects bureaucratic relations'; accordingly more attention should be paid to the study of the vulnerable people outside the Western democratic societies like the United States and the United Kingdom, and how policing of such a population has been affected in different contexts.

This chapter explores relevant social practices and problems featured in a culturally and politically diversified society like China. In the following sections, we first highlight that the issue of vulnerability amongst the population is understood differently in a modern Chinese context, compared to Western understandings. Then we will examine how SLBs operate in China in conceptual terms, and how certain Chinese officials at local level deal in practice with protesting groups within a political system of centralised authority and under-developed legal standardisation.

This chapter examines a culturally embedded practice of 'relational pressure', which is a psychological engineering approach adopted by Chinese frontline officials for policing vulnerable populations. It is suggested that shaping and applying relational repression as a social control approach in targeting the vulnerable social groups, reflects the unique strength of China as an authoritarian high capacity state, yet SLBs in wider social contexts should be enlightened as well that they do have a whole range of social and relational tools too to leverage in executing their public duties. Two problem scenarios will be examined later in this chapter to showcase the discretionary or even indiscrete choices open to SLBs. We conclude that appreciating case examples of mobilising extensive social and economic resources by Chinese SLBs to ensure that policies are carried out dutifully and diligently, could be the key to understanding the phenomenal economic success and relative social stability in countries like China in recent decades.

Vulnerable Populations in China: Targets of Support and Suppression

Underclass people in today's society are normally considered as a modern-day social construction when the social divide in rural-urban, the haves and have nots, grew more rapidly and apparently in the demographic landscape as a result of social and economic development (Wacquant, 2009). Vulnerable social groups are mostly a marginalised aggregate of the working class from a previously underdeveloped or rural sector of the society. China's economic reform and modernisation efforts over the recent decades has not only helped to project China as an emerging powerhouse on the world stage, but has also created a new underclass population in urban areas that increasingly poses a domestic challenge for its various levels of government (Li, 2018). Rural migrants, urban laid-off workers and unemployed people are gradually forming a new class in contemporary China and this is considered to be a hurdle as the country moves towards its next stage of development. Such groups are characterised by socioeconomic disadvantage, destitution and dispossession, and seen by the general population as a potential source of danger to society. Moreover, their very existence leads to active social petitioning and restless protests (Li and Huang, 2008; Chu, 2011; Li, 2016; and Xi, 2018).

The term 'vulnerable group' was initially popularised in 1980s for the World Bank to make efforts on structural adjustment and drew attention to the harm done by relevant social and economic policies to women and other disadvantaged groups (Parpart, 1995). In China, it is conceived in sociological terms as 'the impoverished, lower-stratum of society' aggregated together as unfit for work for reasons of age, education or skills (Solinger, 2011: 4). Yet Chinese culture embodies social life exemplified by collective responsibilities and relational commitments to one's family or local community; this contributes to a complicated situation in which being a vulnerable person or from an underclass social group could attract attention for personal support as much as social suppression for the sake of collective face. Social responses in this regard are very different on three main dimensions in China for the vulnerable population in comparison to the experiences of their counterparts in more individualistic Western democratic societies.

First, a vulnerable group is a relative concept in Chinese society, rather than having fixed connotations and consequences. Culturally Chinese people have long been observed to prefer a cyclic view on one's fortune and fame in life instead of a linear one. This attitudinal tendency affords a different interpretation of vulnerability in terms of time and space variations, and thus implicates social groups in weaker positions as much as stronger ones when it comes to safeguarding their respective welfare. There are certain social groups who are apparently in weaker situations all along, and their weakness is indeed hard to overcome individually. Equally there are many other groups that are just relatively unfortunate, as they are thrown into deprivation or destitution only for a time period individually or collectively. What is worthy of noting is that in the minds of some Chinese people, it would still be a normal thing that such an unfortunate time period can stretch well over 30 or 60 years, a good part or even the entirety of one's life. Poverty alleviation as a contemporary national policy has been, for example, treated continuously as a top priority by central government and its top leaders, and cascaded to various local governments for effective implementation to show that the country does care and wants to share its newly found economic power and resources with vulnerable groups. Nonetheless, of these vulnerable people, the genuinely weaker ones did not cause big concerns to the public as often as the ones who regarded themselves only as being unfortunate, because those who are relatively vulnerable in society have always been the most vocal ones, and they are more demanding and harder to serve in public policies, compared with those who are just too weak to make their existence even noticeable. People of relative vulnerabilities in China often consider themselves as occupying a stronger and better position to stage personal claims, or to make arguments for their collective interests in the society, precisely because of their perceived situation as vulnerable at a certain point in time (Chu, 2011). For such a population, their vulnerability could be leveraged as a tool for promoting their own well-being at the next stage of life, as interpreted according to the cyclic mindset enrooted deeply in Chinese histories and culture, and that it is their due to be well treated when the time comes.

Second, a general reading in the Chinese society on life conditions and remedies for vulnerable people is also contradictory. Such people are considered socio-economically disadvantaged because of lacking access to legal and political resources for rectifying some undeserved social maladies that derail them from being self-sufficient in the first instance, or because of their failure to receive remedies in correcting life-related individual problems of their own making. Help and remedies to address personal vulnerabilities are normally, however, only available once one has been attracting attention of the society or voiced out collectively by the group themselves. This is indeed a social paradox in China, that the very people who need to get together and fight for their collective well-being are politically forbidden to get organised or to have their own voices heard collectively in the wider society. The fact that the social landscape in China over the last two decades, especially in the urban areas, has experienced widening inequity and increased social disorders, is evident enough for most Chinese SLBs. More and more people in China are consequently emboldened, or encouraged even, to seek extra-legal remedies to save them from personal vulnerability and catch up with the development of economy somehow through sharing the fruits of social prosperity under the communist ideology, which is still nominally the orthodoxy on state discourses (Xi, 2018).

Third, at a time when China is rapidly developing economically, the vulnerable population facing social exclusion encompasses any citizen unemployed or with ill health, labourers lacking skills, teenagers in prisons, residents suffering from a natural disaster and peasants in remote countryside, or indeed anybody who is confronting social rejection in general (Li and Huang, 2008). Yet for one reason or another, and in one practical way or another, these people regard themselves somehow as the ones who have missed out, who have been wronged under a government who should look after them for reasons mentioned above, and who can show their strength only by exposing their weakness and vulnerability openly, ostentatiously or even outrageously. Therefore, vulnerable people are arguably positioned better in demanding their entitlement to the fair share of China's development when the country is now more powerful and resourceful. The practical implications for vulnerable people with such an outlook on life means that these people try to seize any possible opportunity to embarrass the government, or to inconvenience other non-caring population in their own community, as the latter are considered as responsible for withholding something from them or leaving them in situations of vulnerability.

In the eyes of Chinese local officials, vulnerable people engaged in self-organising or self-promoting will inevitably pose a threat to social stability and economic prosperity. In exposing their own vulnerable situations to wider audiences, such a population could as well tarnish the individuals with vulnerable life conditions are thus a social force to be reckoned with in their own right by the Chinese government, and the police in particular. 'Vulnerable population' has accordingly assumed different connotations and implications in China, as one's vulnerability could indeed turn into his or her strength for biting back on those public officials concerned with maintaining stability, and polishing the image of that community that they inhabit. Namely, one's personal vulnerability in a group could signify the strength of the individual in jeopardising the group agenda, when viewed from a collectivism point of view. At the local level, it is common to see that the practice on 'rule of law', where everybody is subjected to the equal treatment as specified by the law in terms of their behavioural consequences, has been reshaped into a discourse on justifying the 'role of law' only, in which law is but an effective tool for the officials, and has its role to play in shaping the order of collective life. Any approach that makes a vulnerable person's life harder, even though it is permissible under the strict rule of law when such people have overstepped the line, will be morally and politically inexcusable to the general public in China. Nonetheless, local police and concerned government officials will not hesitate at all in deploying repressive administrative measures of various shapes and sizes fittingly to play out 'the role of law',[1] as long as those approaches are effective in getting the job done if/when the vulnerable people are on the offensive through playing out their vulnerability at the expense of the collective image as explained above.

Jacka (2014) thus draws attention to reconceptualising 'vulnerable group', and opens the way for discussing the passive connotation on the people implicated in such a social grouping. Conventional discourse on vulnerable groups often portraits such people as depending on others for their livelihood, being side-lined by economic modernisation, or even abandoned by their own family members due to old age, bad health or poor wealth. It is worthwhile to shift attention 'from their vulnerability to their agency' though, as recognition and conceptualisation of 'agency' on vulnerable people, such as older women left behind in rural villages due to the urbanisation in contemporary rural China, can indeed contribute to more politically effective strategies for the development and improvement on their own well-being. Constantly being reminded as from a vulnerable group only leads one consequently to a heightened sense of 'insecurity, stress, loneliness, depression and ill-health' (Jacka, 2014: 187). In the case of old women in rural Chinese villages in his study, this notion reproduces a stereotype of them being abandoned, passive and weak, unable to look after themselves. Although there is surely a grain of truth in such a presentation, Jacka (2014: 188) argues that it is also 'empirically inaccurate and misleading' and 'politically dangerous', as they are likely to encourage government policies which further exacerbating a loss of self-esteem and an increase of passivity in recipients. Instead, a 'capability approach' on the part of government officials would provide a broad framework for reconceptualising, evaluating and assessing such individual's social well-being, and the associated social arrangements and policy implementations that emphasising on growth and consumption, and tuning to relevant people's 'being and doing'. This capability approach will broaden the policy delivery to promoting one's personal agency for the vulnerable population, rather than restricting exclusively to responding to the vulnerable situations. As such, it opens the gate for local officials and police officers to seek alternative resources for policy implementation or law enforcement practices.

Street Level Bureaucrats and the Chinese Social Context

For the last half a century, a wide range of research works, mostly carried out in the context of western societies led by the United States, focussed on describing and disseminating how municipal public officials perform their jobs for the sake of improving accountability and efficiency. On the one hand this has helped to generate a reliable though uncommon body of practical knowledge, such as Evidence-Based Practices (EBP) for improving policing as a profession. On the other hand, it also helped to reveal a known secret that local government officials are executing their duties often in ways unexpected by their political masters and the general public. Instead of enforcing laws diligently and universally, police officials could in fact permit its violations at a variety of times, depending on the context of where the interactions between police-public takes place, for example, in the slum areas or with drunken university students (Kosar, 2011). Lipsky's widely cited work therefore draws the attention away from the reasoning and sciences behind the decision-makers at the top, to actual practices of resolving social problems at the frontline by street level bureaucrats (Lipsky, 2010).

Considering SLBs as 'public service workers who interact with citizens over the course of their jobs, and who have substantial discretion in the executions of their work' (Lipsky, 1980: 3), Lipsky turns the process of public policy implementation upside down in bypassing the roles of political elites to focussing on those at the bottom of government hierarchy instead, and emphasising the very interactions they have in engaging the public. This theory subsequently places individual bureaucrats and their relationship to clients, colleagues and supervisors, and the conditions of their work, or indeed anything that helps them to get the job done in any problem context at the centre of analysis. The key argument from Lipsky in such discourses is that discretionary actions of SLBs are the very basis for interpreting and implementing government policies and regulations; however, such policy decisions have been conceived are not as relevant to public at the receiving end as how they are implemented. They become even less a concern when compared to interactional experiences between SLBs and their clients.

Chinese SLBs feel the same pressure from two sides in implementing state policies for the citizens, just like their counterparts in the Western countries. Yet, unlike those SLBs commonly experiencing the restrictions on supply of resources from relevant parts of the state government, and the unlimited demand from public clients, Chinese SLBs are instead confronted on a daily basis with the thorny issue of appeasing the public on behalf of the state for peace maintenance on the one side, and on the other side pushing forward any controversial political directions of the government at whatever cost. Johnston (2012) observed in this regard that for countries like China which fall into the category of the so called

High-Capacity Authoritarian states (the HCA), the unique features of operational contexts always merit some explorations or certain comments, at least in the discussion on how SLBs functioning in that political and social environment.

To understand any HCA, we can examine policy practices of state agents along three operational dimensions: the extent of state capacity, the size of repressive apparatus and the issue of legitimacy. In the case of China, the first dimension refers to the extensive mobilisation capacity and continual internal monitoring of both state institutions and everyday social life. This effectively facilitates the HCA to undertake many resource-intensive tasks that are often treated as unthinkable or unachievable in a western democracy. With respect to the dimension of legitimacy of China as a state, the HCA now offers increasingly more areas of freedom to their citizens and the Chinese government enjoys a level of legitimacy greater than ever before, because of, or in spite of, the first feature being outlined already. As to the size of repressive apparatus and its functioning, China displayed in recent decades to its citizens and the rest of the world a modicum of political pluralism in the form of permitted dissent. That as long as such discontent or protest is expressed within a boundary, in practice people can get away virtually trouble free. The centralised repressive state apparatuses are mostly tasked with decision making and busying itself only with monitoring the performance of relevant organs and personnel at provincial/city level, they are always relying heavily on extensive functionaries at local and grassroot levels in enacting their policies one way or another.

It is also well observed that as a common practice, when striving to implement government policies on the ground, SLBs are more susceptible to the influences on various fronts, rather than simply and rigidly following directives and guidance from within their own bureaucratic machine. Hill (2003: 269) defines implementation resources for SLBs as any 'individuals or organisations that can help implementing units to learn about policy, best practices for doing policy or professional reforms meant to change the character of services delivered to clients'. Mobilisation of, and access to, such non-state resources for help carries, in the Chinese context, more prestige and legitimacy for SLBs in terms of implementing state policies, especially with certain controversial ones implicating economic gains and losses. Such exploratory initiatives will at times be associated with seemingly corruptive conducts or showing favouritism in its forms and consequences, as indeed with the exercising of any personal discretions without the checking of institutional bureaucracy or the scrutiny of the law. In a situation in which there is no commonly acknowledged or accepted set of laws, or, even if there are, not any that are universally enforceable. What one needs is only a powerful patron to promote/protect one's own interests, together with or fight against any others implicated in it. In most such problem contexts, the question of what to do and who is to do it, in policy implementation terms, was decided by personal connections rather than impersonal criteria. The cultural proclivity for relationship networking and social ties thus makes impersonal procedures, as often associated with the concept of bureaucrats at either central or street levels in the West, unworkable in specific problem situations in China.

Policing the Vulnerable in China: A Mission Impossible?

On the face of it, the job of policing seems to be about enforcing laws through scientifically grounded, politically negotiated procedures faithfully and routinely, confronting trivial disputes as well as prominent social challenges in life without fear and favour. Nonetheless, police work always involves problem solving and grappling with contradictory choices that incessantly calls for personal discretion and touches on issues of both fear and favour in reality. Lipsky (2010) identified a number of dilemmas at the individual level for SLBs that make their job most of the time an impossible one instead:

- the social construction of clients who are unpredictable in needs and unreliable in character
- the challenge of giving individualised consideration within a bureaucracy
- the problem of allocating benefits and sanctions with limited resources and supplies,
- the struggle to translate the implement policy amid constraints and ambiguity

As previously discussed, the key to fulfilling a SLB job effectively stays in exercising personal discretion within a rigid bureaucratic system that has long been characterised as impersonal and rational. All personal discretions are by definition carried on the basis of personal connections and stylistic, rather than impersonal calculations and standardised. It springs from the particular social relationship embedded in a web of interactions between institutions and individuals concerned. Inattention to the kinds of police discretion on the frontline has arguably accounted for much of the deficiencies in police officers' job performance when reviewing its fairness and effectiveness, as indeed with most of the other SLBs job in our society (Chery, 2012; Wamg, 2012; Buvik, 2014). Assessment of what police officers achieve in delivering relevant government policies at the local level, in addition to their law enforcement roles, must therefore take account of 'the actions of personnel at the lowest rungs of the organisational ladder – the rank-and-file police and civilians in whom most of the organisation's recourses are vested' (Mastrofski, 2004: 100).

Based on extensive study on social policies and decisions-making practices in a Chinese town government and working closely with the local officials, Wang (2015) shows that China's township government, and their SLBs, have been striving to contain, rather than resolve, social discontent arising from a population that has been increasingly drifting apart in the face of economic conditions and political ambitions. At technical and institutional level, Chinese SLBs, and police in particular, are habitually encouraged to take a short-term perspective on sweeping problems away and avoiding confrontational experiences rather than actually solving problems through strict and effective law enforcement practices. On the practical ground, SLBs are likely to deal with people who are either in need of their help, or desperately avoid them because of the latter's vulnerability and/or violence. There is a general recognition in contemporary China that collective petitioning of any particular group, for instance, is likely to lead to violent protests at the large scale by augmenting certain public feelings and motivating other copycats to challenge the established order, thus it will pose threat ultimately to wider social stability and national economic development. Because of their de facto disadvantaged positions, the vulnerable population are usually desperate enough to test the limits of tolerance of the state and are prepared to withstand any recognisable repression from the local government. Therefore, any effort from the vulnerable group that is co-ordinated and organised at a cross regional scale, will be considered by the related government apparatuses as bad elements, and thus have to be resolutely repressed.

Out of those contradicting considerations, there is a widespread practice in China of using coercion selectively and informally at local government levels, relying on institutional and social mechanisms rather than the judiciary system to address non-political grievances, especially on vulnerable groups who are often protesting for the betterment of their livelihood than proclaiming their entitlement from the state. However, in a society where harmony is highly extolled, individual protest or group violence always manifests itself in multifaceted forms, it can be simultaneously visible and invisible, legitimate and illegitimate, permeate the public and private spheres of everyday life. With such seemingly paradoxical descriptions, violence can naturally be 'productive, destructive and reproductive' (Lam-Knott, 2014: 280), for both the state and individuals implicated, when it involves the acquisition, projection and denial of power amongst different bodies. At the core of it, being violent is not only about the assertation of power by the perpetrator, but also involves the simultaneous disempowerment of the victim who is forced to assume a position of subjugation without being able to exert choice in the matter concerned. This conceptual interpretation could help to turn the power relationship upside down between the vulnerable population and bureaucrats in China, as when those being vulnerable are ready and easy to be violent, the powerful state apparatus at times will be powerless as a result. How one differentiates and displays violent actions within Chinese communities often shaped by ones' life exposure, personal outlook and expectations in the world, but most importantly, it hinges on the extent of one's association with the government apparatus and relevant resources.

Hill (2003) remarked that when the Chinese SLBs implementing state policies in containing the spread of protests of vulnerable people and policing any violent activities implicated, they are often left without guidance on 'what they need to know to do policy'. Instead they are turning to nonstate resources for insights and help on how to get policy done. A network of people such as professional associations, academics, trainers and consultants who act as 'implementation resources' are singled out by the SLBs for reference, mostly focussing on their insights on the efficacy of policy implementation. It can be argued that in a cultural context where interpersonal trust or bond is heavily relying on the so called inter-personal linkage, this 'implementation resources' could be and should be enlarged to include considerations on the emotional side of policy implementation. In Hill's version of 'implementation resources', it has been noted that there are around 300 variables that explains why policy does, or does not, occur as the authors intended (Hill, 2003: 267). He categorised them into four themes. The first class is about policy itself and the policy implementation process; the second is focussing on organisation itself and their milieu; the third is about agents of policy and the leadership quality aspect and the fourth is about the behaviours of groups affected by policy, or overall economic conditions and public opinion. After a careful review on the strength and draw backs of facts from each of those four themed categories, Hill (2003: 269) proposes for the 'development of implementer's understanding, practices and skills', a larger pool of non-state 'implementation resources' shall be made available, rather than only focussing on the 'organisations and milieus in which they work'.

This research call would in theory help to improve the effectiveness of policy implementation, yet it did not sufficiently explain the fourth theme in terms of how the behaviours of the groups could also be shaped by certain elements or practices considered as 'implementation resources', according to Hill's own definition. Policing vulnerable population in Chinese society is a good illustration in this regard. The vulnerable population as public service recipients are not simply the subjects to be acted on by SLBs as typically portrayed in most government policy papers. In China, they can also act on the SLBs as input for considerations on designing the space and pace of policy implementation. Therefore, a detailed investigation on the connections, relationships and interactions implicated in policies on policing the vulnerable groups will be able to conceptually enrich Lipsky's notion of SLB, and contextually ground it for examining its practical relevancy. In particular, the relational pressure posed by the social connections amongst those who are the subjects for the police to act on, could be and have been indeed exploited already as sources facilitating policy implementation in China. This is what we will explore with more details in the next section.

Relational Repression: The Practice of Protecting and Repressing

Repression on publicly expressed dissent by non-democratic states can be reviewed along the dimensions of 'state capacity, size of repressive apparatus and the issue of legitimacy' (Johnston, 2012: 59). Institutionally and politically, the Chinese social governance system harbours permitted dissent as long as such dissent are expressed within the bounds. The competence of state apparatus actually not stays with its important head figures at the power centre, but derives from the pre-existing mobilisation structure that serves as the basis for this ruling party organisation in China, and by extension or augmentation, the entire high capacity of the collective Chinese nation. One of the mechanisms in social governance, enacted by the authoritarian central Chinese government, is to constantly promote fear and distribute favours to the targeted population at the grassroots level.

The Implementation of Repressive Policies

Though China is indisputably one of the perfect examples on authoritarianism, it 'remains far from being a simple police state' (Wang and Minzner, 2015: 339), as local public officials have always been asked to demonstrate a high level of sensitivity to social needs and offer concessions to groups of aggrieved citizens. Because of the social and political recognition that certain personal vulnerability and needs should be attended to by the society as a whole, especially under a nominally communist government, the vulnerable social populations are subsequently endowed with certain rights of social resistances in their petitioning to the central government or protesting against local officials.

Free social spaces invariably exist to varied extent for such discontented people in any community, simply because of the laziness or ineptitude of the security force itself. Chinese police have often shown leniency to certain activists advocating for the vulnerable population and restrained from deploying repressive approaches, they reacted as such mostly out of the consideration that the very existence of an opposition population, such as the vulnerable people, the petitioners and indeed anybody who is complaining about their life conditions or poor treatment by the state, has helped them to define their own role as the police in society. Such people give the police something to do within a community which values internal harmony as high as its external collective image. This recognition helps to make the police respected on both sides in relational terms, as long as the protesters operated within certain constraints outlined either explicitly or implicitly, they will be able to avoid direct suppression from the police out of the pressure to protect the state.

That being said, one should not overlook the fact that the majority of police and security forces at lower levels in a society are often made up of common workers who are happy and content to have a regular job in one's own community, and it is only their institutional role that leads them to certain brutish behaviours called for by situations. When job shifts are over, SLBs and police officials go home to their family, friends and neighbours, and this is so in China as much as in most of the other societies. This normalisation of personal identities has complicated certain moments of political mobilisation or police operation at the microlevel in China though, when it comes to maintenance of order.[2] Police officers are often torn between interests arising in the orders from superiors on the one hand, and on the other hand the social pressure from relations with their family and friends in not following orders to the letters of the law to repress those neighbours and acquaintances. Where possible and plausible, they are happy to stay away from policing those public protests in their own neighbourhood; or addressing bitter complaints of those disadvantaged people whom they know by names, instead they are eager to delegate such responses to any others who could just get the job done. This is different from encouraging someone taking the issue/laws into their own hands or shirking from one's lawful duties though. It is a long tradition in China that a good SLB will perform a duty without asserting his or her own authority but asking the two sides to resolve the issue and keep it to themselves for the sake of not disrupting the whole relationship network in the bigger community, even when the two parties involved are a grieving individual citizen on one side, and the mighty government itself on the other.

Enrooted in the historical Confucian ideology of stressing collective responsibilities, Chinese authorities at various levels, led by the local police at the forefront, are accustomed to mobilising the general public as the first-line defence to reduce criminal opportunities and to nip any element of instability in the bud. Families, schools, communities and work units are mobilised as informal supervisory and educational institutions to assist the government agencies in social control.[3] A whole range of social actors are identified and they work proactively in engineering communal 'pressure and coercion', to seek compliance of any individual with the laws and social norms; and dissuading anyone with a perceived intention to disrupt such order in a given community, will naturally implicate and impact on the vulnerable population first and foremost unfortunately.

Hu (2011) notes that in their governing practice, many Chinese SLBs wish to be given as low a degree of judiciary power as practically possible. They tend to avoid making decisions or solving problems through observing the rule of law expressed in their actions. Instead, a high degree of political and practical elements is introduced or entrenched in their daily activities. For example, the practice of mediation has been well embedded in China's own traditional civil dispute resolutions, and long cherished by both government officials and the general public as the preferred method of resolving disputes and grievances that did not directly challenge the legitimacy of governance itself. Any mediation work naturally involves articulating and acknowledging different individual identities amongst those implicated in conflicts.

The issue of identity management merits further elaboration here, given that we are devoting this chapter to the discussion on policing and protecting vulnerable populations in wider social contexts. Identity information is not only about something that defines who we are at a particular time, but also shapes activities. Presentation of someone's identity in a particular social context will always involve the doing part, in addition to the aspect of being for the person under discussion. It is the doing part of the identity that is often easily ignored in 'identification and authentication of individuals vis-à-vis other people, organisations and increasingly their own things' (Van Zoonen and Turner, 2015: 937). This implies in practical terms that there would be different consequences for people in positions of vulnerability to perform the same course of activities, compared with someone of different identity and status, even though the actions are of the same nature in the eyes of law. Therefore, we need to account for the resilience and the relentlessness of building self not just from distinctive constituent parts that can be objectively exhibited, but through a life story about the person concerned, one's biography or a narrative identity in real-life problem situations. This helps us to make the distinctions between the administration of identity information, as shown in the act of trusting and obligatorily submitting to the state by documenting an ID paper; and the opportunity of broadcasting one's own story to express the personal self, as in sharing family reunion photos implicating certain relatives of fortunate and fame.

A person's identity is therefore not presented as of an information data set, painting out the individuals concerned only as someone who will not change over time in terms of who they are. Any system of identity management should allow human beings to exercise their identity or identities over the course of a lifetime in interacting with other people in a specific milieu, and as such to embrace the life paradox of maintaining privacy and allowing disclosure, voluntary and obligatory disclosing, questing for social linkages and being left alone. In a context featuring strong social connections and collective identity like China, mobilising or managing such identity information will have great implications for SLBs in terms of their chosen approach for policy implementation.

The following two case scenarios of Wukan and Huashui from China, are but illustrative snapshots on how personal identity and social connections are constructed in the format of relational pressure for delivering or destroying relevant government policies.

Relational Pressure to Protect the Vulnerable: The Case of Wukan

In 2011, a series of protests took place in Wukan, a fishing village in east Guangdong Province, and caught the attention of the entire country. Starting as a large-scale march held on September 21, 2011, protesting landgrabs and corruptions (referred to thereafter as the 921 event), problems continued for months after local government rejected villagers' requests to be heard. A grassroots organisation called the Wukan Villagers' Temporary Representative Council, representing the 47 clans of the village, was elected to negotiate with the upper-level government, the Lufeng City government.

Soon, however, local authorities branded the Wukan event as an "illegal event of mass violence" after several instances of violent conflicts as villagers opposed the police. In December 2011, five elected village representatives were detained, and one of them, Xue Jinbo, died in police custody under suspicious circumstances. Following Xue's death, villagers expelled the entire village committee, Communist Party leadership, and the police from the village and reclaimed some of the factories that had been illegally built on village farmland, and instance of the "the exclusion of the excluders by the excluded". On December 14, 2011, more than a thousand police officers from Shanwei City laid siege to the village, preventing food and other goods from entering. When they attempted to force their way Into the village, they confronted resistance from more than 13,000 villagers and had to retreat until next morning. Villagers blocked all entrances to the village and set up checkpoints guarded by 20–30 young men, some holding cudgels. Journalists from Hong Kong and overseas were the only ones allowed to enter. Later, the party secretary and the governor of Guangdong Province got negotiated a truce, allowing the villagers to elect the village's governing body in an open and democratic way.

(He and Xue, 2014: S127–128)

Through their detailed analysis on a saga of a mass protesting event in Wukan et al. (2014) claimed that the restoration of a collective identity in this small village in Southern China helped the local people reclaim the power of self-governance and defend their vulnerability. It is a common expectation that rural villagers in contemporary Chinese society are most likely to expose themselves to hasher economic realities, and thus become vulnerable partly due to their own failing in catching up with the rapid urban expansion and industrialisation building over the last two decades. At the same time, Chinese people are also expected to be submissive towards the local authority and its grand policy of economic development to the entire community, even though their immediate personal interests could well be undermined initially, and any long-term benefits from such development policy are by no means certain and secure either. When people of Wukan were dragged into this kind of situation one time too many, residents there were effectively and efficiently mobilised, by identity formation and relational bonding. Virtually everybody who had the family roots in or traced back to the village, was awakened to participate and reconstitute an overarching collective identity for their own protection. Subsequently, every stakeholder implicated in this event articulated and asserted extended network and kinship connections originated from Wukan; thus, collectively, Wukan residents were able to turn around their vulnerable roles as villagers in fighting against the mighty of local government authority. Forging and fortifying a strong relationship pressure on people who support or supress such an event in this particular context, personally as well as politically, is the key to Wukan's success in achieving what it dues, and signifies something of further value to understand group behaviour of certain Chinese people based on relevant stakeholder's own relational identity.

The notion of personal or social identity can be read here as a fundamental bridging concept for linking individuals and the society at large (Ybema et al., 2009). Being a villager, or having been born or having roots in Wukan, assigns a different meaning once relational references are enacted. Social agents in general draw on a range of discursive sources in pursuit of formation and presentation of respective identities, which are always enrooted in a variety of 'self-other' talk for both themselves and that of the others. This reflects a duality that all such self-other talks are the discursive reflections on the relationship between the individual and sociality, thereby establishing a permanent dialect between the self and the social structure, though not necessarily to the immediate social environment. Ybema et al. (2009: 300) explains that 'Social definitions (and redefinitions) are framed through prescriptive organisational and professional discourse relating to appropriate and desirable role behaviour, as well as the creation of shared beliefs through symbolic violence, or the construction of subjectivity through disciplinary power-knowledge process'.

The clan system in Wukan is based on a relatively small scale and enclosed social network though, characteristics that are instrumental in mobilising members for collective action to strengthen cohesion and solidarity in response to facing conflict with outside groups. Likewise, it can be extended to larger communities characterised by a different relational nature. The assertion of self as villagers and that of local officials finds expression through the process of what Ybema and colleagues refer to as 'role embracing and re-definition, emotional distancing, position taking, meaning making, adopting dress codes and rule breaking' (Ybema et al., 2009: 301). Assuming an identity in a relational network is a transient accomplishment though, in which discursive construction and re-construction emerge as a continuous process. The stability of such relational assumptions appears to reside either in the momentary achievement to reflect on, as evidenced in the case of Wukan villagers' success in fending off the temporary threat to their livelihood. Moreover, it also inspires fictions to be live up to by people implicated in such a network, who may be rooted elsewhere in China. People subscribing themselves to the 'Chinese Dream' drawn by their current leader, President Xi Jingping are examples of this. Subsequently, identity formation is 'a complex multifaceted process which produces a socially negotiated temporary outcome of the dynamic interplay between internal strivings and external prescriptions, between self-presentation and labelling by others, between achievement and ascription and between regulation and resistance' (ibid., 301).

A value regime stemming from the traditional clan system in Wukan, which featured closed social networks, solidarity, mutual trust, self-organising and informal yet stable community norms based on shared identity and property, was threatened, and would have been replaced with the dominant value regime from outside, noticeably the official discourses by the local government. This understandably rendered every villager more vulnerable individually, rather than being valuable to one another anymore. Subsequently, Wukan's communal resistance involves creating and applying alternative discourses for resisting official narratives from local SLBs, and explores alternative discourses in resistance strategies, consolidating social connections and relationship network linkages. Although kinship is often blamed for hindering the emergence of modern society and the spread of industrial capitalism within an established of system of legal and political interests, Hu and Xue (2014) found that it can also be of enormous social, cultural and political importance in societies undergoing economic transition in the modern age. As China is increasingly engaged in the global markets and modern state governance, the backwardness associated with the clan relationship network, could well be transformed into a new source for alternative discourses and life practices in the modern era, to protect those people from the state machine and unsympathetic SLBs.

Relational Pressure to Undermine: The Case of Huashui

In Spring 2005, villagers in Dongyang country, Zhejiang were unhappy. For four years, farmers from eight villagers in Huashui town had been complaining about crop damage and declining public health caused by pollution originating from a nearby chemical park. They had petitioned higher levels again and again, even going to Beijing twice, but to no avail. In late March, disgruntled residents of the most seriously affected village turned to more confrontational tactics. They put up a tent at the entrance to the chemical park and began a round-the-clock vigil, with the hope of blocking supply trucks and force the polluting factories to shut down. Huashui town officials and police dismantled the tent the next evening, but the protesters immediately erected a second one. After villagers raised tents and officials pulled them down three more times, county leaders changed their tactics and formed a work team to conduct thought work.

Over the next 10 days, the team held 135 meetings attended by over 5,000 people to learn about the villagers' grievances and to explain government plans to address them. They also conducted more than 4,000 door-to-door visits, during which they distributed leaflets detailing the new measures to deal with the pollution. The work team initially consisted of about 60 county officials, including some who hailed from Huashui town, some who had relatives in the villages affected by the pollution, and still others who have previously worked in Huashui. The team also recruited village cadres, local school teachers and factory workers, as well as retired town leaders and pensioners with ties to the activists.

Despite the team's efforts and the detention of several protest leaders, the size of the encampment grew, as residents from ten other villages joined the protest, with each village erecting its own tent. County leaders, angered that protesters were "pushing their luck" while the government was "doing everything called for by humanity and duty", decided to turn to a more forceful approach and sent in over 1,500 local cadres and public security personnel to end the encampment. During their efforts to clear out the protesters, violence broke out and over 100 officials or police officers and more than 200 villagers were injured; 68 government vehicles were also burned or damaged. Even after the violent suppression, the protesters still refused to withdraw and the number of tents grew to about 30, representing 22 villages.

The local government at this point opted against another crackdown, partly because the use of force had attracted considerable media attention and higher levels of government, including Beijing, had sent a team of investigators to investigate the protest and the county's response. County leaders quickly switched back to thought work and the floating of possible concessions as their main control techniques. For more than a month, relational repression was carried out daily, and up to 200 people served on a work team that explained the government's new policies toward the polluting factories and urged the tent-sitters to stand down. Promises to address the pollution were made and efforts to buy off the tent-sitters took place, but without a result. Finally, seven weeks after the protests began and several days after the country promised to close the chemical part, the protesters acquiesced to removal of the tents.

O'Brian and Deng, 2017: 183–184

In their account on a mass protest incident above, O'Brian and Deng (2017) revealed that even within a high-capacity state like China, there are times where a version of relational repression is called for and carried out by the states' omnipresent coercive apparatus as well. In a similar style to what happened in Wukan, family relatives, friends or even the next-door neighbours from non-state resources are mobilised to mount pressure on those targets, but they then retreat from protests rather than strengthening them. Precisely because those targets are from de facto vulnerable social groups, outright repressive power from the state in the form of violence and coercions would be not as effective, since those population are the ones who have very little to lose in such situations, be it their personal health or wealth, as captured by the notion 'those with bare feet are not in awe of the one in leather shoes'.

O'Brian and Deng (2013) also uncovered the practices of using relational repression for such purpose are well grounded in evidences from various parts of China. More specifically, relational repression has been mapped out in four consecutive steps in which state and social powers can be combined to serve any repression as necessary, when situations call for it upon SLBs at local levels (Obria and Deng, 2013: 537).

First, information is collected by SLBs about social ties between targets of repression and any individuals who may be able to influence them through personal contacts. Second, people with such ties to the targets are recruited onto a work team championed by SLBs to serve as thought workers, often with their prior consent, yet this is not treated as a pre-condition of the recruitment. Third, members of thought workers with relational ties to the target are organised and deployed to demobilise the latter as a team; and fourth, team members are encouraged to take their respective work allocation seriously and diligently. They will often be reminded individually of the costs of failure to demobilise the target in policy as well as personal terms, and those who show insufficient zeal in the work are at the risk of being disciplined in various shapes and sizes.

Local officials will accordingly learn first who are the key targets posing threat to the harmony of local life, and then from the recruited thought workers they can identity, who might be in a relational position to influence the targeted individual. This is where the merit of the Information User Model constructed by the Chinese police feeds into SLBs' performance, which typically resides in the knowledge of the targets' identities, family situation, social relations and personal contact information. Properly administered, relational repression can help to put an end to popular collective action by the vulnerable groups, as an effective control technique for limiting the scope and length of potential public protests. As observed by O'Brian and Deng (2013: 542), that 'a combination of pressure, skilful emotional work and mediation can soften up protesters and defuse a volatile situation, while channelling demands to the authorities and allowing them to float possible compromises'.

Carrying out thought work on the targets through their social ties stays at the heart of an effective relational repression. Police and local officials are seeking to engineer conducive emotions on the target by mixing practical incentives and psychological pressures together, and tapping into the stressful effects of Confucian values, social bonds and obligations amongst people tied together in a family, in a clan or within a community. Family, friendship and town fellowship based on native place ties can on the one hand draw people together to take actions protecting their vulnerability, like that in Wukan event; or they can equally be deployed to push people away from posing challenges or protests, like in Huashui as illustrated here. In a practical sense, thought work team members leverage their personal ties to influence relatives, friends and fellow folks to stand down from confrontational claims, playing openly on their double-edged image of victimisation in society, or showing as vulnerable in a community defined more by personal relationship than impersonal regulations. Yet it needs to be pointed out that relational repression has never been an open state policy at any stage initiated from the power centre in China, but instead always put in place as a local practice and become more prominent in an era when maintaining social stability is of paramount significance to the Chinese authorities.

Protecting the Vulnerable as Well as Repressing Them

Chu (2011) argues that serving vulnerable groups by SLBs in today's China is nominally enrooted in two of the same measures that are taken for granted in most of western developed societies; one is putting in place a social security system of minimum living standards, and the other is introducing citizen's rights protection and empowering mechanisms. However, the practical consequences of these two are not at all equally favourable to Chinese SLBs, as the dynamics of changing from active innovation by government officials to more forthright citizen's rights is understandably troublesome. A vulnerable population's susceptibility to relational support/pressure in a wider community, makes it hard for their vulnerability to be constrained only to issues of personal interests, as often assumed in many of the democratic countries. Rather, they often become political through the ramifications of such claims from a bigger collectivity, and this implicates many more people beyond the job remits of SLBs.

Within a high-capacity authoritarian government such as China, managing central and local state institutions is different to western states, as local officials have incentives to delegate coercion to third parties, not only due to expediency but also as they are dispensable if things go wrong. Central and upper level authorities in China achieve objectives by relying heavily on top-down policy control and strategies, yet frequently they are issuing conflicting or unfunded mandates to various local authorities. Additionally, the further higher up the hierarchical power ladder in China, the tighter it becomes for one to be constrained by explicit legal and political considerations compare to those at lower and local levels. A multi-layered, decentralised and bureaucratical state administrative structure also constraint local officials mostly in warning them to not deviate from centrally initiated policies than checking on the legality or legitimacy in policy implementation. SLBs are often hesitant in applying formal and straightforward state forces for social control to avoid issues of legitimacy and efficiency, preferring instead to secure help from intermediaries between the government and the public, especially in interactions with vulnerable populations. This becomes even more apparent when officials pursue local or private interests that are likely to diverge from the interests of the central government. Informal coercion is preferable, as it helps to overcome procedural barriers, and avoids scrutiny from central/upper levels too. From a central perspective, it is in the leaders' interest to have in place the relative invisibility of formal state agents in cases of social coercion, as it helps them to cope better with possible international pressure resulted from any high-profile case involving human rights abusing, and overcome any domestic outrage if certain unpopular things have to be done (Wong and Peng, 2015; Chen, 2017).

Considering the factors above will help to explain why local Chinese police implicated in certain social protests of vulnerable populations are often remarkably restrained rather than being violent and forceful in their law enforcement practices, as illustrated in case scenarios introduced in this chapter. On many occasions, the local governments are explicitly forbidden to use police power to enforce local political decisions and restore social order. Local officials in China, particularly SLBs who are interacting directly with the vulnerable people of desperation and needs, are often delegate coercion to third parties, most of the time in the format of employing 'casual workers' (linshigong in Chinese), sometimes contracting out to private security companies or even thugs, occasionally tasking it to those with relational ties, to achieve control or compromise on thorny issues that rendering certain groups of people vulnerable on the first instance, such as 'land expropriation, house demolition, industrial restructuring, urban management, petitioning control or crime fighting' (Chen, 2017: 69).

The rationale for deploying relational repression is not only shaped as such by the power divisions and sanctions within institutions at central and local levels, but also by personal benefits implicated under a populistic power-interest network (Gui, 2017), which is a pre-existing tool for effective social control in China to govern against citizen's uncooperative behaviour. Within this power-interest network, local government authorities, and through them the SLBs, have been the largest resource grabbers and allocators, where personal ties with the SLBs have mainly determined resource decisions. Being accessible to such a network in relational terms will on the one hand get people the benefits to such resource allocations, and on the other hand it will constraint them equally on their cooperative or protesting actions. Gui (2017) provides an empirical account on the effect of such a half-open state control mechanism in operation. He found out that citizens who have intensive interactions with the local authorities in resource allocation terms are under more effective protection and control, and generally responsive to SLBs' requests for relational support or suppression. In contrast, those who are marginalised to such a network in society will likely be the more vulnerable ones, but they will also be behaving more provocatively. It is therefore the mentality of people implicated in such relational interactions that warrants practical exploitation and theoretical elaboration. On the one hand, 'you cannot expect a cadre (namely, SLBs at local Chinese government level) who has abandoned the hope of promotion to work wholeheartedly to pleaser the government'. Thus, those people who are mobilised to repress the protestors into the line out of their relational ties do have some personal motivations to address. With respect to the recipients,

> talking of family ties, it is necessary to consider both the emotional and interest-centric dimensions. This is particularly applicable to people living a hard life. They will not value family ties highly if they see little prospect of reaping benefits from these ties (to the cadres).
> (Gui, 2017: 77)

For the police and local government officials in China, their need to consequently use all of the tools available, and place at the centre the relationship between environment and behaviour of the subjects concerned (e.g., the vulnerable population on protest), as 'extinguishing undesirable behaviours requires understanding the attributions people are making to elements' (Marksman, 2017: 28). It requires an understanding of the User Model itself to expect practical relevance of their efforts, because 'the same treatment applied to an individual at different times will have a radically different influences on their behaviour, and the same treatment will work differently on different individuals' (ibid., 29). Similarly,

> Variability in experience from one moment or affective/relational context to the next derives not so much from being radically divided, cleaved into different states of being at different moments because of an inability to tolerate contact between one state and another.... Rather the variability can be a result of responding wholeheartedly to circumstances that change, and in changing, evoke a changed experience.... The circumstances we encounter are often not simply independent variables that affect how we feel, think, or act; they are also often a product of how we think, feel and act.
>
> (Wachtel, 2017: 548)

A social identity model may also help to understand how relations between agents in a particular geographical environment affect individual and group cognitions. Sechi and Skilters (2018) suggest that one's social identity is generated in an interaction between three different levels of social categorisation. The first one is categorisation of self, which is a core component of the social identify of one's self. The second one refers to the categorisation of direct social groups, such as family members, close relatives, important colleagues and friends; and the third one is categorisation of large-scale social communities in which one asserts or displays political, professional or business-related interests. Of these three categorisations, the first is most significant in social identity generation and is also the most inclusive one, as significant others (both individual persons and groups) are frequently included in the self-presentation. The core idea underlying this conceptual model on understanding individuals in a relationship framework is that 'human selves are flexible and situation dependent, and one and the same individual possesses several selves connected in an interlocking system that activates certain self-aspects in one situation and different self-aspects in different situations' (Sechi and Skilters, 2018: 81).

Kulich et al. (2017) likewise suggest that although assuming multiple identities is a given social fact and may provide a pathway to gain social support and positively influence one's well-being at times, such identities can differ in status and value, and at times create distressing experience which calls for a coping strategy in order to increase people's identity fit. Those Chinese social relationship partners who are called on to do the task of thought work on the targeted person certainly feels this acutely than most of the western scholars who are only researching theoretically on assuming multiple familial, communal or social identities. Besharov (2014) also reports that current literature has affirmed that identification occurs when members perceive their own identity to overlap with their organisation or even nation's identity, and people will be led to define themselves in terms of the organisation and place a high value on organisational membership as a result. This is particularly so in societies that feature collectivism, culturally and follow one-party doctrines, politically. Such an identification emerges, for example, from the combination of bottom-up interactive process among members themselves, and top-down interpretations and enactments by managers charged with engineering such identities.

Conclusion

This chapter has illuminated the unique practice of applying relational repression on and by the vulnerable people in China, and explained thus far on how the particularism and discretion of the Chinese police as SLBs goes hand in hand in an authoritarian Chinese society in both theoretical and empirical terms. It could be argued that conceptualising people in vulnerable positions as a problem as well as endowed with its own strength, and thus need to be dealt with creatively in its own context by the police and other SLBs China. This might be a step stretched a bit too far in exercising discretions for Lipsky's SLBs. Nonetheless, the primary means in which the Chinese authorities deal with the urban underclass is a reshaped social administrative system that imposes constraints on the poor and confine them under the control of managerial justice in the form of discretionary measures of the police, rather than through the formal criminal justice system typified in most of the western contexts (Li, 2016).

Bringing multiple experiences and relational schemes to the surface is not just to get SLBs the necessary exposure to different perspectives in different contexts involving different people, but it also helps them in integrating different perspectives, to see the difference as a spur for developing a more encompassing policy formulation to reconcile differences in reality with such people, to exercise their job discretions accordingly. Guided with a relational model in social practices enrooted in China, we have demonstrated that integration of multiplicity of perspectives and personal interests is not an exercise of diversity management in its own name, but a worthy undertaking in acknowledging and accepting the pervasive presence of others who could have become more vulnerable or violent at the same time, in either real or imaginary sense. Wachtel (2017: 547) suggests in this regard that for 'relational thinking at its best', thinking in a broader range of ways to find practical solutions is better, and one should accordingly open more options rather than close them for the sake of ideology, intelligibility and purity. According to

Wachtel, much of our experiences of the self, others and our very own lives are indeed varying from one setting or relational context to another, as 'it is impossible to envision a singular correct understanding of any piece of human experience, even as an ideal, because human experience is fundamentally ambiguous'.

As long as China remains an omnipotent state in accumulating and drawing on wide range of social resources in the form of a HCA, and personal ties remain to have a great role in shaping the decision about resource allocations and social interactions, the practice of 'relational repression' will be becoming more prominent and widespread in contemporary Chinese society. The weaker institutional setting in legal and political terms has prompted into action of this 'power-interest networks', and it would be self-crippling indeed for the Chinese SLBs to ignore its functioning, either for the general public or for the police who are tasked to keep the public staying in their respective social places for maintaining the order and stability. Social ties can and will be mobilised in facilitating claims of interests from the perspective of the vulnerable groups more and more, for drawing them together as in the case of Wukan. However, we have seen already that social ties can be geared into action by SLBs as well, to drive groups of vulnerable people apart as evidenced in the case of Huashui. As far as the local police officers were concerned, recognising and deploying interest exchanges implicated in social ties is an effective social control tool for policing vulnerable population and regarded as a social norm, rather than bordering corruption or irregularities on the face of it, since it is impossible to separate benefits from emotions in any social ties discourse. Capitalising on personal ties to pursue one's interest exists in its own shape and form in any society, but it is only when it becomes more culturally grounded, socially justified and practically expected in China, to a near perfect standard, that it attracts its due attention as an effective social control tool for SLBs in serving the vulnerable population, even though legally and morally it is still a debated issue from many perspectives. Empirically based research literature shows that up to now, deploying social ties and exchanging relational interests to stop protests of socially disadvantaged or deprived people. Although this may alienate people from the regime's legitimacy more and more, on the contrary is can drive more and more vulnerable people together. The result is that such people will collude with relational partners in positions of wealth and influence in order to better position themselves in terms of seeking benefits via threatening/ inconvenient social order however staying short of jeopardising it. Once this practice was incorporated as the cornerstone or the cutting edge that helps to establish a so-called 'Chinese model of social governance', it deserved to be noticed; further investigation is warranted as well for enlightening commentaries on SLBs within the 'broader contexts of bureaucratic relationships', as Lipsky has envisaged and encouraged.

Notes

1 Such a preference is noticeably exposed in the most recent trade dispute negotiations between the USA and China, for example. While the US trade representatives are pressing China to change its laws to address the US concerns about its faire trading practices, the Chinese negotiators instead ask them to trust China's promises and ability in introducing administrative and regulatory changes. This was rejected by the American politicians, who do not view China's long history of giving pledges and initiative short-lived administrative measures as helpful at all in resolving such a problem between the two nations.

2 One such lessons of profound impact to the Chinese regime and Chinese police is some police officers' sympathetic understanding at the early stage to mass protest incident in China's capital about three decades ago. Wide discussions on the roles of police and local government officials have been carried out and this has arguably contributed to the development of HCA in China.

3 This practice is summarised in China as 'Fengqiao experiences'. Fengqiao is a small town in Zhejiang Provinces, eastern China, which is unknown to most of the people even in its own province before 1950s. Yet, shortly after the communist government took power, the town officials were noted by the central government leaders for have been done very well in mobilising community recourses to contain social discontent and promoting collective well-being of the residents in the town. After promoting Fengqiao's such experiences through the effective communist propaganda machine, Fengqiao was widely known in China in 1960s for its ability of self-reliance and effectiveness of monitoring people on their political and social positioning. However, it fell out of political favour following the notorious cultural revolution episode in China and virtually neglected by the party organs in the post 1980s reform era either. One key practice for Fengqiao public officials is that they are not shirking away from dealing with any civil disputes or even criminal activities directly, rather they took laws into their hands and seek to address all order related issues within the town, rather than passing it on to the judicial system in the county or the province. 'Fengqiao experiences' is brought back again and kicked into fashion by top political and police leaders in China since 2018 though, for easing off the increasingly unequal social distances amongst its population and starve off more and more discontents resulted. This sounds very alarming to any westerner only with the experiences of rule of law and trial by the court in making judgement on other people's rights or wrongs, guilty or innocence.

References

Besharov, M. (2014) "The relational ecology of identification: how organisational identification emerges when individuals hold divergent values" in *Academy of Management Journal*, 57:5, 1485–1512.

Black, A. and Lumsden, K. (2019) "Precautionary policing and dispositives of risk in a police force control room in domestic abuse incidents: an ethnography of call handlers, dispatchers and response officers." in *Policing and Society*, 30:1, 65–80. doi: 10.1080/10439463.2019.1568428.

Chu, S. (2011) "The protection of vulnerable groups in China: from the perspective of local government innovations" in *Journal of Cambridge Studies*, 6, 2–3.

Chen, X. (2017) "Origins of informal coercion in China" in *Politics and Society*, 45:1, 67–89.

Fox, J. (2000) "Common Sense in Shanghai, the Shanghai general chamber of commerce and political legitimacy in republican China" in *History Workshop Journal*, 50, 20–44.

Gittell, J. and Douglas, A. (2012) "Relational bureaucracy: structuring reciprocal relationships into roles" in *Academy of Management Review*, 37:4, 709–733.

Gowricharn, R. and Cankaya, S. (2017) "Policing the nation: acculturation and street level bureaucrats in professional life" in *Sociology*, 51:5, 1101–1117.

Gui, X. (2017) "How power-interest network have shaped anti-demolition protests in grassroots China" in *China: An International Journal*, 15:4, 69–89.

Hammacdk, P. (2008) "Narrative and the cultural psychology of identity" in *Personality and Social Psychology Review*, 12:3, 222–247.

He, S. and Xue, D. (2014) "Identity building and communal resistance against landgrabs in wukan village, China" in *Current Anthropology*, 55, S9 S126–137.

Hill, H. (2003) "Understanding implementation: street level bureaucrats' resources for reform" in *Journal of Public Administration Research and Theory*, 13:3, 265–282.

Hu, J. (2011) "Grand mediation in China: mechanism and application" in *Asian Survey*, 51:6, 1065–1089.

Hupe, P. and Hill, M. (2007) "Street-level bureaucracy and public accountability" in *Public Administration*, 85:2, 279–299.

Jacka, T. (2014) "Left-behind and vulnerable? Conceptualising development and older women's agency in rural China".

Johnston, H. (2012) "State violence and oppositional protest in high capacity authoritarian regimes" in *International Journal of Conflict and Violence*, 6:1, 55–74.

Kjaerulff, J. (2018) "Discretion and the values of fractal man, an anthropologist's perspective on Street-Level bureaucracy" in *European Journal of Social Work*, 1:1. doi: 10.1080/13691457.2018.1553150

Kosar, K. (2011) "Street level-bureaucracy: the Dilemmas Endure" in *Public Administration Review*, March/April, 299–302.

Kulich, C., de Lemus, S., Kosakowska-Berezecha, N. and Lorenzi-Cioldi, F. (2017) "Editorial: multiple identities management: effects on (of) identification, attitudes, behaviour and well-being" in *Frontier Psychology*, 8, 2258.

Lam-Knott, S. (2017) "Understanding protest 'violence' in Hong Kong from the youth perspective" in *Asian Anthropology*, 16:4, 279–298.

Li, E. (2016) "China's urban underclass population and penal policy" in *Criminology and Criminal Justice*.

Li, Z. and Huang, Q. (2008) "Reaching out to vulnerable groups in China: a broad library with social inclusion".

Lipsky, M. (2014) "Assessing government performance through the lens of public sector workers" in *Public Administration Review*, November December, 74:6, 8060808.0

Markman, A. (2017) "Implications of psychological engineering: commentary on De Houwer, Hughes and Barnes-Holmes" in *Journal of Applied Research in Memory and Cognition*, 6:1, 27–30.

Mastrofski, S. (2004) "Controlling street-level police discretion" in *The Annals of the American Academy of Political and Social Science*, 593, 100–118.

Morrell, K. and Currie, G. (2015) "Impossible jobs or impossible tasks? Client volatility and frontline policing practice in urban riots" in *Public Administration Review*, 75:2, 264–275.

Paik, W. (2019) "The institutional of petition and authoritarian social control in contemporary China" in *Issues & Studies: A Social Science Quarterly on China, Taiwan, and East Asian Affairs*, 54:2 (June 2018), 1–28.

Parpart, J. (1995) "Deconstructing the development 'expert': gender, development and the 'vulnerable groups'" in Marchand, M.H. and Parpart, J. (eds) *Feminism/postmodernism/development*, pp. 221–243. London: Routledge.

Pulhamus, A. (1991) "Conflict handling – a common sense approach to appraising supervisory performance" in *Public Personnel Management*, 20:4, 485–492.

Sechi, G. and Skilters, J. (2018) "Social determinants of identity in communities: a social capital-and social categorisation-based approach – findings from Latvia" in *Social Science Information*, 57:1, 77–98.

Solinger, D.J. (2011) "Dibaohu in distress: the meagre minimum livelihood guarantee system in Wuhan" in Carrilo, B. and Duckett, J. (eds) *China's changing welfare mix: local perspectives*, pp. 36–63. London: Routledge.

Van Zoonen, L. and Turner, g. (2013) "Exercising identity: agency and narrative in identity management" in *Kybenets*, 43:6, 935–946.

Wachtel, P. (2017) "A procedural, contextual, action-focused understanding: response to Renn and Westerman" in *Psychoanalytic Dialogue*, 27, 546–556.

Wacquant, L. (2009) *Punishing the poor: the neoliberal government of social insecurity*. Durham, NC: Duke University Press.

Wang, J. (2015) "Managing social stability: the perspective of the local government in China" in *Journal of East Asian Studies*, 15, 1–25.

Wang, Y. and Minzner, C. (2015) "The rise of the Chinese security state, The China Quarterly".

Wong, S. and Peng, M. (2015). "Petition and repression in China's Authoritarian Regime: evidence from a natural experiment" in *Journal of East Asian Studies*, 15, 27–67.

Xu, J. (2013) "Police accountability and the commodification of policing in China" in *British Journal of Criminology*, 53, 1093–1117.

Ybema, s., Keenoy, T. and others (2009) "Articulating identities" in *Human Relations*, 62:3, 299–322.

9 UK Immigration Policy

Asylum Seeker and Refugee Vulnerability

Ian Fitzgerald and Sirak Berhe Hagos

Introduction

> [A refugee is any person who] owing to well-founded **fear of being persecuted for reasons of race, religion, nationality, membership of a particular social group or political opinion**, is out-side the country of his [her] nationality and is unable or, owing to such fear, is unwilling to avail himself [herself] of the protection of that country; or who, not having a nationality and being outside the country of his [her] former habitual residence as a result of such events, is unable or, owing to such fear, is unwilling to return to it.
>
> (Article 1 1951 Convention – UNHCR, 2010)

The United Kingdom (UK) is one of the signatories of both the 1951 United Nations Convention and the 1967 Protocol relating to the status of refugees; this declaration has not only an explicit but also an implicit understanding that refugees/asylum seekers originate from dangerous and hostile environments. Article 1 above makes this clear, but it is disgraceful to note that for many, if not all, in a UK context this vulnerability is only the start of a difficult path to a safer environment. This is because national immigration policy increasingly considers asylum seekers and refugees to be 'unwanted' (Consterdine, 2018). The term 'vulnerable' has also recently been used to seek to '...*map ... insidious divisions between the deserving and ... undeserving* [asylum seeker and] *refugee...*' (Smith and Waite, 2019: 2302). In short Smith and Waite argue that the 2014 Syrian Vulnerable Person Resettlement Programme is part of a neoliberal regime of refugee regulation – essentially the ongoing creation and indeed consolidation of a UK hierarchy of entitlements and rights based upon migrant category (Anderson, 2010).

This neoliberal critic and many of its connotations underpins our argument, although we mainly seek to detail successive governments immigration policy. Introducing into this discussion four North East asylum seeker then refugee first person narratives. Making clear not only how vulnerability arises in a UK context but also how some still do not allow this to diminish their strength of character and community spirit.

To begin with it is appropriate to detail why people have come to the North-East of England:

> I am Eritrean and went to the only University in the country (obtained a degree in accountancy) and became a government employee. I am also a Pentecostal Christian and following the Eritrean and Ethiopian war Pentecostal Christians were persecuted. In fact in 1998 the police came to my house and arrested members of my church who were having a bible study and a prayer session. Hundreds of church leaders and thousands of members were imprisoned, tortured and asked to renounce their faith and religion. Many have been killed or died of mistreatment. People are made to sign a document and promise to return to the old Coptic belief or remain in metal containers for the rest of their lives as prisoners. I instead fled the country to claim asylum in the UK.
>
> (Second author – Eritrean)

> I was active in the Sudan military from late teens and rose up the ranks to become a General, I witnessed though a brutal and corrupt regime and so left to join rebel forces to seek independence for my people. I was captured and tortured with electrodes forced down fingernails then electrocuted to what I thought was the point of death. I accepted my fate and was ready to die as a relief from torture. The lives of my family were threatened and they may have been killed in revenge for my escape. I managed to escape as part of a group of eight men and walked for 3 days in blistering heat to find refuge in a Catholic Mission. I still though suffer as I get flashbacks; sleep poorly and I return each night to that room as the electrodes are inserted into my fingernails.
>
> (AK General Translated – Sudanese)

> I arrived from Czech Republic in 2000 with my family as a 14-year-old as we had faced persecution. We had our house and car vandalised with objects thrown through windows, there was an organized hate campaign against us. My parents were also concerned as education policies were discriminatory towards Roma people, segregating us in special schools for 'mild mental disabilities'. Roma had been persecution for many centuries. So eventually it was decided to leave.
>
> (Gina – Roma Czech Republic)

> So I came to UK because in Iraq every party [political party] had militia that are very violent, I saw many cases. So kidnapping, and militia would come to your house. So they did not like me, as I was a producer, I investigated issues, mainly Middle East corruption.

So they threatened my family, my mother and father and we had to go. My wife and kids and myself. So because of the nature of my work I had visas as I travelled a lot. So we had a multi entry visa to America but when we travelled it was the election of Trump. He banned Iraq so he cancelled our visas randomly so we applied for asylum to UK.

(A.D. – Iraqi)

For us it is clear how each of those quoted can be considered vulnerable as we would argue they each clearly display someone who is '... *persecuted for reasons of race, religion, nationality, membership of a particular social group or political opinion...*'. Each then was vulnerable due to either overwhelming aggressive and violent acts or threat of that. Given this we might expect that a UK government would not only provide a 'safe haven' but also a long-term solution so that they might begin to safely function again and make a valuable contribution to the UK. However, as we show this is far from the truth.

New Labour and a New Favourable Environment for Asylum Seekers?

The Labour Party came to power in 1997 following a number of years of Conservative Party rule. The earlier Conservative period had heralded the introduction of specific asylum legislation, with refugee entry and social rights restricted (see Sales, 2002). Importantly, Consterdine (2018: 6) states that though '...*Labour administrations transformed Britain into a migration state...*' this first, from the start (in 2000), went against public opinion. Second, as noted in our brief discussion of vulnerability, distinct categories of immigrants were created, in short the 'wanted' (in particular European Union migrants) and the 'unwanted'.

The 'unwanted' included asylum seekers, and asylum policy became ever more restrictive. Home Secretary Jack Straw perhaps best demonstrates this when he '...*questioned the utility of the 1951 Convention relating to the Status of Refugees...*' (Mulvey, 2010: 440; see also Table 1, p. 461 that details Labour asylum legislation). Continuing the previous Conservative government policy, Mulvey highlights the emphasis on controlling, or more accurately reducing, the numbers of UK asylum seekers. The 1999 Immigration and Asylum Act began this process via a number of policy initiatives. It also importantly went further than the previous Conservative government legislation in restricting asylum seeker social rights (Sales, 2002). Sales (2002) had also originally discussed the emerging creation of social categories of 'deserving' refugee, compared to an initial 'undeserving' asylum seeker. Even following a review of this new legislation, specifically discussed below are the three main 'restrictive' pillars introduced. These were: the complete removal of asylum seekers from the UK welfare system;

their forced dispersal into local communities; and an increase in immigration officer's powers of detention.

Asylum Seekers and the UK Welfare System

With regard to welfare provision a new section of the Home Office was established called the National Asylum Support Service (NASS) in 2000. This now dealt with asylum seeker applications and administered 'limited' financial and social assistance. Previous to this the local authorities provided financial and, to some extent, social assistance. There is strong evidence that this new 'system' has caused and continues to cause both poverty and destitution (Sales, 2002; Lewis, 2009; Allsopp *et al.*, 2014; Alston, 2018). Underpinning this was and continues to be government policy that asylum seekers cannot work. Mulvey (2010) argues that this legal inability to work means not only forced and diminishing welfare but also isolation and diminishing skills. Some of course are also forced to work informally to survive and indeed this can lead to forced/slave labour (see Lewis *et al.*, 2017). Further, it is important to remind ourselves that asylum seekers are persecuted, hence this the reason why they flee their counties of origin. This often creates lasting healthcare-related mental and physical issues '...*imprisonment, genocide, physical and sexual violence, witnessing violence to others, traumatic bereavement, starvation, homelessness, higher risk of diseases that have increased prevalence in the country of origin...*' (Allsopp *et al.*, 2014). However, UK healthcare provision for asylum seekers has been regularly criticised due to lack of information and access issues (Humphries, 2004; O'Donnell *et al.*, 2007; Allsopp *et al.*, 2014). With O'Donnell *et al.* (2007) stating '*Our research confirms previous important findings regarding issues of access to timely health care and the role of interpreters within the consultation*' (ibid: 10). This of course is amplified when an asylum application is refused, then little or no 'official' support was/is given (see CAB, 2006). On a wider note it should also be said that once granted permission to stay, newer refugee communities also lack employment knowledge compounding asylum seeker disadvantage (Sales, 2002). This can also be a wider issue for all due to both the ongoing decline in funding support for NGOs that have often provided some support during the implementation of the forced dispersal provisions, that we now discuss.

Asylum Seeker Forced Dispersal Provisions

Aa a new system for welfare provision, a new regulatory system of housing asylum seeker applicants was introduced in 2000 following the 1999 Immigration and Asylum Act. Here the new system withdrew any possible choice that asylum seekers might exercise. We detail this new regulatory system as 'forced' dispersal as choice is not evident, asylum seekers were now dispersed to areas chosen for them and not by them. In many ways this new policy continued the previous Conservative government policy (1993 and 1996). This previous Conservative policy had withdrawn the rights of asylum seekers with regard to housing benefits contributing to an increasingly precarious asylum seeker housing framework. Asylum seekers could also no longer access permanent local authority accommodation leading to increased levels of destitution (Sales, 2002). Significantly, though:

> ...asylum seekers were able to live where their communities were residing, receiving support, employment information, advice and emotional support from fellow refugees from the same country. This [new Labour government] policy [of dispersal] created challenges, although the welcome provided to refugees locally [in the north east] has generally been good, there has been some evidence that the increasing numbers and visibility of refugees might be giving rise to an increase in racially motivated incidents and hostility.
>
> (Second author)

An early Home Office study on 'successful dispersal', including local authorities in the North-East, stated, '*...the study clearly identifies a significant association between characteristics related to greater levels of deprivation within host communities and an increased likelihood of poor relations between host communities and asylum seekers*' (Anie *et al.*, 2005: 10). Importantly, though, there were often organisations formed or active in dispersed areas that could provide support to new arrivals. Sales (2002: 469–471) identifies these as refugee agencies such as the Refugee Council; Charities including Medical Foundation for the Victims of Torture; Churches; Campaigning Organisations; and Refugee Community Organisations (RCOs). She highlights though the dependence of these organisations on a variety of funding sources, including national and local government. Campbell and Afework (2015), though in a discussion of Ethiopian and Eritrean asylum seekers and refugees, highlight a decline in RCOs caused by both the cessation of government funding and the policy initiatives, including dispersal. As well as difficult dispersal provisions, the 1999 Immigration and Asylum Act also extended '*...the powers of search and arrest, and detention of asylum seekers...*' (Sales, 2002: 463). This in many ways is the outstanding feature of an uncaring, harmful and often violent policy regime. It is to the detention regime that we now turn.

Immigration Officer Powers and Detention

With the extended powers of immigration officers, a main consideration here is immigration removal centres (IRCs). Bosworth (2014) notes IRCs actually originated in 1970 before the UK even joined the European Economic Community. But as indicated, the Immigration and Asylum Act 1999 played a part in increasing asylum seeker arrest and detention. Thus, this difficult path to a safer environment was made even worse for many. Discussing his story during this period, one of our respondents noted:

> Although I was eventually safe when I arrived in UK I still faced further persecution and injustice in navigating the asylum process. Mistakes, missing paperwork and admin errors caused over 3 years in and out of detention in various centres. In one the governor was corrupt and treated me very badly, lengthening my detention and threatening to extend my stay. This was done to blackmail me to control 'unruly' detainees on my wing.
>
> (AK General Translated)

Doctors and lawyers are in our opinion in the best position to provide ample factual evidence of what can happen in detention due to the consequences of UK asylum seeker policy. For example Arnold (2018), in a recent letter to the British Medical Journal, notes briefly his experience as an independent doctor in detention centres between 2005 and 2011. During this period he dealt with 23 detainees who had poor health due to inadequate detention centre doctors and hunger strikes due to a 'perceived lack of justice'. Significantly, of these 23, 12 were subsequently found to have justified claims to asylum having fled torture, with some receiving 'substantial damages' for the UK government. More graphically, in their response to Clause 22 of a draft of the Borders, Citizenship and Immigration Act 2009. The Immigration Law Practitioners Association provide three cases of individual and family physical and mental harm cased through either 'dawn raids' or whilst in IRCs (ILPA, 2009). Athwal (2015: 52) also states that racism '...*is an accepted fact of life...*' in IRCs and he notes that this has been enhanced due to privatisation. He also importantly details the then known deaths in detention. Twenty-two people had died with 11 of these deaths self-inflicted since 1989, including during Labours period of office.

There was also a wider issue for not only asylum seekers and refugees but also a large proportion of the resident population in late 2007. It was then that the banking sector experienced one of its most difficult periods and the UK Government and Parliament provided it with financial support. The repercussions of this support underpinned future migration policy and contributed to both public disdain for immigration and then to Brexit (Dorling, 2016; MacLeod and Jones, 2018). This will be discussed in more detail in the next Conservative asylum and refugee policy section.

Conservative Asylum and Refugee Policy and the Hostile Environment

The Labour Party period of asylum seeker policy has been termed hostile by many (Zetter and Pearl, 2000; Zetter *et al.*, 2006; Mulvey, 2010; Campbell and Afework, 2015). Whilst the Conservative period has clearly continued with that immigration strategy, it has also been intensified, most notably demonstrated by the Home Secretary's infamous 'hostile environment' interview (Kirkup and Winnett, 2012). Here Teresa May (then Home Secretary) discussed creating a hostile environment for illegal migrant workers, although in essence these measures increasingly affected all immigrants. In fact, as Burnett (2017: 86) states '...*if a hostile environment is embedded politically, why should we be surprised when it takes root culturally?*'. He makes clear this has been the product of successive Labour and Conservative governments, although we concentrate here on Coalition and Conservative policy.

Webber (2019) highlights the full extent of the draconian measures enforced by Coalition and successive Conservative governments. He first notes the creation of an '...inter-ministerial "Hostile Environment Working Group"'. This group devised a range of policies, which were then '...*contained in the 2014 and 2016 Immigration Acts, in secondary legislation and guidance documents, and in operational measures adopted by the Home Office and partner agencies*' (ibid.: 77). In short, these relate to harsher measures with regard to housing, healthcare, education, policing and detention underpinned by a more hostile border including towards 'family life'. As extracts from our refugee witness discussions highlight:

> The hostile environment created a culture of suspicion within communities. Some people felt empowered to blatantly abuse asylum seekers and refugees. Asylum seekers including women and children were detained like criminals. Many were deported and some actually killed upon return to their countries....
>
> (Second author)

> ...there has been increased hostility since 2010 and I do not trust police as I had issues due to ... language barrier. I am now more reluctant to seek activities supporting integration, I am wary of indigenous population, especially those in positions of authority.
>
> (AK General Translated)

More specifically, Webber (2012, 2019) details the main issues with each of these measures. He also notes harsher penalties with regard to work. For example, it is now a criminal offence if you employ an 'unauthorised' worker, such as an asylum seeker. This has led to '...*intensive enforcement through raids on mainly small, minority ethnic-owned workplaces'* (Webber, 2019: 79). We now briefly look at the harsher measures identified above.

Dispersal, Accommodation and Healthcare

With regard to dispersal and accommodation the Conservatives, as with the work provisions, made it '...*a criminal offence to provide accommodation to anyone who cannot prove that they have permanent or temporary leave to remain in the UK*' (Crawford *et al.*, 2019). Webber (2019: 78) states these provisions breach the Universal Declaration on Human Rights and other human and social rights declarations. Whilst Crawford *et al.* (2019) note how this extends border control, an issue highlighted and discussed by others (see Yuval-Davis *et al.*, 2018). A.D. actually details with dispersal that:

> I was sent to a deprived area and had no support at all, apart from a telephone line that never answered ... After my first few weeks here I thought I must get the kids in school. So I went to council and they said "who are you", they don't have any idea who I am they had been told nothing.
>
> (A.D.)

Support was provided by the Red Cross as A.D. contacted them. They remain one of the few organisations that support new asylum seekers in Northumberland as no state agencies now do. A.D. further highlighted that three of his five neighbours were racist echoing the earlier warnings of Anie *et al.* (2005).

Turning to healthcare Hiam *et al.* (2018: 108) note how a stricter hospital regime has led to a number of those who suffered due to the horrendous Grenfell Tower fire '...*decline health care and other public services, fearful of the threat of detention and deportation*'. The key issues being to charge those who could not prove immigration status before non-emergency treatment, this of course includes antenatal checks. Those who are admitted to hospital due to an emergency are allowed treatment but changed afterwards. Returning to Grenfell and overall immigration policy more sinister was the memorandum of understanding (MoU) introduced in 2017 that formalised data sharing between the NHS and the Home Office. This allowed patient details to be shared for enforcement and detention purposes (Hiam *et al.*, 2018 discuss this in more detail). Although Webber (2019) notes that legal challenges led to the MoU being scrapped, the NHS is still legally bound under the National Health Service Act 2006 to pass onto the Home Office information on NHS debts. Other public-sector bodies are also compelled to share data with Home Office enforcement and detention officials, including schools (for further discussion see Webber, 2019: 81).

Detention and Asylum Seekers

Turning to detention, as noted there are unacceptable repercussions due to this, but during the Conservative period of office the high levels of detention remained, nearly 25,000 people in 2018 (House of Commons, 2019: 12). Bosworth (2014) details how detention centres have expanded to include all, including children, with some being housed in police prison cells. Somewhat contrary to the overall assessment of Athwal (2015) she does though highlight some ambivalence with 'front line staff' in detention centres. Thus, some 'front line staff' maintain a belief in fairness and respect when dealing with detainees (ibid: 149). Although others see notes are less sympathetic and are cynical with regard to the detainees' plight. For example, Bosworth (2014) highlights 'pervasive' G4S racism and a critical 2013 coroner's report (see Monaghan, 2013). Importantly, in our neoliberal context G4S is/was a multinational security company contracted by UK government as part of the UK enforcement strategy. They have recently announced that they will not continue to be involved in immigration and asylum removal and detention centres (Busby, 2019). Significant here is a recent House of Commons inquiry that was prompted due to:

> ...the exposure of appalling physical and verbal abuse of detainees by some staff at [G4S] Brook House Immigration Removal Centre (IRC) in 2017 and by persistent reports of the inappropriate use of immigration detention and its damaging effect on the mental health and wellbeing of detainees. Over the course of our inquiry, we have found serious problems with almost every element of the immigration detention system. People are being wrongfully detained, held in immigration detention when they are vulnerable and detained for too long.... The Home Office has shown a shockingly cavalier attitude to the deprivation of human liberty and the protection of people's basic rights.
>
> (House of Commons, 2019: 3)

Specifically, Klein and Williams (2012) discuss how the release of some detainees back into UK communities is not the end of their UK psychological trauma. They highlight how some are not only given curfews in their hostels but are also made to wear electronic 'tags' like criminals. If further evidence is needed of the 'shocking' attitude of the UK Home Office it comes from its 2013 Operation Vaken. Here issues of detention, and indeed the traumas associated with it, were escalated by Operation Vaken, which orchestrated a targeted 'Go home' campaign (see Jones *et al.*, 2017 for an in-depth discussion). Overall, this provides only a brief discussion of some of the trauma caused to both asylum seekers and refugees in the UK since 2010. We want to conclude here by discussing what we believe to be critical to many of these actions, austerity.

Austerity and the Demise of Immigration and Asylum Support

Austerity began of course under the last Labour government, but with regard to migration policy it did not really start to make a difference until 2010. Wintour (2010) reports on the 'scrapping' of the Migration Impact Fund, which was in place to ease the impact of immigration in some areas. This fund supported a range of local council, local police, primary care trust and voluntary body small-scale migration impact projects. On a wider note, austerity also led to the demise of national, regional and local immigration support of all types. This included some direct funding to organisations that were supporting new immigrants, asylum seekers and refugees. More specifically as noted by respondent's:

> ...with the new coalition government's austerity policy, almost all of the funding for vulnerable groups such as refugees and asylum seekers has dramatically curtailed. This affected me personally and as a community, I was working for the North of England Refugee Service as a capacity building worker and lost this job as no more funding. We were supporting small refugee community groups, helping them to run their organisations efficiently and effectively so that they serve their respective communities who are mainly branded as 'hard to reach'. These groups are usually the first point of contact to any new asylum seeker and play a vital role in helping them integrate into the society. The funding cut has caused great pain to many people who were now left with no help whatsoever. Many people became destitute and communities suffer. It seemed that the government took the money from these communities and gave it to immigration law enforcement agencies, which were empowered to detain and deport people in droves. The cut in legal aid and restrictions to judicial review and removal of many appeal rights also left many asylum seekers in a limbo for many years.
>
> (Second author)

> I was able to engage effectively with Czech Roma groups, I built good links city wide and had very good reputation in supporting families with issues such as: housing, benefits, advocacy and form filling and finding school places. However, funding was stripped and services cut back, leaving me redundant and unable to find paid work to support this work. Many Roma families see outsiders as the enemy, see no need for education and are vulnerable to gang masters and modern slavery and bonded housing due to this self-exclusion.
>
> (Gina)

Austerity was due to the failure of the banking sector, a crisis that resulted in total support provided to the failing banking sector of £1,162 billion, of which some £46 billion was still left to repay last March 2018 (NAO, 2019). With the United Nations Special Rapporteur on extreme poverty and human rights commenting: '*The UK is the world's fifth largest economy, it ... thus seems patently unjust and contrary to British values that so many people are living in poverty*' (Alston, 2018). As noted, it also led to the demise of funding for immigration initiatives, including the types of 'grassroots' organisations noted by Sales (2002). However, some have managed to continue, although in some instances they have had to form partnerships with state agencies such as the Home Office. McGhee *et al.* (2016) have investigated a state partnership between Refugee Action and the Home Office. Here the organisation receives funding from the Home Office to deliver certain services including Assisted Voluntary Return (AVR) schemes for refused asylum seekers. Not surprisingly, they note partnership tensions and dilemmas but they also conclude that the organisation can still act independently and indeed challenge Home Office policies. Also, on a more positive note our respondents, including the second author, note that they are continuing to support their communities in these challenging times. Some have setup social enterprises providing employment for refugees. For example, the 'Other Perspective' provides interpreting, catering and cleaning services all geared to serving refugees and asylum seekers. It also provides them with job opportunities as interpreters, cleaners and chefs. Whilst a charity was initially created by the same community leaders:

> A colleague and I set up a charity called Investing in People and Culture (IPC) to work with all small refugee groups in the North East affected by the funding cuts. This now works as a consortium and having originally been set up in 2010 as a community group, it was incorporated in 2015. Overall IPC strives to ensure that refugees settling in the North East are able to attain a good quality of life. I have also set up a consultancy company (Aiba Consultancy Ltd) to provide capacity building service to equip small refugee and migrant groups with tools that would help them run effective organisations; Policies and Procedures; Funding advice; Financial Control Systems; Training on various issues such as Safeguarding and Health and Safety etc.
>
> (Second Author)

Evidence of the usefulness and success of these organisations comes from AK General:

> Since being granted settled status I started my own community group, to support other asylum seekers to integrate and navigate the process. This was difficult to establish, find volunteers with skills

and experience and sustain a management committee; this is when I sought support from IPC.

(AK General Translated)

Importantly, AK General received a community award last year recognising his work and running of this group ('Most resilient community leader') '*...I am very proud of that*' (AK General). Finally, Gina has been able to continue her work:

> Fortunately, my partner was able to support me while I set up a new community group to meet some Czech Roma community needs. So Roma Right Path has received some funding to help run twice-weekly drop-in and support sessions the community. We are also going to apply for charitable status and I am trying to develop my skills to include fund-raising to try and get much needed continued support for our group.
>
> (Gina)

Overall the then successive UK government policy has compounded a hostile, complicated and difficult path to a safer environment. This hostile policy (Zetter and Pearl, 2000; Zetter *et al.*, 2006; Mulvey, 2010; Webber, 2019) has meant increasing asylum seeker vulnerability due to, for example, detention (Arnold, 2018), destitution (Sales, 2002; Lewis, 2009; Allsopp *et al.*, 2014), health issues (O'Donnell *et al.*, 2007) and potential forced/slave labour (Lewis *et al.*, 2017). Therefore, it is not uncommon to find that asylum seekers have been forced into the shadows rather than welcomed. Although it must be repeated that some have been able to display an agency through direct action and activism. This leads us to the overall conclusion to our chapter.

Conclusion

Persecution, struggle and overall vulnerability are part of an asylum seekers life in their home country. But it is sad to note that instead of seeking to support those who flee, successive Conservative, Labour and Coalition governments have withdrawn, sub-contracted or denied support. In fact, it is worth detailing in full the assessment of the United Nations Special Rapporteur on extreme poverty and human rights. Alston (2018: 19) specifically states that:

> Destitution is built into the asylum system [see also Allsopp et al., 2014; Burnett, 2009; Mayblin and James, 2019]. Asylum seekers are banned from working and limited to a derisory level of support that

guarantees they will live in poverty. The government promotes work as the solution to poverty, yet refuses to allow this particular group to work. While asylum seekers receive some basic supports such as housing, they are left to make do with an inadequate, poverty level income of around £5 a day. For those who have no recourse to public funds as a result of their immigration status, the situation can be particularly difficult; such individuals face an increased risk of exploitation and enjoy restricted access to educational opportunities.

In a UK context then vulnerability is all but ensured by government policy but as noted for a period this was to some extent different for EU workers, who were 'wanted'. This, in particular, was clear with Labour government policy and is evident in the approach taken to Central and Eastern European (CEE) workers. These new workers were 'wanted' evidenced by the fact that in May 2004 the UK was only one of three countries to place no restrictions on CEE free movement. More specifically, the Government were positive about the economic benefits of immigration (Secretary of State, 2008) with employers and trade unions both arguing the case of these workers. During this period, there were language, education and information support for new immigrants (including also for asylum seekers/refugees), with initiatives at mainly a regional and local authority level (e.g., I&DeA, 2008). However, there were tensions and at an early stage CEE free movement was described as precipitating the largest ever single wave of in-migration to the UK (Salt and Millar, 2006). Whilst a 2007–2008 House of Lords Economic Affairs Committee was negative towards the benefits of immigration. With the Committees final report (House of Lords, 2008) highlighting in a number of areas that asylum seekers/refugees family/dependents remained outside of any 'managed migration' system. Further, the Government were seemingly positive to EU migrants and indeed to the benefits of immigration. Only three years after CEE accession in September 2007, Prime Minister Gordon Brown, in his first speech to the Labour Party conference, made a point of discussing 'British jobs for British workers' (BBC News, 2007). As briefly discussed, occurring at the same time as this was the start of the economic crisis caused by the failure of the banking sector and the implementation of the politics of austerity and ultimately Brexit.

So, closing on the overall theme of this book, will Brexit affect asylum seekers and refugees? Netto and Craig (2017: 7) note a likelihood that on leaving the EU the UK current obligations:

> ...to adherence to EU directives of the Common European Asylum System (CEAS), which relate to the reception and treatment of asylum-seekers and refugees, may be diluted. If so, this is likely to increase the vulnerability of asylum-seekers to either destitution or participation in precarious employment, exploitation and forced labour.

Waite (2017: 670) agrees arguing that '...*it is clear that Brexit is ... going to have a notable impact on asylum law*'. Whilst one of our respondents echoed these views stating:

> Citizenship cannot be applied for, for six years and you must have a clean record with no offences. So I know someone who had points on his driving licence and he took 12 years. ...I also think Brexit will make this much worse as the UK had to follow many European Union regulations.
>
> (A.D.)

Here it is also interesting to note that it has recently been reported that the hostile environment has made the Home Office a £500 million profit due to an increase in immigration fees (Joiner *et al.*, 2019). We are sure that Netto and Craig (2017) and Waite (2017) are correct in their assessments. This means that asylum seekers and refugees will continue to battle against hostility and racism. However, we would highlight the strength of character that both asylum seekers and refugees display. We should all remember that they are not just victims; they also often assert agency and are leading figures in struggles against this hostility and racism. For example Koca (2016) discusses new social movements, including the Refugees Welcome campaign, and the involvement of refugees in such campaigns. In essence their involvement challenges the assigned category of 'unwanted', bringing them 'out of the shadows' into public life. Meanwhile, MacKenzie *et al.* (2012) discuss the case of the Northern Organisation for Refugees, Migrants and Asylum-seekers, which has grown in significance as state support has diminished. Again they highlight how both asylum seekers and refugees assert agency whilst acting as group leaders and key activists. We conclude, then, with a reminder that some of our own respondents who have suffered due to recent austerity measures have not just slipped into the shadows but have continued to act as key activists and community leaders within both their own and other communities to build a better and more inclusive future.

References

Allsopp, J., Sigona, N. and Phillimore, J. (2014) Poverty among refugees and asylum seekers in the UK: An evidence and policy review, IRiS Working Paper Series, University of Birmingham.

Alston, P. (2018) Statement on Visit to the United Kingdom, by Professor Philip Alston, United Nations Special Rapporteur on extreme poverty and human rights, 16th November 2018.

Anderson, B. (2010) 'Migration, immigration controls and the fashioning of precarious workers', *Work, Employment and Society*, 24 (2), 300–317.

Anie, A., Daniel, N., Tah, C. and Petruckevitch, A. (2005) An exploration of factors affecting the successful dispersal of asylum seekers, Home Office Online Report 50/05.

Arnold, F. (2018) 'Hunger strikes in UK detention centres: injustice provokes desperate protests', *Letters, BMJ*, 361. doi: 10.1136/bmj.k2102.

Athwal, H. (2015) '"I don't have a life to live": deaths and UK detention', *Race and Class*, 56 (3), 50–68.

BBC News (2007) Gordon Brown's speech in full, Monday 24th September, http://news.bbc.co.uk/1/hi/uk_politics/7010664.stm, accessed October 2019.

Bosworth, M. (2014) *Inside Immigration Detention*, Oxford: Oxford University Press.

Burnett, J. (2009) What is destitution?, Positive Action for Refugees and Asylum Seekers Briefing Paper Number 9, February 2009.

Burnett, J. (2017) 'Racial violence and the Brexit state', *Race and Class*, 58 (4), 85–97.

Busby, M. (2019) G4S to leave immigration sector after Brook House scandal, Guardian 24th September 2019, www.theguardian.com/business/2019/sep/24/g4s-to-leave-immigration-sector-after-brook-house-scandal, accessed October 2019.

CAB (2006) Shaming destitution: NASS section 4 support for failed asylum seekers who are temporarily unable to leave the UK, Citizens Advice Bureau, June 2006.

Campbell, J.R. and Afework, S. (2015) 'Ethiopian and Eritrean immigrants in Britain refugee organising, transnational connections and identity, 1950–2009', *African Diaspora*, 8 (1), 98–119.

Consterdine, E. (2018) *Labour's Immigration Policy: The Making of the Migration State*, Basingstoke: Palgrave Macmillan.

Crawford, J., McKee, K. and Leahy, S. (2019) 'More than a hostile environment: exploring the impact of the right to rent part of the immigration Act 2016', *Sociological Research Online*, online first. https://doi.org/10.1177/1360780419867708

Dorling, D. (2016) 'Brexit: the decision of a divided country: blame austerity not immigration for the inequality underlying the referendum decision', BMJ, 354. doi: 10.1136/bmj.i3697.

Dwyer, P. and Brown, D. (2008) 'Accommodating "others"?: housing dispersed, forced migrants in the UK', *Journal of Social Welfare & Family Law*, 30 (3), 203–218.

Hiam, L., Steele, S. and McKee, M. (2018) 'Creating a "hostile environment for migrants": the British government's use of health service data to restrict immigration is a very bad idea', *Health Economics, Policy and Law*, 13 (2), 107–117.

House of Commons (2019) Immigration detention: Fourteenth Report of Session 2017–19, Report, together with formal minutes relating to the report, Home Affairs Committee: House of Commons, 21st March 2019.

House of Lords (2008) The Economic Impact of Immigration: Volume 1: Report, Select Committee on Economic Affairs 1st Report of Session 2007–08, London: The Stationery Office.

Humphries, B. (2004) 'An unacceptable role for social work: implementing immigration policy', *British Journal of Social Work*, 34 (1), 93–117.

I&DeA (2008) Integrating new migrants communicating important information: Guide for local authorities, Improvement and Development Agency for local government (I&DEA), Communities and Local Government.

ILPA (2009) Borders, Citizenship and Immigration Bill – HL Bill 15 House of Lords Committee: Clause 22, London: The Immigration Law Practitioners Association.

Joiner, S., Lombardi, A. and O'Neill, S. (2019) 'Hostile environment: home Office makes £500m from immigration', *The Sunday Times*, August 11th 2019, www.thetimes.co.uk/article/hostile-environments-home-office-makes-500m-from-immigration-fees-vgpbm2h6j, accessed October 2019.

Jones, H., Gunaratnam, Y., Bhattacharyya, G., Davies, W., Dhaliwal, S., Forkert, K., Jackson, E. and Saltus, R. (2017) *GO HOME? The politics of immigration controversies*, Manchester: Manchester University Press.

Klein, A. and Williams, L. (2012) 'Immigration detention in the community: research on the experiences of migrants released from detention centres in the UK', *Population, Space and Place*, 18 (6), 741–753.

Kirkup, J. and Winnett, R. (2012) Theresa May interview: 'We're going to give illegal migrants a really hostile reception', *Daily Telegraph*, 25th May 2012, www.telegraph.co.uk/news/uknews/immigration/9291483/Theresa-May-interview-Were-going-to-give-illegal-migrants-a-really-hostile-reception.html, accessed October 2019.

Koca, B.T. (2016) 'New social movements: "Refugees Welcome UK"', *European Scientific Journal*, 12 (2), 96–108.

Lewis, H. (2009) *Still destitute: worsening problem for refused asylum seekers*, York: Joseph Rowntree Charitable Trust.

Lewis, H., Waite, L. and Hodkinson, S. (2017) '"Hostile" UK immigration policy and asylum seekers' susceptibility to forced labour', in Francesco Vecchio and Alison Gerard (eds.) *Entrapping Asylum Seekers: Social, Legal and Economic Precariousness*, London: Palgrave Macmillan.

MacKenzie, R., Forde, C. and Ciupijus, Z. (2012) 'Networks of support for new migrant communities: institutional goals versus substantive goals', *Urban Studies*, 49 (3), 631–647.

MacLeod, G. and Jones, M. (2018) 'Explaining "Brexit capital": uneven development and the austerity state', *Space and Polity*, 22 (2), 111–136.

Mayblin, L. and James, P. (2019) 'Asylum and refugee support in the UK: civil society filling the gaps?', *Journal of Ethnic and Migration Studies*, 45 (3), 375–394.

McGhee, D., Bennett, C. and Walker, S. (2016) 'The combination of "insider" and "outsider" strategies in VSO–government partnerships: the relationship between Refugee Action and the Home Office in the UK', *Voluntary Sector Review*, 7 (1), 27–46.

Monaghan, K. (2013) Inquest into the Death of Jimmy Kelenda Mubenga, report by the Assistant Deputy Coroner, Karon Monaghan, QC, Under the Coroner's Rules 1984, Rule 43.

Mulvey, G. (2010) 'When policy creates politics: the problematizing of immigration and the consequences for refugee integration in the UK', *Journal of Refugee Studies*, 23 (4), 437–462.

NAO (2019) Taxpayer support for UK banks, National Audit Office. London: United Kingdom Government

Netto, G. and Craig, G. (2017) 'Migration and differential labour market participation: theoretical directions, recurring themes, implications of brexit and areas for future research', *Social Policy and Society*, 16 (4), 613–622.

O'Donnell, C.A., Higgins, M., Chauhan, R. and Mullen, K. (2007) '"They think we're OK and we know we're not". A qualitative study of asylum seekers' access, knowledge and views to health care in the UK', *BMC Health Services Research*, 7 (75), 1–11.

Sales, R. (2002) 'The deserving and the undeserving? Refugees, asylum seekers and welfare in Britain', *Critical Social Policy*, 22 (3), 456–478.

Secretary of State (2008) The Economic Impact of Immigration, the Government Reply to the First Report from the House of Lords Committee on Economic Affairs Session 2007–08 HL Paper 82, London: The Stationery Office.

Smith, K. and Waite, L. (2019) 'New and enduring narratives of vulnerability: rethinking stories about the figure of the refugee', *Journal of Ethnic and Migration Studies*, 45 (13), 2289–2307.

Waite, L. (2017) 'Asylum seekers and the labour market: spaces of discomfort and hostility', *Social Policy & Society*, 16 (4), 669–679.

Webber, F. (2012) *Borderline Justice: The Fight for Refugee and Migrant Rights*, London: Pluto Press.

Webber, F. (2019) 'Commentary: on the creation of the UK's "hostile environment"', *Race and Class*, 60 (4), 76–87.

Wintour, P. (2010) Fund to ease impact of immigration scrapped by stealth, Guardian 6th August 2010, www.theguardian.com/uk/2010/aug/06/fund-impact-immigration-scrapped, accessed October 2019.

UNHCR (2010) *Convention and Protocol Relating to the Status of Refugees*, Geneva: United Nations High Commissioner for Refugees.

Yuval-Davis, N., Wemyss, G. and Cassidy, K. (2018) 'Everyday bordering, belonging and the reorientation of British immigration legislation', *Sociology*, 52 (2), 228–244.

Zetter, R., Griffiths, D., Sigona, N., Flynn, D., Pasha, T. and Beynon, R. (2006) Immigration, social cohesion and social capital: what are the links?, Joseph Rowntree Foundation report.

Zetter, R. and Pearl, M. (2000) 'The minority within the minority: refugee community-based organisations in the UK and the impact of restrictionism on asylum-seekers', *Journal of Ethnic and Migration Studies*, 26 (4), 675–697.

10 Responding to Ageing Demographics

A Positive View from a Public Administration and Public Policy Perspective

Alex Murdock

Introduction

The reality of an ageing demographic in many, if not most, developed countries has been widely reported in the context of being a challenge to both public policy and the expected demands upon public services and public administration. Often too, the elderly are considered vulnerable individuals or groups. Both factors have significantly influenced the public policy debate (Pilichowski et al. 2007, Harper and Hamblin 2014, Pollitt 2016).

There have been graphic accounts of the phenomena and its societal impact, with one author describing it as a 'silver tsunami' (Payne 2015). China, perhaps significantly as a consequence of its past family policy, has responded with policies which create legal duties upon children to visit their parents (Liu and Sun 2015). This represents, perhaps, an example of a traditional intergenerational duty becoming a public-sector requirement. This requirement has often been the case for parents with their children, and it has been re-construed to operate in the opposite direction. Is it a harbinger of replication in other countries as the state finds that public resources are insufficient to meet the perceived needs of an ageing demographic?

The focus of this chapter will be to try and redress the perception of ageing as a social challenge which is generally the line taken in public policy literature in particular the focus on resources such as pension pressures, workforce challenges and social and medical care. Rather we will examine what has been variously described as 'active ageing' or 'positive ageing' and identify trends in the lifestyles of the increasing older generation. We will explore the concept of an ageing demographic as representing an 'opportunity' rather than a 'challenge' (Vincent 1996, Walker 2008, Zaidi et al. 2017). We will also challenge the perceived view that the elderly are always 'vulnerable' members of society.

The trends will be explored in the context of both public policy and public choice and will include lifelong learning, a redefinition of 'retirement' away from a date to a graduated transition, the importance of technology and the likely and emerging changing lifestyle choices of the 'baby boomers' and successive generations (Damant and Knapp 2015, Hyde and Phillipson 2015, Withnall 2015). The methodology will draw on major studies such as the UK Foresight project and Organisation for Economic Co-operation and Development (OECD) studies and will access the growing literature on positive and active ageing.

The implications for public management are considerable in that the positive/active ageing will challenge the traditional user and 'service' driven relationship to older citizens. This may require a radical restructuring of public-sector policies in the light of a changed perception of the older demographic (Albury 2011).

Identifying the Issue of Ageing

In developing countries the population is ageing, and this represents a relatively recent phenomena (especially within the past 30 years). The reality of an ageing demographic in most, if not all, developed countries has been widely reported in the context of being a challenge to both public policy and to the expected demands upon public services and upon public administration. This has significantly influenced the public policy debate (Pilichowski et al. 2007, Harper and Hamblin 2014, Pollitt 2016). This chapter considers the perspective of government and public policy and whilst acknowledging the nature demographic change seeks to challenge the assumption that such changes inevitably represents a threat and challenge. In effect is the proportionate increase in an older demographic a 'vulnerability' or might it be an opportunity.

There have been graphic accounts of the phenomena and its societal impact with it being described as a 'silver tsunami' (Payne 2015). China, perhaps significantly as a consequence of past family policy, has responded with policies which create legal duties upon children to visit their parents (Liu and Sun 2015). This represents, perhaps, an example of a traditional intergenerational duty becoming a public-sector requirement. This requirement has not only been the case in respect of parents and their children but has also been re-construed to operate in the opposite direction. Is it a harbinger of replication in other countries as the state finds that public resources are insufficient to meet the perceived needs of an ageing demographic?

The focus of this chapter will be to try and redress the perception of ageing as a social challenge which is generally the line taken in public policy literature in particular the focus on resources such as pension pressures, workforce challenges and social and medical care. This chapter will examine what has been variously described as 'active ageing' or 'positive ageing' and identify trends in the lifestyles of the increasing older generation. We will explore the concept of an ageing demographic as representing an 'opportunity' rather than a 'challenge' (Vincent 1996, Walker 2008, Zaidi et al. 2017).

The trends will be explored in the context of both public policy and public choice and will include lifelong learning, a redefinition of 'retirement'.

Demographics and Public Policy

The reality of an ageing population has been regarded in public policy terms as representing a potential if not actual demand on public services and public finances. With a younger demographic (such as occurred with the post war 'baby boom') there is a short-term pressures on public provision such as needs for midwives and maternity services and then pressures on education and possibly housing. However, a positive skew in a younger demographic (certainly in developed countries) is seen as having a potential if not actual payback in terms of a growth in the available workforce whose productive capability and tax contributions will, de facto, enable a payback to the costs incurred to public services.

The reality of a younger population demographic is a perception of an asset as opposed to a liability. In the short term it can and usually does present a challenge to the public sector, but this challenge is one usually couched in terms of a clear longer-term benefit. A city (or country) which experiences a loss of a younger demographic (through internal or external migration) would typically assess it in terms of a public-sector problem (such as a lack of perceived opportunities or poverty). The public-sector actors would, in political and public policy terms, endeavour to determine the nature of the problem and endeavour to introduce policies (such as inducements and rewards) and develop services to encourage a younger demographic to stay and not depart.

However, where the skew appears towards an ageing demographic then the public policy discourse tends to take a different path. Such a demographic has, in production and taxation terms, already contributed to the public good. They now represent a demand upon public provision without the attraction of a later return to the investment made in provision of public services. Indeed there is a perspective that the increased longevity represents a call on pension provision, state-funded health and care services and a reduction in what is passed on to the next generation and for the state to lay claim to through inheritance taxes (Vincent 1996, Harper 2010, 2014). This is associated with suggestions (especially in the UK) that the young have become the 'jilted generation' significantly on account of the 'burden of the old' and a failure to share prosperity across generations (Howker, E. and Malik, S. 2013). Willetts (a former UK politician talked of it as 'the pinch' whereby the baby boomer generation has created a problem for successive generations especially in the UK (Willetts 2011).

The implications for public policy of an ageing demographic are thus considerable and have typically been presented in terms of a challenge (Pilichowski et al. 2007, Harper and Hamblin 2014, Pollitt 2016). Some accounts are couched in terms which evoke a spectre of disaster or a potential catastrophic event. Payne in an recent essay talked of a silver tsunami and presented it in public management terms as a sudden wave of baby boomers retirements that could potentially cripple public management networks (Payne 2015). However, the term silver tsunami is one which both evokes a sense of crisis and which is of recent origin. It has become increasing a source of reference in academic literature as shown by the results from a Google Scholar search (Table 10.1).

We argue that the presentation of an ageing demographic as a public management/public policy problem or challenge is well established. This is presented in a number of forms. Here we utilise evidence from the UK Government series of studies called 'The Foresight Programme' which brought together experts and published a series of reports with particular reference to the UK.[1]

The growing life expectancy has increased and is projected to increase. This is demonstrated from the UK Office of National Statistics (ONS) studies.[2] The data indicates that the shape of the projected population of the UK will change to reflect a skew towards an older age profile.

One aspect is simply linked to figures which portray the dependency ratio ... the proportion of 'contributing' workers (usually portrayed in

Table 10.1 The 'Silver Tsunami' in google scholar

Year	Number of citations	Cumulative citations
2000–1	5	5
2001–2	8	13
2002–3	9	22
2003–4	10	32
2004–5	8	40
2005–6	16	56
2006–7	33	89
2007–8	66	155
2008–9	100	255
2009–10	139	394
2010–11	157	551
2011–12	214	765
2012–13	302	867
2013–14	352	1219
2014–15	421	1640
2015–16	477	2017
2016–17	523	2540
2017–18 (to May)	437	2977

terms of a demographic between 25 and 60/65) to an older demographic which are assumed to be consuming and supported by the younger demographic.

The consequences of this demographic change is of particular concern for its perceived impact on dependency ratios. The ONS notes that:

> Despite increases to State Pension Age under existing legislation ... the number of people of State Pension Age and over is projected to increase by 32.7 per cent from 12.4 million in mid-2014 to 16.5 million by mid-2039.[3]

The UK data is broadly similar to that of other countries and in fact the World Bank data suggests that the increase in actual life expectancy over the past 50 years is more pronounced in Emerging economies.[4] To a significant extent this is on account of a low base in such countries. It also is linked to significant improvements in public health (especially in reducing infectious disease)

Health and Morbidity

The issue of ageing is not in itself a problem where health is concerned. It needs to be construed in terms of ageing accompanied by increased morbidity. The key question in terms of health is not so much life expectancy but rather the number of years which are spent in poor health. This has implications for public policy in terms of a demand for services – especially health and social care. It obviously has implications for individual citizens and their families. The Centre for Ageing Better notes the change in number of years spent in poor health (male) when measured from the perspective of the starting point being birth and the starting point being age 65. The factor of geographical location is highly significant with areas of high deprivation being associated with both shorter life expectancy and also relative more years spent in ill health.[5]

The consequence of this comparison is a mixed message. The number of years in poor health when measured as a proportion of whole life have been actually falling. On the other hand the proportion of years spent in poor health post 65 has increased, and it is this group, in some cases more prone to falls, dementia and other health issues that are generally regarded as 'Vulnerable'.

However, the suggestion that longevity implies a longer period of time spent in poor health has been challenged (Beard et al. 2011, Olshansky 2013). The argument is that improvements in public health and living conditions, an awareness of the perils of smoking (and other hazardous activities) and developments in health care diagnosis and treatment have combined to furnish what is described as a 'longevity dividend'. Olshanksy makes the following case for this longevity dividend:

- Treating disease has been effective in the past to extend healthy life but now ageing itself is a risk factor in health
- As people live longer the impact of ageing on disease (or morbidity) will become more important
- Science which focusses on ageing itself and seeks the means to delay or counter consequence of ageing will be the focus
- This will become the priority to avoid an older demographic becoming prone to increased morbidity
- There will be new medical paradigms focussed upon supporting people to live healthier lives in old age (Olshansky 2013).

The argument for a focus upon how to support people living longer lives in good health is seen as unanswerable and just as public health and medical science responded to diseases such as cholera and polio with appropriate remedies so the issue of longevity will also be addressed by a combination of scientific, public health and individual action. Smoking which is accepted as a major risk to health is no longer seen as simply addressed by surgery or medical treatment but rather has increasingly been the subject of public awareness and regulation (discouragement) by state action.

The benefits available through diet and exercise are well known (Elward and Larson, E.B., 1992, Benton 2015). An alternate future scenario is of a healthier old age to accompany the longer life expectancy which is being generally experienced in most countries (McMurdo 2000). Tai Chi has been shown to be beneficial to older people – something which has been known in China for many years (Docker 2006).

Lifelong Learning

The benefits of continuing education are well reported and well established and Jarvis has researched this extensively in a series of highly cited publications (Jarvis 2004, 2007, 2009). It is a global phenomenon and has a number of dimensions which are highly pertinent to public management and public policy.

One key element is economic in that it enables a workforce to be updated in knowledge and skills as the needs of the economy and the market change. Some skills acquired early in life though formal training or education are durable. These are typically 'soft' skills such as language fluency and interpersonal skills. Problem solving and creativity can be acquired through school and the ability is significantly retained typically through implicit usage in everyday life. However, technical environments change and when the nature of technology dramatically changes (such as the emergence of different IT systems and interfaces) then the earlier skills acquired may not suffice. One recent example (which I would suggest represents an expertise which none at the conference possesses) is that of writing in the language of emoji. In 2017 an advert appeared which offered professional expertise in teaching this to the uninitiated.[6]

However, strangely there are some technologies which are relatively impervious to the passage of time and the skills and knowledge acquired by this 60 something year old some 45 years ago is still as relevant now. I refer, of course, to the typewriter keyboard layout I am using that has resisted attempts to update it from its creation in 1873. Another form of technology resistant to change is the steering wheel which is still the prime means of changing direction on wheeled vehicles. Saab tried to replace it with a joystick but the concept proved unacceptable.[7]

The benefits of lifelong learning should not be seen simply in terms of economic benefit whether it be for the student, an employer or the state. As ageing is a particular issue in the land of Confucius perhaps it is fitting to use his own words to represent a concept of what lifelong learning might mean for those who are at a life stage where the economic benefits are not a prime motivator.

> At 70, I could follow the dictates of my own heart; for what I desired no longer overstepped the boundaries of right.

Confucius' observation about life stage is arguably as relevant now as it was when he made it. The pursuit of lifelong learning in older years is not a matter of state policy or institutional direction. Rather it is a personally driven activity which is undertaken in keeping with the individuals emotions and does not seek to have ambitions beyond that of the learning itself. Laal (2011) describes the nature of such learning through a separation into formal, non-formal and informal:

- **Formal learning** consists of learning that occurs within an organised and structured context (formal education, in-company training), and that is designed as learning. It may lead to formal recognition (diploma, certificate)
- **Non formal learning** consists of learning embedded in planned activities that are not explicitly designated as learning, but which contain an important learning element such as vocational skills acquired at the workplace
- **Informal learning** is defined as learning resulting from daily life activities related to family, work or leisure. It is often referred to as experiential learning and can, to a degree, be understood as accidental learning (Laal 2011)

In later years lifelong learning could be seen as moving away from the early and mid-life focus upon formal and informal learning and encompassing a great element of informal learning. It recognises that learning is an activity that happens throughout our life. Some may be viewed as practical to enable re-skilling of people in employment. But it is also viewed as a 'good in itself'. However, it has a civic benefit (a well-educated population is one that does not stop learning and it continues the engagement of citizens throughout their life cycle).

Lifelong Learning does not presume the actual form which learning takes and recognises the importance of informal learning as an important aspect.

University of the Third Age

As an example of this one can draw on the experience of the University of the Third Age. Its origins trace back to France in 1968, with an initiative at University of Toulouse and a consequent programme of learning activities for retired persons. The demand was such that when the programme ended there was pressure to continue it. The Toulouse initiative was associated with university studies on ageing, and admission was a simple form and a nominal fee. Later it expanded elsewhere in France, and the Union French University of the Third Age was founded in 1980 (Formosa 2012).

The U3A was established in UK in 1981 (in Cambridge). It did not link to a 'normal' university but focussed on a self-help model utilising the knowledge, skills and interests of those wishing to learn. There was a strong view that the university of the 3rd Age in the UK should be member led and not subject to the direction or guidance of any formal university or governmental entity.

This almost fierce independence has characterised the UK development since then. The University of the 3rd Age rapidly became an international phenomenon with developments in many countries. Early research suggested that the sorts of activities associated with this were positive for healthy ageing (Swindell and Thompson 1995).

Hence U3A (University of the Third Age) is a UK movement of retired and semi-retired people who come together to continue their educational, social and creative interests in a friendly and informal environment. The Vision and Mission is set out below.

The UK University of Third Age

Vision

To make lifelong learning, through the experience of U3A, a reality for all third agers.

Mission

Our purpose as an organisation and serves as the standard against which U3A weighs actions and decisions. It is to:

- Facilitate the growth of the U3A movement.
- Provide support for management and learning in U3As.
- Raise the profile of the U3A movement.
- Promote the benefits of learning in later life through self-help learning.

There have been a number of studies of the impact of membership of the University of the Third Age on well-being (Mitchell et al. 1997, Hammond 2002). These reports that involvement is beneficial to the well-being of the participants both in terms of self-reporting measures and using standard measures of well-being.

The growth of the University of the Third Age is remarkable. The University of the 3rd Age now has over 400,000 members in around 1,000 locations.[8]

In order to give the comparison with the UK university system one may note that according to official figures there were some 519,000 part time students in the UK university system in 2016–2017. Hence, the U3A has about 80 percent of the numbers of the official university equivalent.

One factor which emerges from research on the membership of the U3A in the UK is that there may be a lack of diversity of members. As with many academic or learning endeavours the benefits are not evenly distributed. Recent research by Patterson and colleagues show that for research undertaken in the North of England there was a clear tendency for less-deprived areas to have a better representation amongst membership. This raises a question as to whether public policy would be served by encouraging a greater diversity of participation in U3A (Patterson et al. 2016).

However, the U3A in membership terms has been a clear success as is shown by the year on year growth in numbers from 1980 to 2016. It reaches further than actual mainstream university provision with, for example, centres in places like the Shetland Islands which have no local university provision.

In public management and public policy terms the U3A is a provision which clearly reaches out to an older demographic (who may obviously also consider a regular university place). However, it is offered at no significant cost to the public purse and is run on a mutual basis by the members themselves. The cost benefit of this provision in terms of healthy ageing and civic engagement should have been explored and there is some literature (from Australia) which has done this.(Swindell and Vassella 1999). This research, however, simply attributes an hourly rate to the voluntary involvement of the organisers of the various U3A branches and attributed some $4 Million per year in value to this aspect (in 1999 Aus$ values). Arguably, this is an imperfect measure because it does not take account of the benefits derived through actual membership and participation in respect of costs avoided for public social and health care.

Redefining Retirement

The emergence of 65 as an age of retirement is long established with the first precedent being set in the 1880s in Germany (Costa 1988). Costa (1998) more recently retirement ages have been raised in a number of countries as a consequence of both increased life expectancy and also of concerns about pension costs.

This section does not propose to examine the detailed research on retirement and the factors which may determine when and how it happens. Rather the focus is upon the extent to which 'cliff edge' retirement has been replaced by a stepping down process by which people continue to work and also the extent to which retirement has become a less prescriptive term. To what extent are people either deferring their pension or taking their pension and continuing to work (as is the case with the author of this chapter).

The evidence (from UK) is that after a dip in the 1980s and 1990s the employment of men post retirement age (65) has shown a consistent upward trend. This is also generally true of other age groups but the pattern of the oldest age cohort has been consistently upward with only a small dip in 2008–2009 (the year of the financial crash).

The pattern is much the same for women except that (perhaps significantly) the financial crash of 2008–2009 was associated with an increase in employment of the oldest cohort.

An interesting aspect from the UK Foresight studies is the tendency for older workers to 'work from home'. The Office of National Statistics in a 2014 survey that over a third of people working 'post normal pension age' were working from home.[9] This could suggest that there was a higher likelihood of older workers either 'running their own business' or perhaps working in the self-employed, 'gig' economy.

> The implications for mental health of working post retirement are to either be not negative or actually positive in an analysis of a range of studies (Maimaris et al. 2010). However a recent doctoral thesis on working on 'post retirement' found that the quality of work itself was a significant intervening variable. Good quality work was associated with positive outcomes for the person working. Poor quality work was not.
>
> (Matthews 2014)

In effect, the reality is a move away from retirement as a 'cliff edge' departure from paid work. There is an increased tendency for people to regard working beyond the 'normal retirement age' as either attractive or perhaps as necessary.

Public policy and indeed public employment needs to acknowledge and take account of this. The public sector itself needs to set an example. In the USA in one small town the author visits the (part time) police chief and the fire chief are both men well into their 70s. This is not regarded as unexceptional in an area with a strong elderly demographic. However, the norm for many public bodies is to regard retirement ages as not subject to flexibility and indeed to see 'retirement' and sometimes early retirement as a solution to budgetary challenges and labour force restructuring.

Use of Technology

The evolution of technology, when it concerns older people, has clearly made a difference to how people live their lives. The usual perception of technology is around specifically designed items such as aids for people who are disabled or modifications to homes or to public and work spaces to assist the older person as a consequence of issues associated with ageing or disability.

However, innovations which are not age or disability specific present particular opportunities for older people to become more socially involved or to continue with employment. 'Driverless Cars' which are becoming a reality of life in a number of countries represent an enormous potential for older people who may confront a situation where they are no longer able to drive (Reimer 2014). This has obvious implications for public policy especially in areas where there are limited potential for public transport which is specifically designed for older people.

The growth of social media is viewed as particularly relevant for younger people. Facebook, Instagram and Skype are all technologies which have emerged in recent years. They are clearly seen as vital aids to communication by young people. However, even in 2009 the extension and adoption by older people was identified and subject to academic discussion (Ellison et al. 2009).

The importance of both these technologies in both communication and engagement of older people is arguably highly significant. The potential and the actuality is that these can enable continued connectedness of older people despite issues of distance and mobility. Loneliness and social isolation in older age is a well-established concern and is a factor of dispersed families, loss of mobility and loss of a partner (Wenger et al. 1996). Older people tend to move home less, and such moves are often associated with disruption and a loss of what local ties a person possesses. The public policy agenda (supported by research) supports 'ageing in place' where this is possible (Gilleard et al. 2007).

The UK Government is possibly the first in the world to recognise the importance of combatting loneliness with the appointment of a Minister for Loneliness in January 2018. Tracey Crouch (a former minister for charities) was appointed and the appointment aroused considerable comment and publicity (including comment from diverse countries such as Mexico and India). The comment from China may be worth noting: The Chinese report quoted the UK Prime Minister

> For far too many people, loneliness is the sad reality of modern life. I want to confront this challenge for our society and for all of us to take action to address the loneliness endured by the elderly, by carers, by those who have lost loved ones -- people who have no one to talk to or share their thoughts and experiences with.[10]

The usual and traditional response to loneliness of older people involves encouraging 'home visits', provision of meals and engagement in various clubs and activities. However, the potential for technologies such as driverless cars and social media to play a key part here is both present and could potentially enhance connectiveness and, for some older people, assist in retention or participation in work activities.

Lifestyle Choices

The final aspect of ageing which we will consider is the decisions and options which current and future older generations may make. The option to withdraw and to live an increasingly limited life with a possible plan to, in extremis, move to supported private or state care (Featherstone and Hepworth 1998). However, current and future older demographics are likely to seek a path in which ageing is viewed as 'positive' or 'active' as opposed to a passive acquiescence in physical and mental decline (Walker 2002, 2008 and 2012).

Active Ageing is acquiring a consensus over its nature and definition. In 2002 the World Health Organisation defined it as optimising opportunities for health, participation and security in order to enhance quality of life as people age (Boudiny 2013). However Boudiny suggested the following division into Unidimensional and Multidimensional approaches.

Type 1 Unidimensional approaches which tend to focus on an economic (typically through employment) engagement through people continuing to be active. These are clearly amenable to a range of government policy measures to encourage continual engagement though, for example, tax and pension incentives. Raising retirement ages (especially for eligibility for state pension) is a crude but effective instrument which aroused obvious and mixed emotions in those affected.

However, positive measures such as reskilling and training for older demographics is also a factor.

However, such an approach has issues in terms of the active ageing concept which the WHO defines as appropriate which enjoins social and cultural engagement and also may not correspond to the definition of positive ageing which people themselves possess. It is also not inclusive as it focusses on the realm of employment.

Type 2 Multidimensional approaches are therefore viewed as more appropriate for conceptualizing 'active ageing'. Here the stress is upon active engagement in a number of domains. Hence leisure activities become important. Active Ageing is viewed along 5 dimensions.

- paid labour,
- care and
- voluntary work
- sports
- active recreation outdoors

The European Commission also devised a multidimensional approach which includes the following (Oxley 2009)

- lifelong learning,
- working longer,
- retiring later
- being active after retirement, and
- engaging in capacity-enhancing and health-sustaining activities

These concepts of active ageing however do not fully capture lifestyle trends and I will conclude by considering a lifestyle trend found especially in the USA and in Australia. This is a trend that changes the concept of ageing in place to one of mobility. The numbers are significant and growing and relate to older people who are often financially comfortable and who are in reasonably good health. In the USA the term 'snowbirds' is used to describe a particular older demographic who, like birds, migrate between different places typically following the weather. So in the winter some South Western USA states find an influx of older people often driving recreational vehicles who in the summer have been in the Northern part of the USA.

In Australia the term 'grey nomads' has become an accepted and widely used term with a semi formalized membership and a detailed web presence.[11] Here the movement is not so much seasonal but just a general desire to live 'on the road' often supported by occasional employment. One such person interviewed by the author had no permanent home address other than a storage facility and was running an online business whilst 'living on the road'.

There has been an emerging body of research into these 'new age' older people.

Shoemaker (2000) identified three distinct clusters or market segments.

- 'An escape and learn group' with a focus on new experiences, relaxation and escape from routine.
- 'A retirees group', who tend to be older and who seek to return to the same destinations rather than explore new ones (these would perhaps describe some of the USA 'snowbirds'.
- 'An active storytellers group' with a stress on socialising, seeking new experiences, physical activities and intellectual enrichment.

In Australia, a study identified motivation patterns among older travellers, five such patterns emerged (Environmetrics 1991).

- 'reunion' (pilgrimage to the past),
- 'recuperation' (rest, peace and quiet),
- 'circulation' (indulgence, comfort, pampering),
- 'reduction' (see it before I die),
- 'exploration' (active involvement)

A slightly later study ion Australian grey nomads conceptualised the motivations slightly differently (Cleaver, Muller, Ruys and Wei 1999) The four largest clusters were:

- 'nostalgics' who travel to renew memories,
- 'friendlies' who seek to socialise and like readymade, safe packages,
- 'learners' who seek new experiences, adventure, new learning,
- 'escapists' who seek carefree fun and relaxation.

The lesson from these studies is that even in one lifestyle choice (to be on the move as opposed to ageing in place) there are a diversity of motivations. This potentially has implications for public policy and public management. There are a range of nuances and motivations in how people choose to 'active actively'. Public policy has to be flexible and creative in order to both utilise the potential of active agers and to develop appropriate responses to meet identified needs. How does the public sector adjust to a demographic which has chosen not to live in any one particular place but which rightly expects to receive the appropriate public services to which they have entitlement through citizenship and from long contributions through taxation (and who may be continuing to contribute through taxation)?

Discussion and Conclusions

The realities of an ageing demographic across most countries of the world is a cause for celebration. It marks the triumph of public health and medical science over the unhealthy conditions and infectious diseases which were generally the lot of past generations, some of whom are still alive to recall them. It also represents a measure of human progress and the acquisition of knowledge about how to live better lives and general improvements in work with the reduction of risk.

However, much of the public-sector policy discourse has focussed on the nature of such longevity as a challenge which involves enhanced pressures on health and social care provision, a growing population imbalance which places burdens upon the younger generation and a perception of the ageing demographic as 'takers rather than givers' now that they are regarded as no longer making an economic contribution to the state.

The focus has been to examine the alternate discourse which views the ageing demographic in a positive light. It is suggested that this demographic will live significantly positive and engaged lives. The 'baby boomers' who are now at or beyond the age of 'anticipated' retirement are significantly opting to continue in work activity. Equally the assumptions about how the current and future older generations will live their lives are based upon current and past experience. Factors such as lifelong learning and technology will probably have a significant effect. The current and future older generations will very probably live in a more positive and informed manner. Factors such as reduction in harmful practices such as smoking and a greater awareness of the importance of diet and exercise are likely to confound predictions of the extent of Healthy Life expectancy. Reduced family ties through smaller family size and geographic dispersion which could lead to isolation and potential loneliness in old age may be offset by the impact of technology which enables greater connectivity.

The lesson for public management and public policy is to be aware of the risk of a 'dependency' mind set, or categorisation as 'vulnerable' in terms of how older age cohorts are perceived. Rather there needs to be a conscious focus upon the positive contribution and engagement in active ageing which may become more typical of this demographic. In some cases this may be associated with the emergence of lifestyles which might be more typical of a young and relatively carefree demographic.

The examples of lifelong learning and the consequent growth of the U3A presents an alternative future of an engaged older population who actively and positively seek out opportunities to continue to learn and be intellectually and socially engaged in their later years. The dramatic expansion of the U3A (which has had no particular encouragement from government or public policy) is indicative of how the choices of individuals and of civil society can bring about change. Perhaps interestingly the government policy and funding focus has offered little or no incentive for the U3A to develop – yet it did.

The expansion of employment (and self-employment) in a demographic which traditionally were seen as 'post work' is arguably generally a positive phenomenon in that work furnishes both meaning and also social engagement. This does not deny the reality that for some the choice to continue working is engendered by a financial imperative. Here government policy in raising the state pension age may clearly have had a role – though the motivation was perhaps not to 'encourage active and positive ageing' but rather the address concerns about balancing the public accounts.

The impact of technology will also play a part. The growth of social media means that people who have mobility problems or who are geographically isolated may have a means to be socially engaged in a way that was previously either technologically difficult or financially costly. The growth of 'driverless cars' seen perhaps as something for the millennials to facilitate a time- or resource-constrained lifestyle may in fact be a major factor for older people who find themselves no longer able to drive especially if they live in rural areas with poor public transport.

Finally there is the whole question of actual differences in the lifestyle choices that the 'baby boomer' generation may make which are different from those of their parents. Intergenerational and co-operative living innovations are on the increase, and these are not being determined through specific government action but through a combination of the desires and resource decisions of the older demographic, many of whom would vehemently rail against any categorisation of themselves as dependent, problem demographics or in need of public policy 'assistance'.

Notes

1 See www.gov.uk/government/collections/future-of-ageing Accessed 18 May 2018.
2 See ONS National Population Projections: 2014-based Statistical Bulletin www.ons.gov.uk/peoplepopulationandcommunity/populationandmigration/populationprojections/bulletins/nationalpopulationprojections/2015-10-29#2014-based-principal-population-projections Accessed 11 Feb 2020.
3 ONS op cit.
4 See https://data.worldbank.org/indicator/SP.DYN.LE00.IN Accessed 11 Feb 2020.
5 See www.ageing-better.org.uk/news/response-ons-statistics-healthy-life-expectancy?gclid=EAIaIQobChMIgaSMjczO5wIVh7HtCh2KWwDQEAAYASAAEgLrZvD_BwE Accessed 11 Feb 2020.
6 See www.todaytranslations.com/news/the-world-s-first-emoji-translator Accessed 18 May 2018.
7 See www.bbc.com/autos/story/20140122-should-we-drive-with-joysticks Accessed 18 May 2018.
8 See www.u3a.org.uk/about/history Accessed 11 Feb 2020.
9 Source ONS (2014) Characteristics of Home Workers, 2014 Release http://webarchive.nationalarchives.gov.uk/20160105160709/www.ons.gov.uk/ons/dcp171776_365592.pdf Accessed 10 Feb 2020.
10 See www.china.org.cn/world/2018-01/18/content_50239439.htm Accessed 18 May 2018.
11 See www.thegreynomads.com.au Accessed 18 May 2018.

References

Albury, D., 2011. Creating the conditions for radical public service innovation. *Australian Journal of Public Administration*, 70(3), pp. 227–235.

Pilichowski, E., Arnould, E. and Turkisch, E. (2007) Ageing and the Public Sector: Challenges for Financial and Human Resources, *OECD Journal on Budgeting*, 7(4), pp. 1–40.

Baars, J., Dannefer, D., Phillipson, C. and Walker, A. eds., 2016. *Aging, globalization and inequality: The new critical gerontology*. London: Routledge.

Beard, J.R., Biggs, S., Bloom, D.E., Fried, L.P., Hogan, P., Kalache, A. and Olshansky, S.J., eds. 2011. *Global population ageing: Peril or promise*. World Economic Forum, Geneva.

Benton, M.J., 2015. Benefits of exercise for older adults. In Sullivan, G. M., and Pomidor, A. K. eds. *Exercise for Aging Adults* (pp. 13–27). Springer, Cham.

Boudiny, K., 2013. 'Active ageing': From empty rhetoric to effective policy tool. *Ageing & Society*, 33(6), pp. 1077–1098.

Cleaver, M., Muller, T.E., Ruys, H.F. and Wei, S., 1999. Tourism product development for the senior market, based on travel-motive research. *Tourism Recreation Research*, 24(1), pp. 5–11.

Costa, D.L., 1998. The evolution of retirement. In Costa, D. L. ed. *The Evolution of Retirement: An American Economic History, 1880–1990* (pp. 6–31). University of Chicago Press.

Davies, A., 2011. On constructing ageing rural populations: 'Capturing' the grey nomad. *Journal of Rural Studies*, 27(2), pp. 191–199.

Docker, S.M., 2006. Tai Chi and older people in the community: A preliminary study. *Complementary Therapies in Clinical Practice*, 12(2), pp. 111–118.

Ellison, N.B., Lampe, C. and Steinfield, C., 2009. Feature social network sites and society: Current trends and future possibilities. *Interactions*, 16(1), pp. 6–9.

Elward, K. and Larson, E.B., 1992. Benefits of exercise for older adults. A review of existing evidence and current recommendations for the general population. *Clinics in Geriatric Medicine*, 8(1), pp. 35–50.

Featherstone, M. and Hepworth, M., 1998. Ageing, the lifecourse and the sociology of embodiment. *Modernity, Medicine and Health: Medical Sociology Towards, 2000*, pp. 147–175.

Formosa, M., 2012. Education and older adults at the University of the Third Age. *Educational Gerontology*, 38(2), pp. 114–126.

Gilleard, C., Hyde, M. and Higgs, P., 2007. The impact of age, place, aging in place, and attachment to place on the well-being of the over 50s in England. *Research on Aging*, 29(6), pp. 590–605.

Hammond, C. 2002. What is it about education that makes us healthy? Exploring the education-health connection. *International Journal of Lifelong Education*, 21(6), pp. 551–571.

Harper, S., 2010. The capacity of social security and health care institutions to adapt to an ageing world. *International Social Security Review*, 63(3–4), pp. 177–196.

Harper, S., 2014. Economic and social implications of aging societies. *Science*, 346(6209), pp. 587–591.

Harper, S. and Hamblin, K. eds., 2014. *International handbook on ageing and public policy*. Cheltenham, Northampton, MA: Edward Elgar Publishing.

Hendricks, J. and Hatch, L.R., 2010. Lifestyle and aging. In George, L. ed. *Handbook of Aging and the Social Sciences, (Sixth Edition)* (pp. 301–319). London: Academic Press, Elsevier.

Howker, E. and Malik, S., 2013. *Jilted generation: How Britain has bankrupted its youth*. London: Icon Books.

Jarvis, P., 2004. *Adult education and lifelong learning: Theory and practice*. London: Routledge.

Jarvis, P., 2007. *Globalization, lifelong learning and the learning society: Sociological perspectives*. London: Routledge.

Jarvis, P. ed., 2009. *The Routledge international handbook of lifelong learning*. Routledge.

Laal, M., 2011. Lifelong learning: What does it mean?. *Procedia-Social and Behavioral Sciences*, Jan 1, *28*, pp. 470–474.

Mann, K., 2007. Activation, retirement planning and restraining the 'third age'. *Social Policy and Society*, 6(3), pp. 279–292.

Maimaris, W., Hogan, H. and Lock, K., 2010. The impact of working beyond traditional retirement ages on mental health: Implications for public health and welfare policy. *Public Health Reviews*, 32(2), p. 532.

Matthews, K., 2014. *Is working beyond state pension age beneficial for health?: Evidence from the English longitudinal study of ageing* (Doctoral dissertation, University of Manchester).

McMurdo, M.E., 2000. A healthy old age: Realistic or futile goal?. *British Medical Journal*, 321(7269), p. 1149.

Mitchell, R.A., Legge, V. and Sinclair-Legge, G., 1997. Membership of the University of the Third Age (U3A) and perceived well-being. *Disability and Rehabilitation*, 19(6), pp. 244–248.

Olshansky, S.J., 2013. Articulating the case for the longevity dividend. *Public Policy Aging Rep*, *23*, pp. 3–6.

Onyx, J. and Leonard, R., 2005. Australian grey nomads and American snowbirds: Similarities and differences. *Journal of Tourism Studies*, 16(1), p. 61.

Oxley, H., 2009. *Policies for healthy ageing: An overview*. Organisation for Economic Co-operation and Development (OECD) Health Working Papers No.42 OECD Publishing, Paris.

Patterson, R., Moffatt, S., Smith, M., Scott, J., Mcloughlin, C., Bell, J. and Bell, N., 2016. Exploring social inclusivity within the University of the Third Age (U3A): A model of collaborative research. *Ageing & Society*, 36(8), pp. 1580–1603.

Payne, A.R., 2015. Intergovernmental management: The Silver Tsunami effect, an essay. *Studies in Social Sciences and Humanities*, 2(2), pp. 88–98.

Pollitt, C., 2016. Be prepared? An outside-in perspective on the future public sector in Europe. *Public Policy and Administration*, 31(1), pp. 3–28.

Reimer, B., 2014. Driver assistance systems and the transition to automated vehicles: A path to increase older adult safety and mobility?. *Public Policy & Aging Report*, 24(1), pp. 27–31.

Shoemaker, S., 2000. Segmenting the mature market: 10 years later. *Journal of Travel Research*, 39(1), pp. 11–26.

Swindell, R. and Thompson, J., 1995. An international perspective on the University of the Third Age. *Educational Gerontology: An International Quarterly*, 21(5), pp. 429–447.

Swindell, R. and Vassella, K., 1999. Money talks: Ascribing a dollar value to voluntarism in Australian and New Zealand U3As. *Australasian Journal on Ageing*, 18(1), pp. 19–22.

Vincent, J., 1996. Who's afraid of an ageing population? Nationalism, the free market, and the construction of old age as an issue. *Critical Social Policy*, 16(47), pp. 3–26.

Walker, A., 2002. A strategy for active ageing. *International Social Security Review*, 55(1), pp. 121–139.

Walker, A., 2008. Commentary: The emergence and application of active aging in Europe. *Journal of Aging & Social Policy*, 21(1), pp. 75–93.

Walker, A. and Maltby, T., 2012. Active ageing: A strategic policy solution to demographic ageing in the European Union. *International Journal of Social Welfare*, 21(s1), pp. S117–S130.

Wenger, G.C., Davies, R., Shahtahmasebi, S. and Scott, A., 1996. Social isolation and loneliness in old age: Review and model refinement. *Ageing & Society*, 16(3), pp. 333–358.

Willetts, D., 2011. *Pinch: How the baby boomers took their children's future-and why they should give it back*. Holborn, London: Atlantic Books.

11 The Important Voices of Care Experienced People in Relation to Services

Stephanie Hunter, Susan Mckenna, Rachel Close, and Rachel Woodley

Introduction

The salient concept of vulnerability is thoughtfully explored within this book. Arguably the most vulnerable group in current society is the young people who have been exposed to the care system and those who have left care. Within this chapter the author will use the term care leavers which was coined in the Children Leaving Care Act 2000. This is a contemporary social issue as the number of children in the care of the local authority in the United Kingdom is the highest level ever at 70,720 (Fostering network, 2018). Indeed, Oakley et al. (2018) described the poor outcomes for "looked after"' children as a silent crisis, lambasting the lack of political action for the 100,000 children who flow in and out of the care system each year in the UK. The increased numbers may reflect the decimation of early help and preventative services for example Action for Children (2018) estimate 1000 Sure Start Centre's have closed in the last decade. It is noteworthy that during the period Sure Start Centre's peaked providing childcare, early help and preventative services in deprived areas, correlating with the only period in history the numbers of children in care reduced in 2006 during a period of Labor government in England (Shoesmith, 2016).

The increase in children in care is perceived by Gupta (2018) to be a consequence of public-sector cuts enforced politically and termed "austerity". A further influence has been increasingly risk averse social work practice since the death of baby Peter in 2007 (Shoesmith, 2016). Baby Peter was killed by his mother's boyfriend during a period of social work involvement. A media moral panic, a term coined by Cohen (1972) followed Peter's tragic death and the figures of children in care rose rapidly after his death while simultaneously preventative services were reduced. Hence, less help to keep children out of care, less help available when in care and continued poor outcomes for those young people who leave care. This will be explored and linked to small scale exploratory research undertaken in 2019.

The Outcomes for Children in Care

The challenges experienced by care experienced children and young people include mental health difficulties, poor educational outcomes, increased risk of homelessness and tragically suicide. Indeed, care experienced young people continue to be more likely to go to prison than University (Nicholson, 2011). Research undertaken by Shelter (2018) indicated 20 percent of care leavers experience homelessness within two years of leaving the care system. Shelter's research also established that the life expectancy of homeless adults is halved. As public health is measured by mortality and morbidity rates, this early experience of displacement and destitution requires the urgent agent of policy makers.

The average homeless person usually dies in their 40s compared to their 70s in comparison to the rest of the population. It is ineffably sad that their lifestyle is challenged by immense vulnerability to hunger, weather extremities and danger from others. Additionally, the homeless are of course at an elevated risk of serious disease, illness, and even death as a consequence of appalling social conditions and poor sanitation arising from the devastating consequences of having no permanent home. The issues of housing stability is salient to the voices within this chapter as all participants have experienced multiple moves and instability in spite of protective factors including intelligence and educational achievement. The absence of a family to provide stability is significant. Currently half of under 25-year-olds still live with their parents, given the high cost of home ownership. Contrastingly most children in care are still expected to leave care by the age of 18. There are positive initiatives, including "Staying Put", introduced in the Children and Families Act 2014 which encourages foster carers to support children beyond 18. However, there is no equivalent safeguard for children in residential care who tend to have the highest mental health difficulties and complex needs. Positively Rachel Woodley who contributed to this chapter reported valuing the staff support in a children's home but did find the transition to independence challenging, thereby echoing related studies which influenced the "Staying Put" policy.

The Scottish Review in relation to Understanding suicide and self-harm amongst children in care published in 2013 highlighted significant statistical risks of suicide. This is of course all of huge political and societal concern. It is also sadly increasingly understood that care leavers are statistically up to 18 times more likely to have their children removed by the local authority (Featherstone, 2017, cited in Hunter, 2018). Tzanakis (2011) reviewed the work of Bourdieu (1977) and his exploration of cultural transmission theories highlighted the social reproduction of poverty and instability from generation to generation. These theories are relevant to the issues children in care face. This process of cultural transmission occurs at a young age. Services need to be intervening early to increase life chances and opportunities.

The concerns that care leavers are more likely to have their children removed are highlighted, within the British Association of Social Work report in relation to Human Rights and adoption (Gupta et al., 2018). This thoughtful and original research drew important attention to the voices of adoptive parents, adopted children as well as the marginalized voices of birth parents, many of whom are care leavers. The voices of the vulnerable parents losing their children to adoption is crucial as they reported they often did not receive appropriate or timely services to help prevent family breakdown and the loss of their children to adoption.

Key Research

It is also understood within Selwyn et al.'s seminal research in 2015 that the ineffable pain and loss associated with this separation hugely impacts on the children with only a third of adoptions appearing to be consistently stable. Worryingly, close to a third of adopted children experience at times quite chronic emotional instability, with a significant number of adoptions disrupting. Figures in relation to adoption disruption vary, but 10 percent is viewed as the most likely figure or percentage of children whose adoptive parent return them to the care system. Children placed for adoption after the age of five are at a particular risk to disruption. The adoptions which involve children attached to birth parents may be the most vulnerable group as it was found that without contact they can hold a misplaced resentment towards their adoptive parents. This is statistically relevant as the age of children placed for adoption has risen since Tony Blair and the then Labour Prime Minister's Cabinet reviewed adoption and placed emphasis on this as the preferred choice of permanence for children in the care system. They highlighted the issues raised by this author in a publication in 2018, focussing on the impact of austerity on children in care children (Hunter cited in Rushton and Donovan, 2018). Gupta (2018) emphasized the need to better understand the most effective way to engage with care experienced voices and how best to help those affected by the care system.

This chapter contributes to important thinking in relation to vulnerability, as it will be authored by adult women who have experienced foster care, adoption and a plethora of contemporary health and social care services. They will highlight strengths and weaknesses in systems which are currently recognized by the Association of the Directors of social services as at breaking point (Bunn, 2019). The three young women can and do comment on services they received or missed in the last decade. It is laudable and a testament to their post traumatic growth that they have navigated services themselves, then worked professionally in helping others. Therefore, this chapter is developed from a unique and credible positionality. Few care experienced adults have acquired sufficient opportunity to develop the social and educational capital to make published observations in relation to their life path. Theorists including Bourdieu (1984) and Nicholson (2011) are referenced; the latter's work focusses on deracination and the trauma resulting from constantly uprooting vulnerable young people. Bourdieu also commented upon the complex ways in which power is created in society and generationally transferred. He developed the term described as symbolic violence which illustrates the injurious impact misused power can have upon individuals. This theory is of course highly relevant to care leavers as they are probably the most marginalized and stigmatized groups in society. It is argued that Bourdieu's theory is relevant as it is a type of violence which ejects young people from residential care aged 18 to live mainly alone and unsupported in often substandard social housing in socially deprived areas. It is perhaps not unsurprising that many become homeless and criminalized misusing substances as inappropriate self-medication. Rohner (2004) studies involved magnetic resonance imaging of rejected adult's brains he found the Dorsal Posterior Insula the "pain centre" of the brain was activated. This study in some way explains the physical and emotional challenges for children in care. All three co-authors, whose voices are articulated within this chapter, described professionals changing their interactions negatively in relation to their status as care leavers. Within this chapter I will apply these theoretical explanations to the challenges that children in care and care leavers face.

Methodology

A life history approach advanced by Mannay et al. (2019) was the chosen methodology as this is designed to empower these important voices. Crucial themes in relation to placements, social work support, access to services and the fluidity of vulnerability will be examined within this chapter. Important theoretical frameworks in relation to attachment and trauma will also be explored.

Corresponding with Mannay's model (2019) the themes were loosely agreed with the three research co-authors. This was designed to reduce power imbalances that exist in society and may be replicated in research. It was important this work represented the experiences as the participants perceived them. To ensure the themes were identified by those with a positionality in which they genuinely have experienced services. Reflexivity also developed within the writing as the topics were explored during a meaningful dialogue. The participants are also co collaborators and co-authors within this work. The involvement of only women was co incidental. In relation to gender the only observation I can note is all the participants had brothers who they loved and felt attached to but were unable to be placed with them long term, creating disruptions in their important sibling bonds.

It was agreed the work would be edited as a collective to ensure power was evenly distributed. Data was collected face to face during semi-structured interviews with two participants and via telephone with a third, due to practical challenges. All three participants invested in the research as they were keen to highlight the voices of children in care and all three sent written data, which is also included.

The term co-production has been included within policy from the vital white paper "Putting People First" (Department of Health, 2007) then more recently featuring within the Guidance for Care Act (2014). There is a significant body of literature in relation to co-production. Bovaird (2016) asserted co production was much more than engagement with service users and should aim to be a meaningful partnership.

This co-production involved providing interventions which are co-produced to encourage full participation and reduction in power relations. This model of working also influenced the approaches to this research. It was an endeavour to harness and value the expertise of the individuals involved (Dix et al., 2019). This cannot be overlooked as without the participant's contribution these findings would not be possible.

The lead author also has relevant experience of services as she qualified as a social worker in 1997 working in CAFCASS, Children's mental health services and latterly as an academic. Therefore, the leading author can comment and make relevant observations on contemporary social work services in relation to staff changes, data protection and policy breaches. Modern social work is conducted within the challenge of austerity, budget cuts, and social work retention challenges. It is also a concern, that in spite of contemporary changes to legislation including Practice Direction 12J clarifying how to address domestic abuse cases introduced in Family Proceedings rules in 2017. It is still considered by Women's Aid and women's charities that domestic abuse in still overlooked or minimized due to complex issues including misogyny and patriarchy. These issues are currently under review by the Ministry of Justice in August 2019 after a number of child deaths following court ordered contact (Woman's Aid, 29 child homicides 2016). The latter is relevant as being re-abused is a greater risk after survivors leave the perpetrators, and unfortunately this small-scale research identified the fact that co-authors had experienced domestic abuse then re-abuse as a consequence of variable responses from services.

All of the health and social care issues identified must influence outcomes and the "felt" experiences of service users. The impact of the social work recruitment and retention challenges must ultimately impact on outcomes and the well-being and recovery of service users. The author herself is also a social worker, as is another participant. Of the other contributors one works in army social welfare. The other two women are studying, one to PhD level. Ethically the participants were able to choose the research topics and withdraw consent should they choose to do so. It was also agreed that any sensitive data they felt was too personal could be withdrawn, as ethical considerations outweighed the sharing of the data collected. While all the participants had painful and challenging childhoods, to their credit, they wished to contribute to a greater understanding of social care concerns to help others.

Findings

In line with Mannay's (2009) collaborative research model the themes were identified together and developed reflexively. These are the themes within the findings:

1 The need for professionals to be trauma informed:
   "I needed Trauma informed professionals, who could acknowledge what I had been through" (RC).
2 Services:
   "I did not always get the help I needed. I would love to write a book about my experiences, a book to help others overcome adversity" (RW).
3 Attachment relationships:
   "The ineffable pain of wanting to be found and not lost. I so wanted attention and it costs so little" (RC).
4 Impact of adverse early childhood experiences:
   "In spite of knowing what I deserved I still could not ask for what I needed" (SM).
5 Unfair judgements:
   "Remember the relationships are not equal and they never stick around anyway. They judge and move on and I was left" (RW).
6 Seeking a home and keeping a home:
   "I have done what I have to. As I have had to be adaptable and resilient" (SM).
7 Stigma:
   "There felt like many nasty voices when I was in care. So much judgement. One kind voice would have been enough" (RW).

Themes were developed collaboratively during the early stages of this research. The topics were not imposed on participants but decided together. In order to be ethical and supportive services were sometimes discussed in these life history conversations. For example Lemn Sissay, the poet, public speaker, actor, and care leaver, runs a Christmas initiative for fellow care leavers to reduce social isolation and feelings such as the co-authors movingly described. This has developed to a national level but none of the co-authors were aware of it.

The themes will be linked to research and theoretical frameworks to best understand the data; however the voices of the participants need full attention as they are moving and relevant to modern discussions on vulnerability.

1. The need for professionals to be trauma informed

The theme in relation to trauma informed responses was identified as the most important. This is unsurprising as all of the participants felt they had no voice at times to express their feelings and recover from trauma and abuse.

All participants understandably described struggles with emotions, relationships, and feelings of loss. Of concern services were not always available or sufficiently trauma informed as one co-author explained.

> I needed trauma informed people who would stick around and ac-knowledge how difficult it had been. As well as acknowledge the trauma, I needed them to understand and reflect how difficult signif-icant life events can be, Christmas, birthdays are difficult, birthdays are difficult. People offer to have you but they do not seem able to acknowledge the pain that you don't feel you belong.
>
> (RC)

2. Services

Some of the co-authors were not fully aware of some of the provision for care leavers, including higher education practical and financial sup-port. Given that the local authority is viewed as a corporate parent to children in care it is a corporate failing if care leavers are given insuf-ficient information in relation to support services. Lack of information may influence the proportionately small numbers of care experienced young people who go to University, which rose to 12 percent in 2017 from 6 percent the previous year; however, this is still very small com-pared to the 42 percent of the general population of young people who go to University. Harrison in 2017 conducted research with 212 care experienced students in Higher Education and found they were over a third more likely not to complete their studies. Positively, if they did complete the degree courses they were as likely to receive high grades as their peers. Harrison (2017) argued for more support for care leavers and flexible further education routes to higher education. Concerningly Allen Kinross (2018) reported an 8 percent cut in funding for learners aged 16–18.

This is an important area for consideration as services for students with emotional difficulties or care experiences need to be promoted and easily accessible and non-stigmatizing. Currently all require proof of care experiences. Other University benefits may be accessible, such as considering, disabled student allowance which is designed to meet the extra costs associated with studying with a disability this can include emotional difficulties. Some student services are developing and areas such as Sunderland with high numbers of care leavers have developed dedicated support for care experienced students. There is a bursary for care experienced students in England. In Scotland this is developed further, and accommodation costs up to 105 pounds is available outside of term time. One co-author noted, "It was more generous when I lived in Scotland. I got my fees paid. I didn't know I could get a bursary in England" (RW). The findings will now be developed further in categorized themes although it is apparent that the themes are interlinked and many understandably relate to the importance of children having access to reliable, caring emotionally intelligent adults.

3. Attachment relationships: The ineffable pain of wanting to be found and not lost (RC)

Attachment theory developed by Bowlby (1907–1990) has significantly influenced contemporary social work practice. The negative impact of ruptured relationships on children is now much better understood and academics including Nicholson (2011) have considered the impact of deracination on looked after children. He proposed that the constant uprooting increased the risk of emotional instability and even future incarceration. He argued that relationship ruptures must be minimized to avoid the care system being re-abusive. One participant said, "I had few connected people as a child. Sometimes my disobedience was acknowledged but it was more effective if they acknowledged my determination. I so wanted to be paid attention and it costs so little" (RC). The participant elaborated that education was a positive force as "they looked for me if I went missing" (RC). Clearly as a child she equated being looked for as being connected and cared for. The power of attachment seeking behaviour may be illustrated here. It is clearly possible that some young people go missing in care to be found not lost. The tragic reality given the figures of children missing from the care system is that for many they are sadly found by predators and paedophiles (RBSCB Overview report in relation to Rochdale. 20th December 2013).

Certainly all the co-authors had lived in multiple geographic locations and only one had sufficient financial capital to purchase a home. Given the cost of housing and the reliance many young people have on their parents to join the property ladder, this is perhaps unsurprising. While some councils had agreed in 2018 to reduce council tax for children in care, not all have accepted this as their corporate responsibility. This policy was probably influenced by the Children's Society report entitled "Wolf at the door", highlighting issues with council house debt as sadly this debt can be a precursor to homelessness. The Children's Society and other charities active campaigning has influenced one in six councils to currently exempt care leavers from council tax. It is a small step in bridging the habitus issues which can plague children in care (Bourdieu, 1984). Children in care are often placed in areas of deprivation with insufficient independence skills or resources to avoid homelessness or at the least chronic housing instability.

Contemporary professionals in relation to children in care comment on the importance of mental health services which do not rely solely on talking therapies (Armiger, 2019). He emphasized it may be the carers and staff who need the mental health advice and training. This was borne out poignantly by all participants. The painful, early experience of unmet needs meant "In spite of knowing what I deserve I still could not ask for what I needed" (SM). Each of the participants echoed the point that they needed caregivers who were skilled in almost mind reading or second guessing their needs as they may be unable to articulate what they deserved as the imprint of care experiences meant they may think or understand they are worthy or "deserving" but on a primitive, unconscious level feel undeserving. Fonagey (2006) and other psychiatry experts indicate what may be needed are caregivers skilled in mentalization or the ability to understand the mental state of oneself or others and the influence on overt behaviour. Interestingly all the participants appeared highly aware of the mental states and perceived emotional states of those around them and made consequent and often exhausting adaptions. For example they had at times grown used to making adaptions and accommodations to parents/care givers who were unable to meet their needs, then continued this at times within adult relationships.

Put simply, children gain an understanding of themselves and emotional world as a consequence of caregiver's reaction to their behaviour. Participants who experienced unreliable care and reactions indicated they had learned to second guess what people were communicating in relationships. They were all intuitive about the fact that past relationships had been fear based, which impacted on their capacity to trust attachment figures fully. Therefore until children in care have an experience of care givers who "second guess" or "wondering" as Dan Hughes (2008) advocates to help them begin to develop self-awareness and identify what they need emotionally. They may not develop the capacity to feel worthy enough to ask past carers or indeed friends to come to graduations or similar important events. This of course then magnifies and resonates with former losses.

Examples were repeatedly given of co-authors working tirelessly to not over depend on adults and the appreciation they placed on help other adults may take for granted. In some instances carers who were reliable were almost elevated to being placed on a pedestal level. However the limitations are the participants then had to ensure they remained on this pedestal and this involved not asking too much. Participants expressed themes of "enough". Not being enough for past family figures or being "too much". It is possible if these extremes of feelings reflect experiences of neglect "never experiencing enough of the care they needed" or abuse "getting much too much or more than enough" abusive care.

4. Impact of adverse early childhood experiences

In recent years an interest has developed in research in relation to the impact of adverse childhood experiences. It is linked to morbidity and early mortality (Filelitti 1998). The original study explored the potential impact of traumatic childhood experiences occurring under the age of 17. The impact was highlighted within this research: with sadness one co-author said, "I can hear my birth parent almost say to me: I know you're not good enough" (RW). So tangible were the experiences of abuse and rejection, all recognized the value of counselling, therapy, and trauma informed adults to help them recover. However, access to therapy was not easy to achieve, they reported. One participant said, "I was never seen alone by a social worker. I did not know it was my right". She lamented the lack of opportunity to talk privately and said sadly, "I needed them to say do you want to be seen alone? I did not have the self-esteem to ask to be seen alone and feared repercussions if I was honest in front of caregivers" (RW). This captures the experience of feeling not valued, not enough of a person to request help themselves and needing professionals to allow genuine opportunities for meaningful dialogue to develop these skills. Many serious case reviews have highlighted the need to see children alone to keep them safe. It is of course more than this: it is the tangible expression of valuing the voices of children in care. There are also many published findings on carers' conflicted feelings. Chard (2019) summarized key messages from research that carers can feel conflicted, loyal, caring but also burdened and self-sacrificing. It is recognized that care experienced children have learned to read adults minds and second guess their feelings to try keep safe. Then consequently they will be acutely aware of the carers conflicted feelings and cannot possibly make any comment that could be perceived as criticism in their presence. Their experience of ruptured relationships may mean they cannot believe they are loved, sadly increasing their fear of speaking freely. One even said with ineffable sadness, "You know as a foster child you're inevitably disposable". It is evident that carers and professionals need much support to enable the children in their care to feel of worth and valued. To ensure they do not suffer feelings as unbearably painful that they are disposable as a human being.

5. Unfair judgements: Remember the relationships are not equal and they never stick around anyway. They judge and move on, and I was left" (RW)

With regard to receiving what has been termed "good enough" care, the level of value and gratitude demonstrated by participants was tangible. Conversely, when navigating health and social services they all commented that assumptions and unfair judgements were made about them. One (RW) described experiencing a relationship characterized by domestic abuse and perceiving that the police negatively judged her for her relationship choice with another care leaver. Consider that not only was she victim blamed, the implication was she should have known he was an abuser, as he grew up in care. The message from professionals imprinted on the co-author was that professionals view care leavers as either victim or abuser. They indicated that this was unwise relationship choice and emphasized if there were children involved it would be a safe-guarding situation almost predicting the transmission theories Bourdieu (1984) described. From these discussions other themes emerged, which we called unfair judgements.

To the co-authors' credit, all had a capacity to self-reflect. They all in different ways concluded "I don't express my emotional needs well" or "I find it very difficult to ask for help" (SM). At important developmental stages they lacked parents who provided the opportunities for social and emotional development. It is also a painful paradox that all encountered professionals in their adult lives made pre-conceived judgements about them as a consequence of their knowledge of their care experienced status. Dimes, cited within Dix et al. (2019) discussed the assumptions and ageism attached to social work with elderly people. The author would argue similar discrimination and assumptions take place when an individual's care experienced status is known. As a professional the author has witnessed greater scrutiny of care leavers in relation to education, parenting and other rites of passage or transitions young people experience and are celebrated rather than scrutinized. One participant described contrasting midwifery experiences:

> One midwife did not ask if I had been in care, I would have answered honestly. The other midwife who did seemed to judge my parenting capacity entirely on what happened to me as a child. It was horrendous and I was made to feel the scum of the earth.
>
> (SM)

The author has heard this from many care experienced adults in her career but remains shocked that professionals do not utilize strengths-based approaches advocated by Cameron and Maginn (2009). The capacity to recover from abuse, to hold down employment, and to maintain your own tenancy are laudable for children in care who may lack permanent attachment figures to support them. All of the attributes care leavers must possess in abundance to survive such as courage, bravery, adaptability deserve highlighting. This positive psychology approach is far more empowering than the victim blaming experiences reported by survivors of abuse and trauma.

6. Seeking a home and keeping a home: "I have done what I have to. As I have had to be adaptable and resilient" (SM)

I was so impressed by the dialogue that emerged from the topic of moving. One of the co-authors discussed thoughtfully the care she took if she and her daughter moved with her employment in the armed forces.

Without realizing she seemed to be underpinning theories in relation to transition to her practice. She described for example visiting settings and using a transitional object. She endeavoured to prepare to help her precious child to achieve liminality. The process of successful transition is hard for many but potentially harder for those who have been in care as they may not have the attachment figure to guide them.

In relation to housing stability, the importance of warm, stable relationships as a pre-requisite for good emotional health is now more widely understood (Cameron and Maginn, 2009). Some local authorities have invested in additional training for their professional workforce. Models based on evidence which enhance the parent/care/dyad have been developed and some areas have achieved increased capacity in the workforce. Some councils, since 2018 have sought government funding for edge of care projects targeted to reduce the vast care population £180 million (one hundred and eighty million) is currently shared between councils with high populations of children in care to try to reduce the figures and help children remain living with birth family. The importance of trusting professional relationships cannot be emphasized sufficiently and was echoed by all the co-authors.

All participants described the value of attachment relationships. It is noteworthy Maginn (2009) recently entitled this work as attachment science, drawing on the use of magnetic imaging resonance utilized in Rohners (2004); research referred to earlier. They emphasize the need to understand the neuroscience impact of attachment relationships. For example, rejection can cause physical pain and mental health difficulties. While this is a recognizable need, it sadly, for many, remains unmet. The journey for these brave co-author's, to receiving appropriate attachment figures who could meet all or some of their needs, was fraught with challenge, uncertainty, loss, and change. One participant within this study experienced a number of foster care moves, a frequency exceeding government targets, until stability was found within residential care. She stated

> I guess I struggled fitting into a family setting as it was something I never had. I had gone from a broken, abusive family home, where my siblings and I were abused and neglected. I struggled with the concept of strangers loving me. The three moves in the space of a year led me to the children's home. This was the best for me as I got emotional support and help with independence and relationship building.

> (RW)

The positive experience in residential care probably reflected the small group home statement of purpose and attachment focus of the staff. Ruttle et al. (2011) found cortisol levels abnormally high at the peak of emotional distress and then abnormally low when the distress was sustained for a long time. Put simply the body adapts to long-term stress and blunts its responses. They provide a simplistic but helpful example if someone sees a bear in the yard, that person experiences a fight or flight reaction. If you see a bear in the yard every day for a year the stress response is lowered and blunted and eventually cortisol is abnormally lowered impairing appropriate stress responses. This ground-breaking research is powerful as leaving children in the wrong environment or placement will change them physiologically, psychologically and bodily, and the capacity to "know whether a bear is dangerous" leaves them vulnerable to re-abuse. The removal of the stress of family-based care may have reduced cortisol levels for the co-author, who feared that foster carers saw her as disposable. The residential home may have provided more emotional security.

The value of independence skills was acknowledged by another co-author who said

> When my peers where honing their executive function skills such as learning how to drive or manage finance, I was concentrating on surviving. My primary concern in adolescence was to have enough money for food and essentials. I lacked stability, I had mental health issues and numbing behaviours took precedence.
>
> (RC)

This co-author was discharged from care prematurely without access to care leaver support, which breaches legislative and policy frameworks in place. While shocking it is not wholly surprising as performance indicators for local councils in 2015 suggested that just eight (8) out of a total of one hundred and fifty one (151) local authorities knew the whereabouts of their care leavers (Elvin, cited in the Guardian July 20th, 2015). Overall the data concluded that local councils had no information at all on the whereabouts of 17 percent of their 19- to 21-year-olds. Elvin bravely commented on the gravity of this corporate parenting failure. He speculated that the readers should imagine the public outcry if 17 percent of parents lost their teenagers.

Linked to this, the Fostering Network (2018) reported a huge shortage in foster careers which inevitably limits placement choice and matching. One participant reported placements in which her sibling felt favoured, whereas she felt unloved and unwanted. The importance of placements which do not resonate the feelings which result from the original abuse is of vital importance. Linked to independence skills, such as driving, only one participant had a license. This would be valuable practical skills for care leavers; one that I understand may be provided on a discretionary basis and may have been impacted by austerity. It is questionable if all children in care are advised this was a possible provision or given the information to query this, themselves. Given the difficulties for this vulnerable group to express their voice, Barnados (2019) conducted extensive research with young people and concluded that many felt vulnerable and excluded, lacking in hope for the future. This is relevant to care leavers as they are so vulnerable to mental health difficulties and feelings of hopelessness, which is a risk factor for suicide. Consequently, many children in care do not get matched to the right placement with the right support or the right information and provision of opportunity to express themselves to change things. It is documented that many of the children in care self-medicate with substances to cope with their mental health difficulties. Alderson et al. (2017) undertook the first longitudinal study in relation to substance misuse and children in care. The aim is to divert young people from illicit substance use, utilizing evidence-based motivational relationships. The findings are yet to be published; however it is laudable that responsivity is being applied to risk to help these vulnerable young people achieve longed for stability.

7. Stigma: "There felt like many nasty voices when I was in care. So much judgement. One kind voice would have been enough" (RW)

All the participants identified that they experienced different treatment as a child, as a pupil, as a mother and as an employee, resulting from growing up in care. Given the growing understanding of the impact of adverse childhood experiences, one would have hoped for more compassion-focussed responses. Compassion-focussed therapy, developed by Gilbert (2014), is increasing in use and interest in the United Kingdom, and at least two Universities have developed postgraduate courses in response to this training need. Clearly work is required to educate professionals and indeed the general public.

The co-author who least identified with stigma experienced the longest family placement and identifies her foster careers as long-term family figures. The value of this to enhance resilience cannot be overestimated. Conversely, she felt sad and responsible for family members who had not had such a positive experience in terms of placement. It is evident a stable placement with experienced carers is a buffer against discrimination both with the advocate role they provide and their capacity to support young people with thoughtfulness and a compassionate care.

All three described the feeling that their care leaver status meant assumptions were made of them. One co-author speculated, "You know people are wondering do they have a real family". (RW). To their credit many could apply this painful experience in a positive way to their own employment. One explained

> Children in care need the space to wonder, to explore how they feel. What it means to them. Let children be curious. Trauma informed adults should wonder about the things that children do feel. For example, do you worry that you are not a favourite? "Haven't we all longed to be someone's favourite?

(RC)

This final comment perhaps highlights the value of capturing care experienced voices. They truly know how it feels to not feel a favourite, and to struggle with identity and relationships. Yet in spite of this to find the strength every day to push forward. "To keep going. To fight the stigma" (RW). To push against stereotypes, unfair judgements, and preconceived ideas.

Summary

The experience of producing this chapter has been moving and enlightening. Thoughts the author held in relation to the training needs for professionals in relation to trauma and abuse were confirmed. These thoughts were also developed further. To heal from abuse, the impact of the abuse needs to be acknowledged and young peoples' emotional needs really need to be anticipated. Plans for graduations, Christmas and birthdays needs the consideration and care that the general population of young people experience. The message is then transmitted that you deserve, you are valuable. The focus on attachment and compassion focussed therapies and metallization will enable these crucial workforce skills to be developed (Allen and Fonagey, 2006).

More work is required to train professionals and the general public about the strengths of children who have grown up in care. This could reduce the stigma co-authors experienced. It is positive organizations like Become (2019) that represent the voices of Children in care have linked their manifesto to the United Kingdom's general election upcoming the participants struck me with their thoughtfulness, self-awareness, and capacity to mentalize. The need for work with children in care and care leavers to be a genuine co production between them and professionals is vital, as the young people know what they need. For example, the young woman who thrived in residential care benefitted from a choice of placement. She had reached her capacity to manage family settings, too many had been unreliable and poor matches.

Finally, the clinical upskilling of careers and professionals will require policy and practice development as Arminger (2019) thoughtfully suggested. Professionals need to interpret young people's behaviour as behaviour really does tell the story. As one participant explained she ran away to be found. She was seeking attachment relationships inappropriately through risk-taking behaviour. Help young people understand the meaning of their behaviour and provide what they need and harmful behaviours will reduce. As the co-authors all indicate genuine, loving relationships would be the best intervention we could provide for children who have been denied this due to abuse or neglect. Consequently, policies, including "Staying Put", which financially enable foster carers to extend placements beyond 18 need developing for children in residential care.

Recommendations

1 Positive awareness raising in relation to children in care to reduce stigma.
2 Ensuring access to training in relation to the emotional needs to children in care is easily available for all professionals and carers. To enable them to understand the "Behavior tells a story. It may be a story of loss and pain but these needs to be heard and understood".
3 Strengthening access for care experienced adults to access further and higher education and remain in studies until they are completed.
4 Ensuring access to trauma informed therapy for all care experienced children, young people and adults.
5 Increasing the professional and public understanding of the impact of adverse childhood experiences. Furthermore, develop connected thinking/networks in how to promote recovery from these difficult experiences utilizing the important voices of care experienced adults as they are the ones with the relevant knowledge.

Acknowledgements

It remains my duty and privilege to thank the co-authors they have already changed my direct practice with young people in care. More time is spent wondering how the young people may feel, how they are anticipating transitions and how their carers can best anticipate their needs. It is hoped readers will also embed these important themes identified and improve their practice.

"The final stage of healing is using what happens to you to help other people. That is healing in itself" Gloria Steinem.

The Co- Authors Include

Rachel Close is a qualified social worker currently working therapeutically with children and families. Rachel was adopted as a baby from Romania by British parents. During adolescence, following a breakdown in family relationships at home Rachel was placed in emergency foster care before living independently from the age of 18. Rachel went on to study social work and postgraduate study in systemic practice in the hope of supporting children and families experiencing relational difficulties.

Susan McKenna is 39-year-old woman who was placed in Local Authority Care on two occasions, once at 10 years and then from 14 years until joining HM Forces at 18 years. Susan aspired to employment within the Police and as a Social Worker due to the wish to support those affected by child abuse and domestic violence. She has attained those life goals within the specific roles she has undertaken and continues to undertake within HM Forces. She continues to find the lack of understanding and empathy regarding the enduring impact of traumatic childhood experiences heart-breaking.

Rachel Woodley is a 29-year-old woman living in Essex. She was born and raised in Darlington. Rachel was raised in the care system from the age of 3 to 21 as she stayed in higher education until the age of 21. Rachel works full time in accounts and studies part time for a degree in criminology and law. She has admirable aspirations to work as a police detective within the field of domestic abuse. She has laudable aspirations to share the challenges she faced growing up in care and how these impacted on her transition to adulthood. Rachel states "I have faced many difficulties from childhood but these difficulties and the stigma I face from being in care have not and will not define me".

References

Allen JG and Fonagey P (2006) *The handbook of mentalization –based treatment.* Chichester: John Wiley.

Alderson H, McGovern R and Raghu L (2017) Supporting looked after children and Care leavers in decreasing drugs and alcohol. *Pilot and Feasibility Studies* 3, Article 25 2017.

Armiger M (2019) Teachers are not experts they need tools to talk about mental health Times Educational Supplement 16 February 2019.

Bourdieu P (1986) The forms of Capital in J Richardson Handbook of Theory and Research for the sociology of Education (New York, Greenwood) 241–258.

Bovaird T and Loeffler E (2016) User and Community Co Production of Public Services: What does the evidence tell us? *International Journal of Public Administration* 39(13) 1006–1019.

Capron L and Ayre D (2015) The Children's Society: Wolf at The Door: How Council Tax debt collection is harming children March 2015.

Care Inspectorate (2013) A report into the deaths of looked after children in Scotland 2009–2011 April 2013.

Dix H, Hollindrake S and Meade J (2019) *Relationship based social work with adults.* St Albans: Critical Publishing.

Cameron and Maginn (2009) *Achieving good outcomes for children in care.* London: Sage Publications.

Chard (2019) cited in Dix H, Hollindrake S and Meade J (2019) *Relationship based social work with adults.* St Albans: Critical Publishing.

Cohen S (2002) *Folk devils and moral panic.* London: Routledge, Taylor & Francis Publishing.

Elvin A (2015) We cannot allow young people leaving care to be forgotten by councils. *Guardian Newspaper* 20th July 2015.

Featherstone B and Gupta A (2018) The role of the social worker in adoption-ethics and Human Rights an enquiry BASW January 2018.

Fostering Network (2019) Foster Care Winter 2019.

Felitti, VJ, Anda, RF, Nordenberg D, Williamson DF, Spitz AM, Edwards V, Koss MP and Marks JS (May 1998) Relationship of childhood abuse and household dysfunction to many of the leading causes of death in adults: The adverse childhood experiences. *ACE study American Journal of Preventative Medicine* 114 248–258.

Gilbert P (2014) The origins and nature of compassion focused therapy mental health research Unit, Asbourne centre Kingsway Hospital Derby UK.

Hughes D (2008) Attachment focused family therapy. *Journal of Family Therapy* 30(3) 320–321.

Mannay D, Staples S, Hallett S, Roberts L, Rees A, Evans R and Andrews D (2019) Enabling talk and reframing messages: Working creatively with care experienced children and young people to recount and represent their everyday experiences. *Childcare in Practice* 25(1) 51–63. Routledge.

Nicholson C (2011) Relational Ruptures: The psychodynamics of leaving care www.researchgate.net/publication/289062792.

Oakley M., Miscampbell G and Raphael G (2018) Looked-after children the silent crisis, Social Market Foundation August 2018.

Putting People First (2007) A shared vision and commitment to the transformation of adult social care 10 December 2007.

RBSCB Overview report in relation to Rochdale 20th December 2013.

Rohner RP, Khaleque A and Cournoyer DE (2008) Parental acceptance-rejection: Theory, methods, cross cultural evidence and implications. *Ethos Journal* 33(3) 299–334.

Rushton P and Donovan C (eds) (2018) *Austerity a bad idea in Practice Palgrave.* Cham: Palgrave Macmillan, Springer International Publishing.

Ruttle P, Shirtcliffe EA, Serbin L and Fisher B. (2011) Stack D and Schwartzman Disentangling psychobiological mechanisms underlying internalizing and externalizing behaviour in youth: Longitudinal and concurrent associations with cortisol. *Hormones and Behaviour* 59(1) 123–132.

Saunders H (2016) Twenty nine child homicides: Lessons still to be learnt on domestic violence and child protection February 2016.

Schiettecat T, Roet G and Vanderbroek M (2018) Capturing life histories about movements into and out of poverty: A road with pits and bumps. *Qualitative Social Work* 17 384–404.

Scott J (2011) The impact of disrupted attachment on the emotional and interpersonal development of looked after children. *Educational and Child Psychology* 28(3) 31–43, the British Psychological Society.

Selwyn J, Wijedsa D and Meakings S (2014) Beyond the adoption order: Challenges, interventions and adoption Disruption University of Bristol April 2014.

Shelter research- In work, but out of a home. (2018) Shelter 2018.

Shoesmith S (2016) Learning from baby Peter Jessica Kingsley Publishers.

Smith G, Sylva K, Smith T, Sammons P and OMoniggho A (2018) Survival, decline or closure? Children's Centres in England 2018 University of Oxford and Sutton Trust.

Sissay L (2019) *My name is why.* Edinburgh: Cannongate Publishing.

The final report of the National Camhs review (2008) Children and Young People in Mind 18 November 2008.

Tzanakis M (2011) Bourdieu's social reproduction thesis and the role of cultural capital in educational attainment: A critical review of key empirical studies. *Educate* 11(1), 76–90.

Winkler A (2014) Resilience as reflexivity: A new understanding for working with looked after children. *Journal of Social Work Practice* 28(4) 461–478.

12 Lesson Drawing for Theory, Policy and Practice

Developing a Future Research Agenda

Joyce Liddle and Gareth David Addidle

Introduction

In the field of public policy, there has been a long tradition of literature on policy transfer and learning with a recent renewed scholarly interest (Dunlop, Radaelli, and Trien, 2018) in learning from comparisons, after identifying where to look for lessons to be learnt.

Despite the need for caution because of the normative assumption that learning is always a good thing, we take the work of Rose (1993, 2004) as a starting point. We also acknowledge some of the difficulties in importing and applying policies from one domain to another, but argue that at least in highlighting issues, it is possible to create awareness on policy problems and also point out potential pitfalls for evaluating future consequences on policy action. The aim of this collection was not to perfect theory on either Vulnerability, policy transfer or lesson learning, but instead to encourage each contributor to add empirical, practical, theoretical and policy insights that could aid future research directions in studying the topic. The researchers were deliberately chosen for their multi-disciplinarity in approach, and all were academics and policy/practitioners drawn from a variety of social science disciplines such as public leadership and management, social policy and social work, criminology and policing, IT and cyberspace, and contributions were invited from front-line professionals who are, or were, in direct day-to-day contact with vulnerable individuals and groups; nationally and internationally. A primary concern was the continual appraisal of existing theoretical concepts and models and their application (or not?) to policy and practice in the second decade of the 21st Century. Each chapter facilitated deeper reflection and reflexivity on current ways of defining, analysing, understanding and operationalising this significant concept of 'Vulnerability' in a variety of jurisdictions and contexts.

Lesson drawing within, and between, policy fields is a useful way of highlighting issues, and even if lessons may seem desirable and the pressures on events create demands for action, this does not always guarantee that the lessons can be applied in another policy domain or jurisdiction. Often the right lessons can be applied to the wrong institutional context, but the foundation of policy learning needs to be grounded in pragmatism of what works. For policy learning to succeed there must be space to introduce a new programme of action, resources committed to it, and clarification that any misunderstandings on lessons learnt must match existing beliefs and practices (or ideologies).

Politicians; civil servants; and, increasingly, academics with an interest in the impact of their research (author emphasis and italics) are concerned with practical solutions to immediate problems and they need to search for lessons and feasible ideas on policy problems across space and time. Usually they seek out new ways of addressing problems when there is current dissatisfaction with existing programmes of action. Rose makes the case for the significance of learning from experiences elsewhere, and the policy and academic value of studying how lessons can be drawn (Rose, 2004).

Much has been written in academic literature over the past 25 years on learning, lesson drawing and policy transfer, and the impacts may have been political, social or instrumental. Moreover, the importance of evidence-based policy making has waxed and waned from a policy and practical perspective, with varying degrees of success. In essence, despite some of the difficulties and constraints on learning from other jurisdictions, holding up a lens to identify solutions on research questions and practical problems can offer comparisons and new perspectives on policy issues such as the one to which this manuscript has been devoted; the 'wicked' and escalating problem of vulnerability. A contentious and contestable concept it could be regarded as one of the most significant policy issues of the early part of the 21st century, with no ready solutions. The topic lends itself to analysis and offers useful pointers for policy transfer, lesson drawing and learning in different jurisdictions. It is an important and growing topic of enquiry for the individuals and groups experiencing vulnerability; for policy makers seeking solutions to any consequences, for front-line professionals responding to vulnerable people, and, for wider society and the general safety of citizens. The rise in Vulnerability can be costly due to drain on already strained public finances, and on the time front-line professionals devote to the issue. Furthermore, the political and social consequences can be long term and detrimental to the social fabric of many communities and neighbourhoods.

In future there will be a greater need for research projects in this growing and important field of enquiry, if we are intent on filling gaps in current knowledge and understandings of transnational-local linkages, connections and consequences, but also to increase the knowledge base of some of the major, underlying and contested explanations of who the vulnerable individuals and groups in society are. We also need to interrogate the causes and consequences of a rise in Vulnerability, and more significantly address the issue from policy and practical perspectives. From a UK perspective and despite the 2019 General Election Party Political

Manifesto (December 2019) promises, it is clear that public expenditure cannot keep pace with the levels of demand being placed on public services. A rise in 'wicked issues', many that remain outside of state control, places considerable strain on service providersdeliverers. Furthermore, the constraints on public finances is not a wholly UK problem due the universal problems resulting from the hollowing out of state forms of delivering public services, and the need for stronger economic management. Greater citizen demands for action are severely testing current state capacities to deliver on vulnerability and other policy concerns.

At the outset when this edited collection was proposed, the overall aims were to:

- Locate the issue of 'vulnerability' into an international context, within public-sector reform processes, and to go beyond conceptualisation of existing concepts of policing and vulnerability (to include multi and intra-agency working)
- Examine the withdrawal of state forms of service delivery, and a policy shift from the collective/community to stigmatisation of the 'individual'
- Identify and explain many competing, contestable and contradictory conceptualisations of the phenomenon of 'vulnerability'
- Illustrate how a variety of agencies prioritise and operationalise the concept in practice
- Examine the growth in multi-partnership arrangements for responding to the vulnerability agenda. In particular we assess the inclusion of non-state forms of provision (business and third sector/community and other agencies)
- Draw out policy and practice learning from comparative research and across multi-disciplinary professional boundaries, and identify key issues for further research
- Define a future research agenda for managing this important topic for the 21st century

Both editors are confident that the chapters, from each author perspective, have satisfied these aims and highlighted new areas for future research and enquiry, for professional practice and policy learning. Each chapter has enabled authors to specifically focus on different contexts for collecting empirical data, and to draw on diverse understandings of the concept. The European, international and cultural dimensions highlight the varied ways that vulnerability has been conceptualised and operationalised, and most contributions are set within a context of public-sector reform, and persistent delivery of public services through partnerships, collaborations and networked forms. However, the chapter on China, offers a useful contrast due to a wholly different approach to conceptualising vulnerability, and to demonstrating how the police respond to it.

From the beginning the editors wanted to offer overall guidance on structure and format, at the same time as allowing each author the autonomy for innovative thinking and reflection on existing multiple disciplinary theoretical and empirical approaches. In emphasising the need for understanding current, multiple types of research investigations, it was anticipated that many of the contested definitions of vulnerability from social policy, criminology, policing, public leadership and other perspectives would surface. A primary concern was identifying the potential for adapting approaches to dealing with vulnerability by altering current understandings. Limited theory or empirical work exists on this policy area, it is a very complex field of enquiry involving many stakeholders, multiple agencies, professional values, as well as crossing numerous academic, policy and professional boundaries.

Chapter contributions were deliberately drawn from combinatory empirical, theoretical, policy and practice fields and diverse academic and policy/professional authors. Editors and authors deliberately cast their nets widely to provide integrative scholarship, with contributions from international perspectives confirming the complexity, and how socio/cultural, political and historic antecedents shape the definitions and responses to vulnerability. Cross-national studies can aid understanding and empirical data has the potential to alter perceptions of the phenomena under enquiry. Many contributors set their chapter findings in public-sector reform processes and Western models of democracy and public service provision, by stressing the importance of state and non-state partnerships, collaborations and networks. Significantly it is evident that vulnerability is no longer just the preserve of either police of social work front-line professionals, and the withdrawal of solely state forms of delivery have emphasised and a policy shift from collective, community or societal responsibility to demonisation or stigmatisation of the 'individual'. The Chinese case was refreshingly different from Western analyses, due mainly to the particular central system of authority, culturally embedded practices, and quite contrary definitions and understandings of what it means to be vulnerable.

In drawing out policy and practice learning from some comparative research, and across multi-disciplinary professional boundaries, the editors have been able to identify some key issues for further research, and the list that is shown at the rear of this concluding chapter will go some way towards developing a future research agenda for investigating this hitherto under-researched topic. First of all, as editors, we turn attention to some of the key findings and reflections drawn from each chapter in turn.

Theoretically, in Chapter 1 the authors (the editors) set the context for discussions in subsequent chapters by analysing literature on conceptualising, defining, analysing and understanding vulnerability as well as empirically examining the types of individuals and groups defined as vulnerable. Readers were introduced to many and varied definitions on a very contentious and politically charged concept. The articulation of a strong historical narrative of how different individuals and groups have been categorised as vulnerable from different professional, policy and academic perspectives, drew out antecedents of what it is to be considered as Vulnerable in 2020. The authors not only examined the importance of the topic for academic enquiry but also considered how policy makers and front-line professionals respond to a rise in vulnerable individuals and groups across society. The concept is certainly a slippery one, and shifts in understanding are dependent on specific contexts; who is attempting to define it; but more importantly, the choice of policies and decisions for implementation in response to this 'wicked issue'; one that can result in many unintended consequences of policy action (or inaction). In the subsequent chapters each author (s) was encouraged to operationalise 'Vulnerability' in a variety of jurisdictions and specific contexts.

In Chapter 2 Murdock and Barber provide an excellent overview of the changes to public-sector service delivery and further contextualise the way that any discussion of vulnerability must be seen in terms of rapid reform of the state. The authors reinforce the point made earlier of a multitude of state and non-state providers of services in a period of austerity and squeezed finances. Their starting point is to suggest that public services exist to support the most vulnerable in society, and it is important to define what constitutes 'public services' prior to deciding how services could be delivered. They discuss 'narrow' and 'broad' interpretations that, on the one hand limit service delivery to only those mandated or legally obligated (such as police and fire services), or on the other hand involve a range of actors, not all formally engaged. The authors develop a refreshing notion of New Public Populism due to (what they perceive to be) inadequacies of earlier explanatory models of reform. Their re-appraisal of public service delivery goes way beyond earlier research and confirms many of the problems inherent in existing perspectives and theories. New Public Management (NPM), as an example, was modelled on private-sector ideals and became the dominant model to describe the management and delivery of public services in the 1980s onwards. Its theoretical foundations cannot be attributed to one single strand of thinking, instead, it was reaction and antidote to traditional public administration, and ideas underpinning NPM were influenced by a range of diverse writers and thinkers (Liddle, 2018). The term was used to describe the way of re-organising public-sector organisations to bring their management processes closer to business methods, but in the period following the 2008 financial crisis, Murdock and Barber concur with Liddle (2018) in arguing that NPM was an insufficiently robust explanation of service delivery. Nor indeed did it, or the later explanations of New Public Services and New Public Governance adequately account for the changing nature of state and non-state interactions as mechanisms for coping with vulnerability.

In asking the question 'Who are public services for?' and suggesting that market solutions are incapable of addressing welfare issues alone, the authors use three examples of New Public Populism to demonstrate how citizen discontentment poses challenges to existing top-down, professionally driven services. With social divisions and anti-elitism as driving forces to their thesis. They argue that citizens, including vulnerable groups reliant on welfare services, are ready to challenge traditional, or new service delivery mechanism based on outdated bureaucratic approaches and, instead readily take to the streets to voice their concerns. The era of populism requires a fresh appraisal of public services for the people who rely upon them most, but also deeper analysis of leaderless civil disobedience and localist 'bottom up', more contradictory solutions.

In Chapter 3 Liddle and Addidle (the editors) use Brexit and its potential aftermath to draw out some of the transnational and local linkages within security, criminal justice and policing (those with the potential to impact on levels of vulnerability). They argue for better understanding and targeting of resources on 'left behind' localities, those disproportionately affected during Brexit negotiations and future trade deals. Policing, security and criminal justice remain un-discussed and under-researched elements of Brexit, and for Liddle and Addidle, adopting a transnational lens can identify relationships and inter-connections across spatial levels, especially those with potential to detrimentally impact on vulnerable groups. Moreover, it is possible, they argue, to appreciate consequential agency responses to the problem.

Research is already developing on global shifts and impacts on local areas and their socio-economies, but more needs to be understood on the rise in terrorism, borderless crime, people trafficking, drug smuggling and other issues facing Police (and other emergency and Blue Light) Leaders as they cope with austerity, on top of a multitude of domestic policing and security issues. Under-investigation of new technology and an increase in cross border criminal activities impacting on local vulnerability levels has created a weak knowledge base and authors call for enhanced research in this area. Moreover, they argue, a need to understand embedded structural issues in former industrialised localities; how states and non-state agencies use institutional channels to broker cross border connectivity and partnership working; how communications and information is exchanged across national borders; and connecting transnational to local processes would all improve empirical data in the field.

A reduction in front-line service personnel dealing with vulnerable people in an era austerity and on-going Brexit negotiations, is happening at concurrently with increased hate and race crime, Islamophobia,

Anti-Semitism and cyber-crime. Other vulnerable groups, such as the homeless, rough sleepers, refugees and immigrants, are living in poverty and leading to larger numbers seeking assistance. The real financial consequences of Brexit are difficult to predict, so no one quite knows how Emergency and Blue Light services, and statutory social and welfare services, still reeling from budgets cuts, will fare in a post Brexit world. Furthermore, many essential services for vulnerable people depend heavily on foreign workers, but there is limited research on this aspect of vulnerability.

There are many challenges in identifying the multi-scalar (transnational, national, regional and local) impacts of Brexit on policing and other emergency services and responses to greater levels of Vulnerability, but no-one really knows the full extent of how many non-state, charitable, voluntary, church and other civic organisations are stepping in to support the vulnerable once the statutory agencies withdraw coverage. Table 12.1 indicates a selection of initiatives where faith-based and charity groups are taking over service provision from traditional public service providers (literally thousands of these organisations have sprung up since Prime Minister David Cameron's (ultimately failed) Big Society initiative in 2010).

In Chapter 4, Brookes, a senior academic with many years of practical experience as a police commander, considers whether vulnerability is a collective/societal issue or the responsibility of the individual, who is increasingly blamed, demonised and stigmatised for the unfortunate positions they find themselves in. He uses examples from sex work (prostitution), modern slavery and youth extremism to demonstrate how each transcends the criminal justice system. He calls for all public leaders to collectively tackle the contextual social, political and economic determinants of vulnerability. In his view Public Leaders need to properly appreciate and frame the issue by looking beneath the problems for root causes, as well as mapping the historical contours of situations, based on a strong evidence base.

Brookes argues for vulnerability as a central element of community safety strategies, through a collective form of community-based leadership,because he believes that agency leaders have a duty of care to victims, and must solve these societal and 'wicked issues', with public interest and public value at the very core of all strategies and plans.

In Chapter 5, three separate professional and practice contributions are included from Emergency and Blue Light service personnel; those working at a strategic level, but also familiar with front-line service provision (Knox and Downs, Ambulance and McMillan, Police), together with a contribution from Murphy, an academic who provides consultancy for Fire and Rescue Services, who draws on long experience as a Senior Civil Servant and, also first responder in dealing with emergencies and crises across the East Midlands region of England. All writers

Table 12.1 Source: Authors' own research findings

Some examples of charitable/faith based and third sector agencies plugging the gap in service provision for vulnerable groups	
Railway Mission	Provides Rail Pastors to support vulnerable staff and passengers on rail services
Pop up Prostitution, Buxton- Derby	Police working with this body to identify international people trafficking
Buzz Huddersfield	Community charity set up by a Syrian Refugee (former University Professor) to help vulnerable people use Bee keeping as a way of doing something valuable and reducing mental health issues
Clear Vision Research	Set up by a black individual who was wrongly convicted of an offence and found not guilty-helps to steer young black guys away from a life of crime
Grenfell Tower Support Groups	Community based/faith groups helping to look after homeless after the disaster
Sutton Trust	Recent report on the inability of disadvantaged and vulnerable teenagers getting into University
St Giles Trust	Vulnerable people being used as drugs mules-they work with hospitals to identify children as young as 8 seeking a glamorous life as drug mules
Care B & B	Families paid £1000 to look after discharged hospital patients (seen as an example of innovative public services)
NACRO & Groundwork Trust	Helps young, vulnerable ex-offenders to get into employment through various initiatives
Samaritans	Connect with high risk groups, also formal and informal partnerships/MOIs with, for example police, probation and prison education services, NHS Mental Health Trusts, Universities, and Rail authorities to deal with a variety of vulnerable people e.g. after a tragedy such as Manchester Arena, Grenfell, suicidal students, people throwing themselves under trains, vulnerable prisoners or mental health patients
Street Pastors in the Evening and Night time economy (teachers, vicars, off duty police officers and social workers)	Keeping vulnerable people safe in city centres. They receive a small grant per annum from local authorities, to reduce the case load of the statutory agencies such as police and social workers by working across city centres caring for vulnerable people. They also work with nationally organised charities such as Age Concern, Mental Health Charities to deal with increased demands from homeless people, drug users, and isolated people

provide a different dimension on the role of front-line professionals in day-to-day dealings with vulnerable groups and individuals, but each addresses the European and national policy imperatives on how Blue Light and Emergency service agencies prioritise and operationalise responses to the 'wicked issue' of vulnerability, within given statutory requirements and available resources.

Each service has experienced a rise in the numbers of vulnerable people seeking assistance, and all three use a different mechanism for categorisation. They do this in the interest of providing the best support for individual safeguarding, risk or potential harm and to highlight any perceived welfare concerns. At the forefront of their thinking, whether adopting a Triage process (Ambulance), the THRIVE list provided by the College of Policing (Police), or Risk Assessment (Fire and Rescue), all services are continually making choices on whether callers have a health, criminal or fire and safety issue of concern. Additionally, Fire and Rescue Services have a duty to achieve risk reduction and prevention. As all the services featured here work with other statutory and non-statutory agencies in collaboration and partnership, a decision must be made on whether to deal immediately with any issue if its within their line of responsibility, or whether it warrants referral to other welfare services. Interestingly, all services recognised how under-represented they are in relation to minority and ethnic groups, and all are making efforts to recruit and train personnel more reflective of the populations that their activities are affect.

Brown and Cook, both senior practitioners with years of experience in social work academic and practice worlds, consider in Chapter 6, the changing nature of professional roles as they too respond to escalation in the numbers of vulnerable people. Their core message is the need for more comparative research on front-line service deliverers who daily confront vulnerable individuals. These professional groups are experiencing higher levels of stress related illness and absenteeism, in comparison with other professional groups. According to these authors, excessive working hours, low staff coverage, poor support mechanisms lead to a negative work/life balance, with many professionals experiencing mental health difficulties, so as a group they are as 'vulnerable' as the vulnerable individuals and client groups they joined their respective professions to support.

Central Government recently acknowledged how vulnerable and exposed some front-line emergency service professionals were, and this included police officers, fire and rescue workers, prisons and National Health Service personnel but social workers who are also exposed to daily risks and dangerous situations were omitted from this timely legislation. Brown and Cook therefore argue for more research on the day-to-day hostile, risky and dangerous experiences of social workers, and for more understanding of training and practice needs of these groups. In support of this, and to reduce the stress levels, anxiety, poor mental health, staff turnover and ultimate burnout, the authors have developed a very useful Vulnerability Map to assess, and unpick the dynamic elements of very specific organisational accountability, workload, emotional and threat contexts that impact on the daily practices of social workers. They suggest that this group occupies a unique position at the interface between the organisation's legislative function and the needs of service users; they continuously respond to a variety of stakeholders, as various threats and forces impact on their activities. They urge new thinking on complex social work activities and delivery mechanisms.

Phippen and Bond in Chapter 7 examine the concept of 'vulnerability' in a new digital world of social media, and their findings show how abuse traditionally occurred in face to face encounters or in written form, but the advent of social media has questioned our views on geographical boundaries on space and situations, on who is now vulnerable, and where vulnerability can be seen. Abuse and therefore a rise in vulnerable individuals can literally take place anywhere in the world now, and the anonymity afforded by the web allows abusers to access potentially millions of vulnerable people through a multitude of personas.

They show how online targeting of vulnerable people has challenged criminological norms but failed these individuals, because those responsible for safeguarding don't fully understand the changing wider context in which abuse occurs. Policy documentation and statistics are used to support evidence based on the increased use of a range of social media within cyberspace and illustrate that rapidly changing technological landscapes have blurred boundaries between public and private spheres and dramatically altered the contours of risk in relation to self-identity in late modern society.

Virtual space is a very real concern as vulnerable people experience abuse, victimisation and online crimes, identity theft, online scams, image-based abuse, fear of being stalked and harassment online are on the increase. Therefore, Phippen and Bond argue that our understanding of risk has changed in late modern society, from being focussed on natural hazards to becoming unintended consequences of modernisation itself. Digital technology, according to these authors, redefines the nature of vulnerability, and the Internet has reshaped the environment where anyone can now be vulnerable. They make a plea for government to appreciate the need for challenging abusive and complex social behaviour, because technological interventions alone cannot solve this policy problem. To protect victims from online abuse, a variety of stakeholders and their relationships need to be put under the spotlight; without this fundamental challenge neither the criminal justice system nor any new legislation can protect vulnerable individuals online. The reach of abusers is now extended, and anonymously hidden from view. The consequences for victims demand human behaviours and responses, rather than inadequate technological fixes.

In Chapter 8 X Jian Xu author (an academic with long and senior experience as a police officer and trainer in the Chinese Police) changes the focus towards an international dimension of vulnerability in a different jurisdiction and political system. Theoretically he adopts the lens of Street Level Bureaucrats to frame the research design and analyse illuminating, comparative case findings. In exploring the daily interactions of Chinese police officers with citizens he shows how much personal discretion police officers have in adapting tailored responses, executing activities and developing different routinised procedures. Xu explains that on the surface, it may appear not dissimilar to Western social and legal contexts because the way vulnerable individuals and groups are treated is very much conditioned by deeply embedded cultural and political factors. However, within a political system of centralised authority and under-developed legal standardisation, vulnerability is treated much differently in a Chinese context.

Xu examines how SLBs operate in China in conceptual terms, and how certain Chinese officials at local level deal with protesting groups on a more practical level. Drawing on data from two illuminating cases, he investigates the culturally embedded practice of "relational repression", which in essence is a psychological engineering approach adopted by Chinese frontline officials for policing vulnerable populations and maintaining social control. Police use a variety of social and relational tools but the primary means to maintain control is by imposing constraints on the poor and vulnerable, rather than through the formal criminal justice system typified in most of the western contexts. Weak legal and political institutions enable police and other authorities to use flourishing 'power-interest networks' and 'personal and social ties' to facilitate order. The police were able to effectively capitalise on existing culturally grounded personal ties, as these social norms ensure social order and maintaining control.

Fitzgerald and Hagos, in Chapter 9, show how asylum seekers and refugees in pursuit of a safe haven have been dealt with by successive UK governments With the use of up to date narratives, the authors use the voices and experiences of vulnerable individuals on arrival in the country, to examine how immigration policy rules have created categories of the 'deserving' or 'undeserving', though for a short period they noted that some EU workers were welcomed to serve economic purposes. People at perhaps the most vulnerable point in their lives largely experienced a hostile, complicated and difficult journey to safety, as many faced detention, destitution, health issues and potential slave labour.

A culmination of the consequences of the 2008 economic crisis, on-going austerity and Brexit may have exacerbated problems experienced by asylum seekers and refugees, though Fitzgerald and Hagos did find evidence of direct action and activism. They found many who became key activists and community leaders within and beyond their own communities, and on a positive note, despite some of the still unknown effects of Brexit, new social movements and campaigns have sprung into action, and brought vulnerable people 'out of the shadows' into public life, thereby overturning the perception of victimhood.

In Chapter 10 Murdock provides a reality check on the issue of ageing and elderly. He challenges the perceived wisdom of this demographic as a 'problem' or as 'vulnerable' because in many, if not most, developed countries there is a widely reported view of increased demands on public services. Too often the elderly were designated as vulnerable, and this has significantly shaped public policy debates. Recently these have focussed on whether or not public resources are sufficient to meet the perceived needs of an ageing demographic.

The author makes a convincing argument that the elderly should be seen as an 'opportunity' rather than a 'challenge'. He asserts that the elderly should not always be treated as 'vulnerable' members of society, though he does acknowledge that some are. Rather he examines 'active ageing', 'positive ageing' and identifies a series of lifestyle trends (lifelong learning; University of the third Age, redefining retirement; use of technology, and lifestyle choices) that he thinks demands a radical restructuring of public-sector policies for this older demographic, and calls for a more societal perception of the positives rather than negative aspects of ageing.

Hunter and co-authors in Chapter 11 change the focus again by concentrating on the 'voices' and 'narratives' of three female individuals; all have experienced first-hand what it feels like to be defined as 'vulnerable' and exposure to long periods within the social care system. Three contributors provide life histories of their individual trajectories towards re-entering society after experiencing varied institutional histories, and Hunter, an experienced social worker, offers useful commentaries throughout, and valuable recommendations for social work training and education.

Hunter refers to the large and increasing numbers of children in care in the UK as a silent crisis and offers some thoughts on why this might be the case. Importantly she suggests that insufficient support for children in care and those leaving care lead unsurprisingly to poor overall outcomes. Many children who are in or leave the care system experience mental health difficulties, poor educational outcomes, homelessness and suicide, and they are more likely to go to prison than university. She arrives at a series of recommendations that could be usefully adopted in training and educating social workers and front-line providers. In no order of importance she highlights the need for training on dealing with trauma; how to help vulnerable individuals navigate services on offer; the nature of attachment relationships; the impacts of early childhood experiences, how care leavers can find accommodation; and finally helping carers to understand unfair judgements and stigmatisation exemplify the experience of being in, or leaving the care system.

Hunter makes a heartfelt plea for more understanding and cooperation on the part of professionals and the general public to stress the strengths of children who have grown up in care; many, she argues fully understand their own particular needs, and large numbers have overcome sever adversity to make a success of their lives, as demonstrated by the three life stories she presented.

A Future Research Agenda

The following proposed research topics shown in Table 12.2 have been derived from the composite findings on which each chapter is based, and though it is far from an exhaustive list, it does offer useful pointers towards some key areas in need of future investigation and research. Both editors recognise that Vulnerability is a multi-faceted topic field and scholars are at a very early stage of discovery and exploration of the varied and numerous theoretical, conceptual, empirical and practical parameters in this important area.

Table 12.2 Potential research topics for the Future-Source-Authors own

Potential research topics for the future- in no particular order of importance
Understanding competing and contradictory definitions of what it means to be 'Vulnerable' in the 21st Century in different contexts
Multi-disciplinary approaches to 'Vulnerability' as scholars from numerous disciplines are engaged in on-going research in the field. Public Leadership and Management, Policing, Social Work, Social Policy, Information Technology and Cyberspace, and many scholars from wide disciplines are employing both quantitative methodologies to investigate the phenomena
Comparative research on how 'Vulnerability is conceptualised and operationalised in different political/judicial/legal jurisdictions
Comparative research on how 'Vulnerability is conceptualised and operationalised in different political/judicial/legal jurisdictions
How Vulnerability can be contextualised within state reform processes, and the consequential new forms of delivering services (through state, non-state and other agencies)
What is the full extent of non-state, charitable, voluntary, Church and other civic organisations stepping in to support the vulnerable once statutory agencies withdraw from coverage? Capacity issues?
Global and transnational shifts and the impacts on Vulnerability at local scales of analysis
How policies to deal with 'vulnerable' arise or move up political agendas? What are the explanations for a rise in Vulnerability?
Who are the Vulnerable groups and individuals and how are they being dealt with?
Examining the differences between Vulnerability as a collective/societal issue or an individualised 'stigmatised' phenomenon

Potential research topics for the future- in no particular order of importance

---

The trajectory from Community Safety to Vulnerability, and the importance of New Public Leadership

The trajectory from Community Safety to Vulnerability, and the importance of New Public Leadership

Contextualising the social, economic, political and cultural determinants of Vulnerability- framing the symptoms, causes and inter-connections of the issue

Ethnographical studies investigating the day-to-day activities of front-line professionals in dealing with vulnerable people, and in responding in collaboration with other agency professionals (state and non-state)

Street level bureaucrats and their levels of discretion in dealing with Vulnerability

Case studies reflecting the 'voices of the vulnerable' across different groups and populations

How front-line services or Street Level Bureaucrats define, identify, prioritise and respond to 'Vulnerability' -key issues arising e.g. training/support mechanisms

Are Emergency and Blue Light Services and other agencies reflective of the Vulnerable groups they serve?

How are front-line deliverers working in partnerships to respond, and issues of accountability, responsibility and where non-statutory services fill gaps in provision?

Juxtaposing negative connotations of Vulnerable Groups with positives (i.e. refugees who become community champions and campaigners, elderly people who are not a drain on public finances)

How are Vulnerable people (e.g. refugees, children in care, sex workers) processed through the systems and how are they perceived (hostility/ stigmatised)?

How might Brexit impact on Vulnerability? For example, are there increased levels of criminal activity and /or vulnerability in evidence, and what impact will the reduction in free movement of people and potential foreign workers have on essential public service delivery?

References

Dunlop C A, Radaelli C M, and Trein P (eds) (2018) *Learning in Public Policy: Analysis, Modes and Outcomes, International Series in Public Policy*. Palgrave Macmillan, Springer International Publishing AG, Cham, Switzerland.

Liddle J (2018) Public Value Management and New Public Governance: Key Traits, Issues and Developments (Chapter 49) in E. Ongaro and S. van Thiel (eds.), *The Palgrave Handbook of Public Administration and Management in Europe*. Palgrave MacMillan, part of Springer Nature Ltd, London.

Rose R (1993) *Lesson Drawing in Public Policy: A Guide to Learning across Space and Time*. Chatham House Publishers, Chatham.

Rose R (2004) *Learning from Comparative Public Policy: A Practical Guide*. Routledge, Taylor & Francis, Abingdon, Oxfordshire.

Index

Note: **Bold** page numbers refer to tables and *italic* page numbers refer to figures.

Printed in the United States
by Baker & Taylor Publisher Services